P9-DYZ-485

McCLURE

To Joan & Don,
with warm regards,

Robert B. McClure

May 23/82.

2 3

4

5

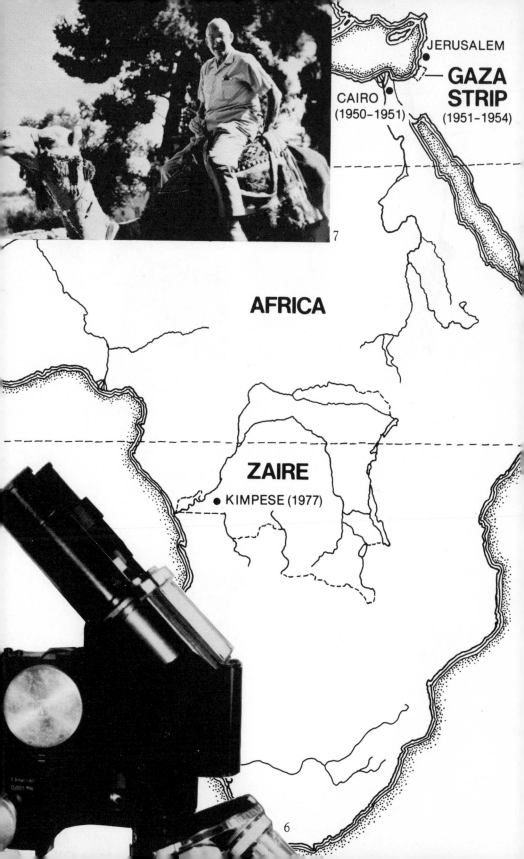

JERUSALEM

GAZA STRIP
(1951–1954)

CAIRO
(1950–1951)

AFRICA

ZAIRE

● KIMPESE (1977)

7

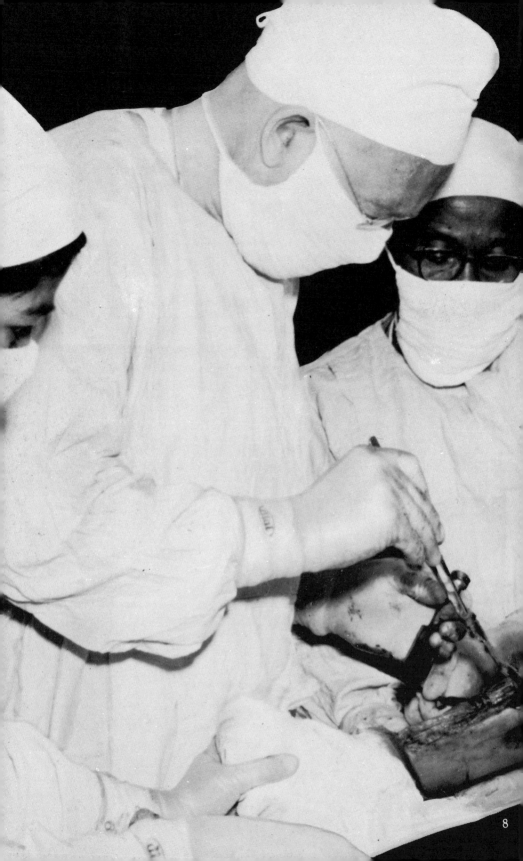

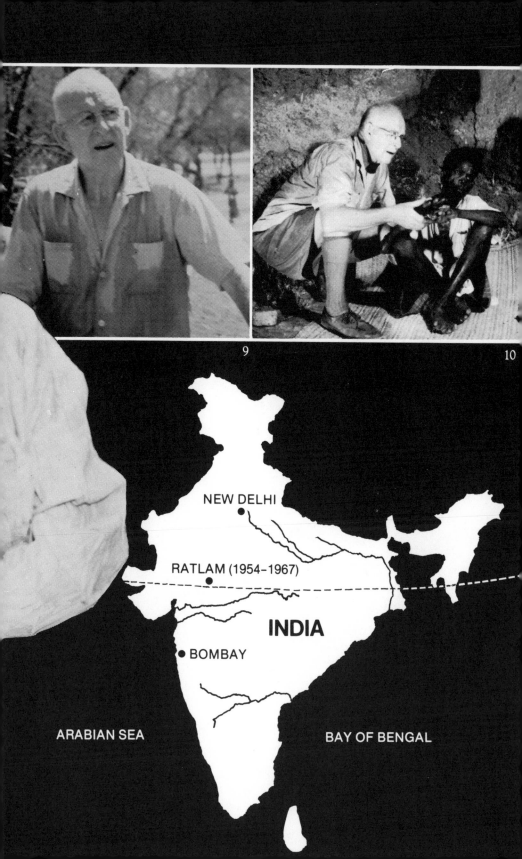

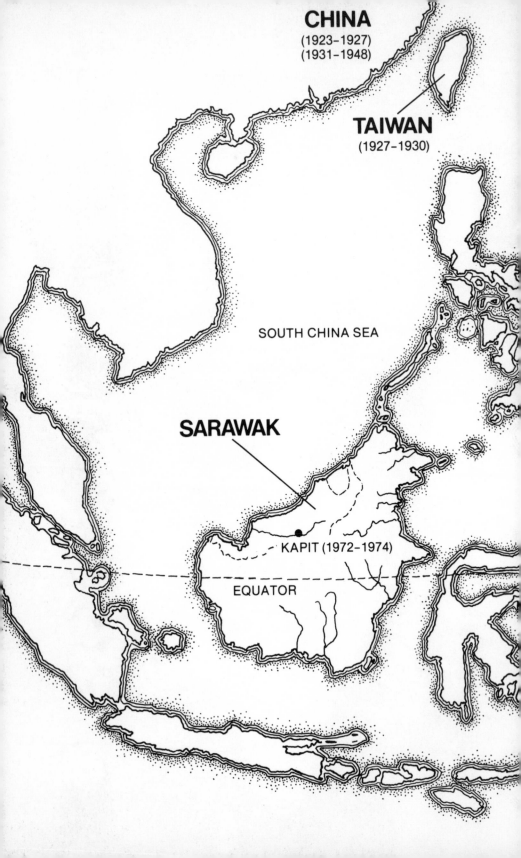

CHINA
(1923–1927)
(1931–1948)

TAIWAN
(1927–1930)

SOUTH CHINA SEA

SARAWAK

KAPIT (1972–1974)

EQUATOR

11

12

CANADA

●PORT SIMPSON (1978)

MODERATOR OF
THE UNITED CHURCH
(1968–1971)

TORONTO
(1949–1950)

13

14

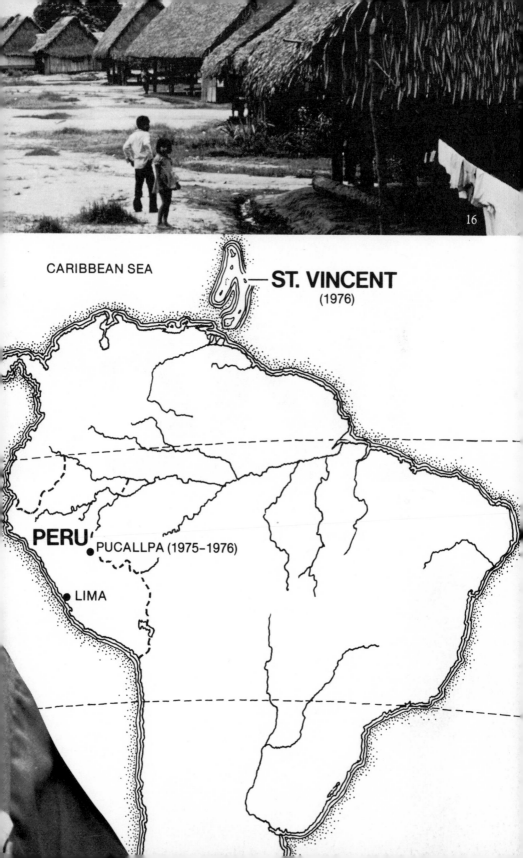

16

CARIBBEAN SEA

—**ST. VINCENT**
(1976)

PERU

PUCALLPA (1975–1976)

LIMA

McG

YEARS OF CHALLENGE

lure

Volume 2 of a biography by Munroe Scott

Canec Publishing and Supply House, Toronto

Copyright © 1979
Munroe Scott Presentations Limited.

All rights reserved. Except for review purposes,
no part of this publication may be reproduced,
stored in a retrieval system, or transmitted
in any form or by any means, electronic,
mechanical, photocopying, recording, or otherwise,
without the prior written permission of CANEC
Publishing and Supply House.

Canadian Cataloguing in Publication Data

Scott, Munroe, 1927 –
McClure

ISBN 0-919000-13-4

1. McClure, Robert, 1900 –   2. Missionaries,
Medical — Biography.   3. United Church of
Canada – Biography.   I. Title.
BX9883.M24S362   266'.025'0924   C79-094650-5

Printed in Canada for
CANEC Publishing and Supply House
47 Coldwater Road, Don Mills, Ont. M3B 1Y9

Book design by Bryan Mills & Associates Ltd.

Printed and bound in Canada by the Hunter Rose Co.

PHOTO CREDITS

Photos 1, 2, 11, 15, 16 — Lorne Direnfeld, M.D.
Photos 3, 8, 9, 10 — Berkeley Studio/Canadian Broadcasting Corp.
Photo 5 — Toll of Toronto
Photo 6 — Studio Hrant, Gaza
Photo 7 — N. Bruce McLeod
Photos 4, 12, 13 — Berkeley Studio
Jacket cover photo: Ken Elliott, *The Canadian*
The publisher regrets that photo 14 could not be attributed
to its photographer.

ACKNOWLEDGEMENTS

Quotations from *The Koran* (pages 72 and 73) courtesy J. M. Dent
& Sons Ltd., publishers, Everyman's Library Series.

Quotations from *The Discovery of India* by Jawaharlal Nehru (page 93)
courtesy Harper & Row.

To Ian, who journeyed with me.

CONTENTS

Foreword

Once upon a time I embarked, innocently, upon the task of writing a biography of Dr. Bob McClure. The project grew from one book to two, from one year of labour to three, and from research that centred around Canadian-based interviews and perusal of archival material to research that took me journeying to England, the Middle East, India, Sarawak and Hong Kong.

I know now, in retrospect, that when Bob McClure was Moderator of The United Church of Canada back in '68-'71 he was undoubtedly the least-known popular public figure in Canada. Those people who knew a great deal about his life and adventures in China knew very little about his work in India and vice versa. Neither the "old China hands" nor their counterparts from India knew anything at all about his dynamic few years in Gaza. At one stage in this project some very knowledgeable people assumed that I could probably compress everything following 1948 into a few chapters. Towards the end of this book, I have managed at least to compress the years after McClure's *retirement* into a few chapters!

It is my hope that you will enjoy reading about the McClure "years of challenge" as much as I have enjoyed exploring them. I hope you find, as I did, that one can grow in deepening admiration for the man without being impeded by undue reverence. The McClure personality denies pomp, reverence, or sophisticated ornamentation. It is no accident that this biography carries few footnotes, no appendices, addenda, glossary, or other academic frills. I would be lacking in courtesy, however, not to acknowledge a great personal debt to other authors, principally

Percival Spears, *India*; Anthony Nutting, *The Arabs*; Martin Gilbert, *The Arab-Israeli Conflict*; Joan Rawlins, *Sarawak 1839-1968*; Jawaharlal Nehru, *The Discovery of India*; and J. M. Rodwell for his translation of the *Koran*. I am indebted to Rev. G. Lucas and his staff at The United Church of Canada Archives, to Mr. W. I. Smith and the staff of the Public Archives of Canada, and to Matt Blajer of CBC Programme Archives. I also wish to express my sincere appreciation to the Humanities and Social Sciences Division of the Canada Council that provided a grant that not only made this second volume possible but enabled me to travel abroad following the McClure spoor. There is, unfortunately, no suitable way to express my appreciation to the many many people in Canada and of a variety of nationalities and religions in far away corners of the globe who invariably offered me warm friendship and a fund of information upon the mere mention of the McClure name. I trust they will forgive me for errors or omissions. There will be many of the latter; few, I hope, of the former.

Several people have read the manuscript with an eye for accuracy and since I appreciate their co-operation I will protect them with anonymity. One who cannot escape identification, however, is Norman K. Vale who has been associated with the project since its inception and who underwent heart surgery upon its completion. I thank him for his assistance but disclaim responsibility for his arteries.

The United Church and Dr. and Mrs. McClure have, once again, given great support and encouragement without interference and my extraordinary secretary-wife has been, as usual, unsung and unparalleled.

M.S.

Lindsay,
Ontario.
May 1979

McCLURE

Prologue

It was late December, 1948, and the Doctor was homeward bound across the Pacific to Toronto. He had celebrated his 48th birthday a few weeks earlier at Hankow, in the heart of China, little thinking that he would soon be flying out of Shanghai with a 'plane-load of Canadian families being summoned home by a Canadian government nervous for their safety in the face of the pending Communist take-over of North China. No government was ordering the Doctor home. No Canadian government would have had the effrontery and no Chinese government could intimidate him in the wake of the 48 years he had already survived.

He had been a child in China back in the latter days of the Manchu dynasty. He had seen criminals beheaded by broadswords when he was only eight. He had travelled the Trans-Siberian Railway through Russia and had crossed Europe when he was only ten. As a teenager in China he had seen the surge of nationalist pride and accomplishment that followed the First Revolution of 1911. At "home" in Canada he had completed high school and had graduated in medicine but had been back in North Honan as a doctor in time to be further educated by the anarchy and butcheries of the Age of the Warlords in the 1920s. As a young doctor he had learned to treat parasitic diseases in children, to mend broken femurs on soldiers and to give wounded bandits a twenty-four-hour head start over policemen. He had learned that in the interests of smooth hospital administration it was wise to make police and bandits check their weapons upon admission and that sometimes a surgeon had to carry a Colt .45 along with the tools of his trade.

The Doctor had married a Canadian girl just in time to flee from China in the face of the anti-foreign purge that accompanied the Second Revolution and the rise of Chiang Kai-shek. He had worked in Taiwan where he learned to cope with a demanding Chief Surgeon as well as with three hundred leprosy patients every Saturday morning for three years. He had studied in Edinburgh and had become a Fellow of the Royal College of Surgeons before heading back to China in the early 1930s.

In the cities and villages of the North Honan plains he had pioneered with X-ray and with family planning, had introduced the "loop" and radium to inland China and had established a rural medical system built around peasant "doctors" whom he had trained himself.

When the Japanese had invaded China in 1937 the Doctor had left his mission hospital to become Field Director for the International Red Cross along the Yellow River battlefront. When the North fell he had gone to South-West China and had organized a Red Cross trucking fleet. He had been one of the first men to drive a truck the entire length of the Burma Road. In those same mountainous regions he had been Commandant of a Quaker Ambulance Unit staffed by an international collection of gutsy and often eccentric young men and women who stuck to their pacifist principles in the midst of a violently disintegrating social system. He had struggled with bureaucracy, had learned to disarm both high explosives and bandit soldiers, and had fought cholera and the bubonic plague. He had collapsed from relapsing fever, had had eighteen bones cracked in one accident, had parachuted into the Himalayas, and had performed major surgery in jungle hospitals.

The Doctor had pioneered in post-war rehabilitation. As a master of the *fait accompli* he had established an UNRRA hospital almost a year before UNRRA heard about it. He had been well acquainted with Generalissimo and Madame Chiang Kai-shek, had met Mao Tze-tung, Chu Teh, and Chou En lai in their own remote headquarters and was known to General Stilwell, Lord Mountbatten, General Chenault, and a host of others.

Now, at the end of 1948, he had completed a year as the prime mover in the establishment of a cancer clinic in Hankow—a clinic that was the only one of its kind in Central China and that served an area containing 200 million people.

The Doctor spoke Chinese with a North Honan accent. His Chinese name was Lao Ming-yuan. He spoke English with a Canadian accent and a Chinese lilt. His Canadian name was Robert Baird McClure.

McClure was a Canadian citizen and a United Church of Canada missionary but, unlike the other citizens on board that trans-Pacific flight in December of 1948, he was not being summoned home by a nervous government. He was being summoned home by his wife. A telegram in his pocket told him that his eldest daughter was in hospital, seriously ill. He was expected home "immediately".

McClure had a vague feeling that he was leaving China for the last time but no instinct told him what lay ahead. The old days of adventure and high risk had probably gone; the days when he had learned to define "adventure" as "risk with a purpose". Common sense told him that no physical adventures could possibly top what he had already crammed into the first forty-eight years of his life! There could be, of course, adventures of the heart, the mind and the spirit.

The entire world had changed. It was now the Atomic Age. He himself was changing; his red hair had turned sand colour and was now graying; he was not quite as tall as he once was, his shoulders not as broad. But his eyes still sparkled blue and his drive was undiminished. He was middle in years but youthful in spirit. Along with energy and enthusiasm he carried another major and unconquerable asset—optimism. So powerful was the McClure optimism that he himself sometimes described it as being glandular in origin. Be that as it may, Dr. Bob McClure viewed the China years as mere prologue to the life which now lay ahead.

1

108 Strathallan

For Bob McClure the homecoming in December of 1948 was not a pre-planned, highly anticipated trip. Everything happened so quickly he had not even packed all his belongings. The telegram from Amy had informed him that their eldest daughter, 21-year-old Norah, was seriously ill in Toronto and he had responded with dutiful haste. He had taken a few clothes but had left most of his belongings where they lay, in Dr. Dalziel's house in Hankow. The Dalziels would no doubt see they were put to good use in a city that was in the grip of enormous inflation and corresponding shortages and that was overflowing with refugees moving southward in front of the Communist take-over of North China. McClure had had the good fortune to arrive in Shanghai just as a 'plane destined for Toronto was preparing to leave.

During the long hours aboard the crowded aircraft, as it lumbered its noisy, heavy way across the Pacific, McClure's mind was divided between anticipation of seeing his family and concern for the fate of the international staff back at Hankow Union Hospital. It was more than a year since he had seen his wife, Amy, and their four children. His surgeon's mind probed ahead through the Pacific night considering the things that could be wrong with his dark-haired daughter, his first-born, the one who looked so much like her mother. Thinking of things medical and surgical sent his mind hurtling back to China and to the hospital at Hankow. At least the cancer clinic that he and Dalziel had laboriously built from scratch during their year of rehabilitation work was still in good hands. If the work could be carried on, Doug Dalziel was the man to do it.*

Refueling stops came and went and hours blended into two overlapping days and then McClure was in Toronto. Inside the wretched huts that were Toronto's excuse for an air terminal he was greeted with hugs and kisses and a babble of voices. Fourteen-year-old Josephine and fifteen-year-old Patricia were bubbling over but Douglas, the quiet young man who was his son, seemed even quieter than usual and Amy was never one to be demonstrative in public. McClure wondered whether she and Doug had always been that quiet, or were they feeling the weight of Norah's illness? He wondered and worried but the terminal was no place to ask questions.

The house at 108 Strathallan had not changed. Its hardwood floors boomed to their feet as the family entered the central hallway. His father was there to meet him. The old doctor was now 92. He moved carefully, but with precision. His eyes were still bright, his mind alert, his memory good.

In the living room the Christmas tree lights were aglow. The floor beneath the tree was piled with gaily coloured, gift-wrapped packages waiting to be opened. It was, in fact, Christmas morning.

For Bob McClure, that Christmas Day, 1948, was composed of kaleidoscopic impressions. There were friends, relatives, chatter, laughter, warm handshakes, gifts, trees, tinsel, baubles and food, but McClure could not force from his mind yesterday's memories of Chinese families scattering before the shock waves of continuing war and revolution. So many people without homes, without adequate clothing, without food. Still fleeing.

They went to the hospital to see Norah and she looked pretty and fresh as one should look on Christmas Day and he was relieved because the problem was neither medical nor surgical. But, even though he was told, McClure could not quite understand what her problem really was, not today, not in a country that obviously had no problems, that was having the biggest Christmas blow-out since 1929, with its war well over, its boys all home, and its post-war economy booming. Or was that part of the problem; Norah's problem; his problem?

*Dr. Douglas Dalziel hung on in China in the face of escalating harassment until December, 1950.

The euphemism was that Norah had suffered a nervous break-down. The fact was that she was suffering from mental illness and it was a fact that was, for awhile, almost beyond the comprehension and the experience of her own father, a surgeon.

McClure's only clinical experience with mental illness had been in his undergraduate days when he had worked one summer at a provincial mental hospital in the town of Whitby, Ontario. That summer his attention had been distracted from his work by Amy Hislop, an attractive young female resident of the same town, who later became his wife. It was true that as Commandant of the Friends Ambulance Unit along the Burma Road he had had one of his own doctors go insane and had had to shepherd him out over the Himalayan Hump to India. But that insanity, which proved fatal, had been medically induced by a new anti-malaria drug. Another member of the Ambulance Unit had once attacked a companion with a microscope, but a short rest had put him right again. Incredible as it might seem, McClure—who had been through two civil wars, several revolutions, the Age of the Warlords, and the Sino-Japanese War— had had no practical experience with mental illness. He had removed forty-pound ovarian cysts, had done delicate eye surgery, had fought epidemics, had straightened TB spines, had become famous for his handling of fractures and was still a neophyte when it came to disorders of the mind. Wars, he had decided in his own clinical way, do not bring on mental illness. Affluence brings on mental illness. He felt the same way about stomach ulcers.

But what had brought on Norah's illness? Or was she really ill? Was the remedy, he wondered, merely a matter of "pulling herself together"?

Norah had been having difficulty putting the world into any context that made sense. At university Norah was a social activist. She was involved with the Student Christian Movement and was a leader in the Canadian Girls in Training programme. She pinned her political faith on the socialist C.C.F. Party and had a nagging suspicion that the really practical answers to the world's inequities lay with communism. In the summer of 1948 she had travelled to Europe, on a journey of self-discovery. It was a journey that would be taken by thousands of young North Americans in the years that followed, but the Europe of 1948 was still clearing away the rubble of war and was just moving into the initial stages of reconstruction. Norah had returned home more confused and depressed than she had gone away. "Depression" was the key word. She anguished over the plight of a society that could do to itself what Europe had done. She proclaimed herself to be a Christian-Communist and stoutly declared she would abandon neither faith. But the Toronto newspapers carried sensational stories of atrocities being committed by the rising Communist masters of China and the younger girls would be awakened at night by the sound of Norah's tears as she wept in fear for her father.

Amy had conferred with her brother-in-law, Dr. Stan Montgomery, and they had signed Norah into Toronto Psychiatric Hospital.* To bring Norah out of her acute depression, electrical shock treatment was prescribed. It was not a pleasant prospect. Amy summoned Bob from China.

McClure could understand the problem of having a social conscience. What he could not understand was that a social conscience could make anyone sick. That was what the church was all about. The world was a depressing place *only* for those who had no Christian faith. What, he wondered, were the Student Christian Movement members doing to let one of their number get into such a state as this? Where was the church? Where were the spiritual leaders of his own Bloor Street United Church congregation to let Bob McClure's daughter so slide in the faith that a mere trip to Europe could disorientate her? He himself, as a Christian missionary, had always been out of tune with the larger society around him. He rejected much of that society's values yet had always managed to function within it by clinging to the areas that reflected his values—the hospital, the mission, the Red Cross, the Friends Ambulance Unit. His single-minded drive to render immediate assistance to people in physical need had made it possible for him to go all these years without ever wrestling with the big philosophical issues of how a modern, complicated society should be organized. At first glance it looked to McClure as though a little more of the optimism that comes from a strong Christian faith could have saved his daughter from all her tribulation.

Unless the problem lay elsewhere.

*The forerunner of The Clark Institute of Psychiatry.

There was a slender young man from Montreal who was introduced to Bob as Norah's boy-friend. His name was David Busby and he turned up at Norah's bedside bearing white chrysanthemums. David and Norah had met during the summer and anyone who knew anything about hormones could see that nature's old magnetism was still operating between the sexes. McClure knew all about hormones. He had them himself. McClure asked potential-father-in-law questions of the young Busby concerning his intentions and prospects for the future. David was enrolled in Arts at McGill and was heading for Theology. He was an Anglican. McClure decided the young man's intentions were honourable and that his career prospects were negligible but not to the point of causing Norah acute depression.

There was another possibility that had to be considered. Could Norah's break-down have anything to do with being raised in a home where the father had been almost consistently absent for the last decade, and longer? McClure was already known in his daughter's church and college circles as something of a legend, a man of incredible energy and decisiveness whose name placed a certain weight of responsibility upon those who bore it. He did not know it, but there was a reverse to that coin. Among the children's peer group there were some who assumed that the McClure parents were incompatible. The father's long absences were construed as being mutually agreed upon separations—a poor man's divorce. The fact that family and close friends knew the idea to be nonsense made it no less of an irritant to sensitive daughters.

All these pressures could have been affecting Norah.

McClure thought of gathering the family around him and leaving town. They would go en masse to British Columbia. He was licensed to practise in that province and it had always recommended itself to him as a base, being so much closer to the Orient. They would go as soon as Norah could be released from hospital. They would make a new start all around. That was the remedy.

McClure discussed his proposed prescription with Norah's psychiatrist, Dr. Mary Jackson. Dr. Jackson told Dr. McClure exactly what she thought of his remedy and was not complimentary. She said Norah was suffering from a form of schizophrenia and that the cure had to be carried out in Toronto. They had abandoned electrical shock in favour of insulin shock and were making good progress. Fleeing to B.C. would help no one, least of all, Norah. Dr. Jackson assured McClure that she and the other doctors at the hospital were convinced Norah should aim at moving back into her studies at Victoria College and completing them. Only then would they feel a cure had been effective.

Dr. McClure, the surgeon, had come face to face with Dr. Jackson, the psychiatrist, and he had suddenly realized that in her field he was a layman. He also had that instinctive feeling that here was another professional who was as good at her job as he was at his. McClure experienced, for the first time in his life, that great sense of relief that comes when one can freely put one's implicit trust in a doctor. He consigned his daughter to the care of Dr. Mary Jackson and her associates and he returned home to 108 Strathallan to survey the future.

2

Doctor at Home

Bob and Amy McClure had been married for twenty-three years. Except for short intervals he had been absent for the last twelve years. Paradoxically, distance had never separated them. Now, as McClure moved in as head of the family, the reins of authority seemed to shift effortlessly from one to the other. There was never any conflict, any suggestion from Amy that he had been away "shirking" his family duties and that she had had to "bring up the children" by herself. Even so, ever since the telegram had been sent off to recall their father young Jo and Pat had been under the impression that their mother expected "things to change around here", but what exactly was to change they were not too sure. Their mother had always seemed to rule with a reasonably firm hand. And Grandpa was always there, a quiet but strong male presence, occasionally bringing them up short with, "What would your father say!". Doug, it was true, was more in tune with Grandpa than were the girls, but even now at 92 the old gentleman could still unravel the mysteries of mathematics and somehow or other cause their homework to make sense. And their mother had always read Dad's letters out loud at the dinner table. They were strong letters. Even though Bob McClure had been away from his family he had never been totally absent.

McClure moved easily back into the niche that had always been his and from the portals of 108 Strathallan he took stock of the new scene.

In the early months of 1949 it was an interesting world that McClure looked out upon from the vantage point of Toronto.

There were no soaring communication towers in those days and
no skyscrapers that a later generation would consider worthy of
the name but Toronto boasted the largest hotel in the British
Empire, a hotel that then, as now, proudly clung to the title
Royal. The city also claimed the tallest building in the British
Empire and that building was, reassuringly, a bank. The city
fathers were preparing to build a subway from Front Street to
Eglinton Avenue and no one was really blanching at a prospective price tag of some forty million dollars. There was a certain
euphoria in the country as a whole. The young men and women
who had returned from service in World War II and who had
seized the heaven-sent opportunity for a university education
were now graduating from the crowded halls of venerable institutions such as the U. of T., McGill and Queen's and from the
newer upstarts like Carleton, in Ottawa. The new graduates
were enthusiastic and optimistic. Their country had entered *the*
war as a callow agricultural youth and had emerged as a young
industrial giant. They knew that the *per capita* efforts of Canadians in the recent trials had been as great, if not greater, than
that of any other people on earth and they were looking ahead
now to the creation of the brave new world. The majority of the
graduates fervently believed that at last Sir Wilfrid Laurier's
maxim that the twentieth century belonged to Canada was finally about to be verified, and they turned a blind eye and a deaf
ear to Ottawa where the energetic Minister of Reconstruction
and Supply, the Hon. C. D. Howe, was busily selling off the
national assets to the highest bidders, most of whom were
American.

McClure had never cared much for the Liberal government
in Ottawa but his antipathy had been more against Mackenzie
King than against the Party. Mr. King had retired the previous
autumn and Prime Minister Louis St. Laurent was now piloting
the country towards a general election. It seemed pre-ordained
that "Uncle Louis" and the Liberals were going to win. Only a
few radicals were wondering out loud why the "emergency"
measures of wartime controls were still in effect. Besides, there
were exciting things in the wind. The Speech from the Throne in
January had promised an investigation into the feasibility of the
Canadian Broadcasting Corporation moving into the exciting
new medium of television. Surely a new world was coming—
a world in which men would communicate as brothers, and
work toward a stable, peaceful society.

For Canadians in 1949 the signs of international co-operation were everywhere. In March, Newfoundland, amidst much goodwill from all sides, left the British colonial orbit and joined the Canadian federation as its tenth province. In April, the Minister of External Affairs, "Mike" Pearson, a man who symbolized brotherhood and goodwill, signed Canada into the North Atlantic Treaty Organization. In the middle of April, southern Ireland became independent as the Republic of Ireland. At the end of April, India, already independent, became a republic but elected to remain within the British Commonwealth, mankind's largest non-political political institution.

Even farther east more changes had been underway. Burma had become an independent republic outside the Commonwealth. Ceylon had become independent as Sri Lanka, within the Commonwealth. The French were still clinging tenaciously to Indo-China but the Indonesians were struggling towards independence from the Dutch.

McClure's thoughts often turned towards China. By the Spring of '49 Generalissimo Chiang Kai-shek had withdrawn to the island of Taiwan and the Kuomintang troops on the mainland were engaged in obviously hopeless rearguard actions against Mao Tze-tung's Communists. Word came through mission channels that the Generalissimo's takeover of Taiwan had been preceded by the extermination of many of the island's political and cultural leaders. Apparently the purge had been carried out by an enthusiastic governor, without the Generalissimo's direct consent, but it saddened McClure to think of the Generalissimo and Madame trying so desperately to maintain the fiction that they governed China. He had met them first in 1938 when they were two beacons of morality and hope. Now the old warlord and his remarkable lady were clinging to decayed illusions and championing a degenerate cause.

The ordinary Canadian was interested in China in that spring of '49 but was more interested in the Middle East where the new state of Israel had recently been formed.

Canadians were emotionally for Israel. Canada had formally recognized and supported Israel's application for membership in the United Nations. In Canadian eyes the United Nations was the great hope for mankind. Somehow or other the UN would sort out any puzzling moral dilemmas. Canada would support the UN and in the meantime Canadians could get on with the more interesting challenge of building an affluent society.

It was in the context of this perhaps naive and somewhat euphoric Canada of the late 1940's that Bob McClure made a seemingly major decision. He decided to plug into the new society. With Norah ill, with old Dr. McClure living to such an incredible age, with two children in university and the other two approaching university age, it seemed obvious that his place now was at home. The mission fields of the Third World would have to get along without him for a few years. Having made that decision he moved quickly to remove himself from Mission Board salary and to get himself installed in the medical profession in the city that some folk still called "Hogtown" and that others still referred to as "Toronto the Good".

McClure had no hurdles to cross in being licensed for practice in Ontario. He had complied with all such requirements years ago. His F.R.C.S. from Edinburgh was universally recognized. He had acquired an F.I.C.S.* back in the Thirties. It was true that among the high-powered medical fraternity of Toronto neither set of degrees stood like a beacon the way they had in the interior of China. It was also true that Toronto doctors were not particularly impressed by his pioneering achievements in the Orient. It did not impress them that McClure had introduced spinal anaesthesia to Taiwan at the same time it was being introduced to Toronto. The majority of them neither knew nor cared about his pioneering efforts abroad with cancer treatment and family planning. His achievements teaching Chinese "quack" doctors were not appreciated. In Toronto, McClure was just another doctor. There were some observers who thought he would find the experience an interesting lesson in humility but that was a cynical view.

McClure decided that trying to build a private surgical practice was out of the question. A specialist's practice depended upon general practitioners referring their surgical cases to him. People in the know estimated that it took about ten G.P.s to support one surgeon. Some estimates went as high as twenty. Even if cases were referred to McClure there would still be the problem of breaking into the establishment to gain access to hospital beds. The process could take years. McClure was not

*Fellow of the International College of Surgeons.

established. He had not been in the medical queue ever since graduation, becoming known to his peers. He had not been on the staff of any major teaching hospital. To McClure there was something bizarre about the whole system. He had been accustomed to working in a society where the need was great and where the doctor served. Here the doctors seemed to compete. There was nothing particularly sinister or unusual about the medical profession in Toronto any more than in any other North American city but, although it was not exactly a closed shop, the profession certainly looked after its own. Those doctors who had hospital privileges did not demonstrate undue haste in voting to extend the same privileges to newcomers. The entrenched members of the profession talked about the need to protect standards. Cynical outsiders wondered if the protection had more to do with income and status.

McClure's problem was solved for him. He was invited to join a group practice. The idea of group practice was one that was just beginning to catch on. It had been experimented with in various countries. Not far from Toronto the Oshawa Clinic was drawing a great deal of interest as a model. To McClure it made good sense that several specialists and a G.P. should pool their talents under one roof, refer patients to each other and share the costs and, presumably, the rewards. The obvious efficiency of such a system should benefit both doctor and patient. Such a clinic was functioning in Toronto and included an internalist, an obstetrician, and a general practitioner. There was also a surgeon but he was moving to Saskatchewan. The clinic had its own laboratory and X-ray facilities and a pharmacy. When McClure joined as the new surgeon he was walking into a practice that was ready made.

The clinic served a largely immigrant section of Toronto's rapidly increasing post-war population. To McClure it was a worthy challenge. Not only was he going to be practising in an under-privileged area of the metropolis, he was going to be working almost exclusively among New Canadians, whose need would be great.

McClure entered upon the new job bubbling with enthusiasm and proclaiming to family and friends that group practice in Toronto was going to be the most challenging thing he had ever tried.

One of the first illusions to be shattered was that of efficiency. What may have been efficient for the patient was not so
for the doctor. McClure lived in north Toronto. The clinic was on
Bathurst Street. The clinic doctors had privileges at Toronto
Western Hospital and at Toronto East General, some six miles
apart. It soon became apparent to McClure that he was spending
more time in transit between home, clinic, and the two hospitals
than he was spending with patients. It seemed absurd. And
then he discovered that he was also spending more time in
consultation in his office than actually putting his skills to use in
an operating room. Moreover, in his opinion, far too many of the
patients being referred to him were not in need of his services.
His "quack" practitioners in China had screened patients more
thoroughly than did his fellow M.D.s of the clinic. It seemed to
him that many patients were being referred to him simply because the patient wanted the reassurance of actually talking to a
surgeon. From where McClure sat too many of those patients
were merely suffering from being too fat, or too thin, or from
hypochondria.

McClure's reaction was understandable in terms of his past
experience. In the mid-Thirties in China his Hwaiking Rural
Medical System had been functioning in such a manner that
only the cases of real need turned up in his office. Those of
McClure's fellow missionaries who had been his patients knew
that one had to be in a bad way to merit much of his sympathy.
Now, when he would spend an hour in consultation with someone who was merely neurotic he would be chafing inwardly
because he knew that in that same sixty minute period in China
he would have helped three or four people who were in serious
need. As for actual surgery now, in Toronto, with access to two
major hospitals, he was doing in a month what he would do in
a day in a well run mission hospital.

McClure became irritable and frustrated. Although still in
the prime of life and physically fit the man who, a few years
before, had been able to bicycle a hundred miles and finish the
day doing heavy surgery was arriving home exhausted at the
end of a Toronto working day.

Then came the final disillusionment.

McClure began to suspect that the clinic was not being
administered in a completely honest manner, that all its income

was not being accounted for and that distribution of the profits was not strictly equitable. He was convinced that some private patients were being permitted to pay cash at discount rates by foregoing receipts and that those transactions never showed up on anybody's books. He reluctantly came to the conclusion that the clinic was set up to make the most profit from group practice rather than to give the best service from group practice.*

By the summer of 1950 McClure had had enough and was once again looking abroad. His eyes fell upon India.

The Canadian Presbyterian Church had established a mission field in Central India in the 1870s. Part of this field had been inherited by The United Church of Canada in 1925. Medical work was an important part of the Canadian thrust in India. Now, in 1950, the field was badly in need of male doctors. The Secretary of the Board of Overseas Missions of The United Church of Canada was delighted to know that Dr. Bob McClure had had enough of his secular experimentation and was ready once again to work with the church. Machinery was put in motion to elicit from the Indian Church an "invitation" to McClure to join the staff of the mission hospital at Ratlam, in Central India.

The Board Secretary† had been delighted by McClure's decision but had not been surprised. Amy McClure was not particularly delighted but neither was she surprised. She knew that it was merely a matter of time before her husband rebelled. By now, the summer of 1950, Norah had made a full recovery and had graduated from university. Doug was living at home but was studying for his B.A. at Victoria College. The two younger girls were still teenagers and at home. Grandpa McClure was still a responsibility. Once again it appeared that Amy would be left to tend the hearth while McClure went foraging.

Amy raised no arguments. There was no way she was going to put shackles on Bob McClure. Besides, Central India, although remote, looked reasonably peaceful when compared with most of the other places her husband had served.

And then a cable arrived for McClure.

*The clinic and its founder have both passed on.

†The title "Board Secretary" will appear frequently. Its use represents any one of five people—Rev. David Gallagher, Rev. Floyd Honey, Rev. Jesse Arnup, Rev. Roy C. Webster and Associate Secretary Miss Wilna Thomas.

The wire was from a former member of the Friends Ambulance Unit. He was still associated with the Quakers and was working among Arab refugees from Palestine. The telegram said that there was a great job for Bob McClure doing surgery at a Church Missionary Society (C.M.S.) hospital on the Gaza Strip. The hospital was serving refugees and was functioning under a United Nations' contract. The same message assured McClure that if he accepted the job he would not be a well paid UN employee but would be a C.M.S. missionary and suitably underpaid, with money deducted at source for room and board. The idea of being able to serve refugees by practising surgery in a situation as unstable as the Middle East was too much for McClure. He approached the Board Secretary and suggested a change in plans.

The arrangements with India had not yet been completed and since long experience had demonstrated that no such arrangements were ever completed speedily the United Church agreed to second McClure to the British Anglicans in Gaza for a period of one year. They also agreed to supplement his salary to keep it in line with the Board's standards so that his family could survive in Toronto.

In October of 1950 McClure headed for Egypt en route to the Gaza Strip. It was to be, so everyone thought, a temporary detour on the main journey to India but it was a detour that was destined to escalate in length and that would lead, within three years, to Bob McClure making a decision to part company with The United Church of Canada.

3

Egypt

In October of 1950 a ten thousand ton Norwegian freighter nosed her way out of New York harbour. In addition to her customary crew and her miscellaneous cargo she was carrying five passengers. Her rambling journey took her south-east for several days and when she finally struck across the Atlantic she was in warm water and under balmy skies.

During the early watches of the night one of the passengers could usually be seen on deck with an inexpensive naval-surplus sextant in one hand and a notebook in the other. He would take celestial readings then retire to his cabin and transpose those readings onto a chart and eventually would go to the bridge to compare his findings with those of the ship's navigator. This apprentice navigator was Bob McClure. He was following what had become a lifetime habit of seizing any opportunity to add an additional skill to his already formidable repertoire. By the time the ship reached the eastern Mediterranean he was plotting her position accurately to within two miles.

Navigation was a skill that could be of use to McClure only if he were to take to sea in a small boat or decide to cross a desert on a camel. Neither possibility could be ruled out but he was now fifty years old and such adventures were unlikely. He was acutely aware that the big adventure facing him now was one of the mind. Only a portion of the vast experience he had gained in China would be applicable to the Middle East. He would have to learn a new language and adapt to a different culture. Thanks to the hours spent contemplating the rhythmical complexities of the stellar skies and struggling with the abstract world of mathematics, by the time McClure arrived at his destination he had managed to change mental gears. He had unwound his mainspring, rewound it, and had charged his batteries. He stepped ashore feeling he was truly launched into the second half of his life; into the second half of the amazing twentieth century. McClure was looking with optimism into the future. He stepped ashore at Alexandria, a seaport of the ancient world. He caught a train and headed inland along the Nile. His destination was a hospital in Old Cairo. Here, in Egypt, he was to spend a brief period of acclimatization and orientation before continuing on to the Egyptian protectorate known as the Gaza Strip.

The Harper Memorial Hospital in Old Cairo was run by the Church Missionary Society of England, the same missionary organization that was luring McClure to Gaza. The Egyptians, who had trouble with some of the sounds in "Harper Memorial" shortened the name to the more euphonious "Harmel". The Harmel Hospital was an institution of approximately five hundred beds. It was divided into men's wards and women's wards with a courtyard separating them. It had an enormous out-patient capacity, being able to handle several thousand out-patients a day. This capacity was made possible by a large staff of qualified Egyptian doctors. McClure was to work in both the men's hospital and the women's hospital.

His Chief in men's work was Dr. Fletcher Lunn, from England. His Chief in the women's work was Dr. Charlotte A. Stuart from Northern Ireland. Dr. Stuart's medical qualifications were impressive. She was fluent in Arabic. She had developed great insight into the minds of Arab women. In addition she was associated with the C.M.S. hospital in Gaza. Here, in Cairo, Dr. Stuart was McClure's chief mentor in preparing him for Gaza and McClure considered himself privileged.

Bob McClure had never been in a country quite like Egypt. He was accustomed to the teeming multitudes of the Orient but he was not used to those multitudes being concentrated in one ribbon of settlement along one major river. Nor had McClure ever seen anything to equal the intensive farming methods used by the Egyptian peasants whose fields were watered by irrigation channels from the Nile. They made the irrigation-wise peasants of North Honan look like amateurs. But here the irrigated lands only stretched about two miles on either side of the mother river. Beyond that was the desert.

The past was everywhere. What was more, in a powerful, cultural sense, part of it was *his* past. That was a feeling he had never experienced in China. Old Cairo itself was said to be the very community to which Joseph and Mary had fled to save the infant Jesus from the swords of Herod's troops. An island not far from the hospital was said to be the place where Pharoah's daughter plucked the baby Moses from the bulrushes. On the tip of that same island was the oldest Nilometer, a measuring stick by means of which men had measured the seasonal rise and fall of the River Nile for three thousand years. They had kept detailed records which existed now just as they had in the days of Joseph, son of Jacob. McClure could well believe that Joseph, after perusal of centuries of those records, had been able to prophesy seven fat years followed by seven lean years. Joseph had capitalized on the Pharoah's dreams in order to drive home his predictions but his predictions were soundly based upon scientific observation. McClure could believe, too, that during the time of the biblical plagues the waters of the Nile had indeed run red. The public urinals in Egypt still ran red; red with blood. It was a result of a disease called bilhartzia.

Bilhartzia was a disease of the bladder caused by a parasite which penetrated through the skin. A few minutes swimming in a canal was a sure way to guarantee infection. It seemed to McClure that at least 98 per cent of the Egyptian peasantry had bilhartzia. Every two or three years the victims would go for a cure. The cure involved a series of intravenous injections administered over a period of ten days. It was because of bilhartzia that the Harmel Hospital out-patient department was so large.

McClure's interest in bilhartzia was not so much in the disease itself as in the great reservoir of genito-urinary complications that arose from chronic infection by the disease. One of these complications was cancer of the bladder. McClure had spent many years battling cancer, particularly the ones that attacked females—cancer of the breast, the uterus and the cervix. What intrigued him now was not the presence of cancer of the bladder but the fact that it was virtually the *only* cancer.

While McClure was amazed by the general lack of cancer he was equally amazed by the prevalence of hernias. It seemed to him that every Arab had or once had a hernia. The men had them in the groin, and sooner or later on both sides. The women had them midline and femoral. When he inquired about this phenomenon he was told, only half facetiously, that the presence of a hernia, past or present, was a good way to tell whether a person was a true Arab. It set McClure to puzzling over the mysteries of the geography of medicine and to wondering impatiently why researchers had not put more time and money into exploring the global picture. Why had he seen so much cancer in China and so little here? Why so many hernias here?

There was another mystery.

In his gynaecological work in the women's hospital he was seeing no unwed mothers. Their absence was a social phenomenon that was much harder to believe than the medical ones. He sought an explanation for this phenomenon and was informed that any girl unfortunate enough to become pregnant out of wedlock ran the risk of being taken for a ferry ride across the Nile by an uncle or a brother. The ferryman would be bribed to turn his back at an appropriate moment and the girl would "fall" overboard. The crocodiles would do the rest.

McClure had expected Arab women to be in a repressed situation and this story only confirmed his expectations. His opinion, however, was gradually revised. A few years later, looking in retrospect, he would come to the conclusion that the women of Egypt, and of Cairo in particular, were among the most urbane and sophisticated in the Arab world. In hospital, whether as visitors or patients, the Egyptian women were refreshingly uninhibited and would discuss operations and ailments, complete with sexual detail, in a frank outspoken way that would have reduced their Western sisters to blushing confusion.

Harmel Hospital was situated in an area of the city that was inhabited by Coptic Christians, members of the oldest of all Christian sects. The Coptic Church had broken away from Rome in the fifth century in an effort to remain orthodox and to escape Roman heresies embodied in the Nicene Creed. The Copts rejected the doctrine of the Immaculate Conception as well as that of the Trinity. For them, Christ was totally divine. As had so often happened in the past Bob McClure found himself marvelling at the richness and diversity of beliefs that went by the name "Christian".

He also marvelled at the Moslem world around him. Several times a day the whole society would come to a halt while the devout would kneel and pray toward Mecca. The less devout and the non-Moslems would stand by, patiently waiting for the end of the hiatus.

There was another religion in evidence and one that McClure had already learned to treat with respect. It was Nationalism. McClure had witnessed several revolutions in China and the leaders of all had been high priests of Nationalism. The root causes of those revolutions were commercial exploitation and poverty. But there had also been the mortifying affront of foreign domination and, inevitably, when the revolutions had come, the faithful had rallied around the banner of Nationalism. Nationalism had become both creed and battle cry.

When it came to tasting revolution McClure was a connoisseur. He looked with a practised eye at the society around him. Never before had he seen such contrasts of rich and poor side by side as he saw in the streets of Cairo. Never before had he seen the well-to-do so oblivious of their impoverished brothers. Although the heavy hand of the foreigner was more benign than it had been in China it was, nevertheless, still there. The smell of revolution was in the air. He wondered that anyone could miss it.

Intimations of revolution did not prevent McClure from wallowing in the pleasure of a six-week stint as Chief of the Harmel Women's Hospital while Dr. Stuart was away. He worked in the operating room almost twelve hours a day and enjoyed every minute of it. An internationally renowned specialist, Dr. Charles McIntosh Marshall, who was visiting Egypt accepted an invitation to demonstrate his techniques to the Harmel staff. One of his major contributions had been the development of a technique for doing low segment Caesarean sections. McClure was elated to be able to learn it from the master himself.

As was usual with McClure, as the surgical load increased his spirits soared. "I do not think I have ever had so much major surgery before with so few accidents," he wrote to the Board Secretary. "With all the heavy work we have only had two post-operative deaths in four months and each of those was easily understandable." He said he was heading for Gaza by the end of March and for India at the end of the year. "When thinking of India in December I hope to either buy a small boat and sail to India from Suez or else go overland by bus through

Iran. Both can be done and there is nothing original about them but it would serve to make life more interesting without any additional expense. The only expense one can think of that might crop up would be funeral and they have those very cheap in Moslem countries."

The Board Secretary was not amused and told McClure that if he persisted in the small boat plan to "come home and kiss your wife goodbye". He alerted the Indian Church to be prepared for a McClure onslaught "toward the end of this year".

In the meantime, his Egyptian apprenticeship having been completed, Bob McClure was off to Gaza.

4

Among the Philistines

In the spring of 1951, McClure found himself in the city of Gaza which was already an old city when Samson, the Israelite strong man, was captured by the Philistines. It was in Gaza that the mighty hero, blinded and enslaved, had felt his strength returning and had pulled the temple of Dagon down upon himself and upon his tormentors "*so the dead he slew at his death were more than they which he slew in his life*". Samson was one of the great raunchy heroes of the Old Testament who had rather fascinated McClure in boyhood days. McClure had never closely questioned the strong man's motivation. Samson was an Israelite and a hero and that was that. Now, however, he took a look at Gaza and the surrounding country and also took a fresh look at the Old Testament. It became difficult to know who were the heroes and who were the victims. Had Samson been a hero or a monumental public nuisance? When "the Spirit of the Lord" used to come upon Samson he would do strange things, like paying off a gambling debt by killing thirty innocent men to get their wealth. The Lord moved him so mightily that he slew a thousand Philistines with the jawbone of an ass. It was only after Samson had come whoring into Gaza and had then carried off the city gates that the Philistines really put their minds to the task of laying him to rest and *that* had a messy ending for everyone. It was quite possible to glory in Samson's prowess, to writhe in sympathetic agony as his eyes were gouged out, and at the same time to feel deep sympathy for the Philistines. In that story, as in so many of the Old Testament chronicles, everyone wound up being victim. McClure peered out upon Gaza and the Middle East and wondered if anything had really changed.

The little stretch of land known as the Gaza Strip was no more than twenty-five miles long and about five miles wide. It was a stretch of fertile soil, bordered on the east by the sand sea of the Negev Desert and on the west by the salt-water sea of the Mediterranean. Its borders were political rather than natural and until recently had stretched another fifteen miles or so farther north, along the Mediterranean coast, toward the city of Tel Aviv.

In 1947, when the United Nations had decided to divide the State of Palestine* (a British Protectorate) into a political Siamese twin, one-half to be Jewish and one-half to be Arab, a coastal strip of Palestine surrounding the city of Gaza had been designated to become part of the proposed Arab portion. The Jewish residents of Palestine endorsed the proposal but the Arabs, like the mother who came to Solomon for judgement, refused to let the baby be split. The Arab reaction to the partition plan was violent and swift. Within the next twelve days they slew 79 Jews within Palestine. The Jews and the British police killed 32 Arabs.

That was neither the beginning nor the ending but it was the point at which the Arab-Israeli conflict erupted into open and almost constant violence. As the date for the official birth of Israel had approached, the British began to withdraw from many towns and villages and Arabs and Jews fought to be first to fill the vacuums. Among the Arabs were regular soldiers from Syria and Iraq.

The State of Israel was born on Thursday, May 14th, 1948. The following day six Arab armies attacked Israel. They belonged to Iraq, Lebanon, Syria, Transjordan, Egypt, and Saudi Arabia. During the next ten days the combined Arab armies almost achieved their avowed purpose of driving the Israelites into the sea. Then, in a military come-back worthy of Joshua, Gideon and David, the modern Israelites turned the war around. By January of 1949 they had not only recaptured the areas the United Nations had designated as theirs, but they had extended Israel's borders across the Negev Desert to the Gulf of Aqaba in the south and up the Mediterranean coast to Lebanon in the north. As for the parts of Palestine that were to have become the new Arab state, the somewhat shrunken "West Bank" area of the Jordan River was occupied by Transjordan,†

*"Palestine" is from a Greek word meaning "Philistine country".
†In 1950 the amalgamated territory was renamed *Jordan*.

and Egypt was occupying a somewhat shrunken "Gaza Strip".

The rest of the world was under the impression that Palestine had vanished. It had not. The West Bank was annexed by Transjordan but Egypt never annexed the Gaza Strip. Egypt, the refugees and the original inhabitants still thought of the Gaza Strip as being Palestinian.

Nor had the *people* of Palestine vanished. The United Nations estimated that during 1948 close to three-quarters of a million Arabs had fled from their Palestinian homes. The morality of the United Nations putting an existing state on the chopping block as a kind of offering of atonement for the crimes of Christendom would be debated for the next thousand years, but there was no doubt about the immediate effects. By the time McClure arrived in Gaza, the tiny Strip was sheltering about a quarter of a million Palestinian refugees. They outnumbered the original inhabitants by almost two to one. There was a barbed wire fence and minefields, manned on both sides by armed patrols, running along the northern and eastern borders which were shared with Israel and along the southern border which was shared with Egypt. Egypt was the occupying power but had no desire to let many refugees into Egypt.

The hospital McClure came to had been established by the Anglican Church Missionary Society in 1891. It had been started in a rented house. In the beginning most of its patients were Arab pilgrims on the way to Mecca. The hospital had soon grown into permanent quarters. During World War I it had been occupied by the Turkish Army which thought a hospital would be good cover for an ammunition depot. Although it was a British Anglican Mission it had been shelled by the British Army which somehow managed to separate church from state long enough to miss the ammunition and blow the second storey off the main building. The hospital had struggled through a period of repair and rehabilitation during which time, so it is reported, the O.R. roof leaked rain into abdominal operations. In spite of its problems, by 1929 the "English" hospital, as the locals called it, had established a firm reputation for surgery under two generations of doctors named Sterling. From then until a few months before McClure's arrival the hospital had been under the administration of a colourful Anglican missionary, Dr. Alfred Ridley Hargreaves.

As a doctor, McClure had never before followed a predecessor quite like Hargreaves nor, as a missionary, had he ever entered a society quite like this Moslem one. It was no accident that the Anglican missionaries in the 1800s had opted to concentrate on medical work. The followers of Islam were a very tough-minded people. They had never taken kindly to the thought of anyone being turned away from Islam. In the 14th and 15th centuries both the Franciscans and the Dominicans had tried to convert Moslems to Christianity and had given up. Even St. Francis of Assisi could make no impression. Their failure was easily understood because death was the penalty for success, and it applied to both missionary and convert. The same penalty still held unofficial sway when McClure went to Gaza in 1951.* Moslems would attend Christian schools. Moslems would attend Bible study classes. But Moslems would not convert and they took unkindly to any suggestion that they should.

The Church Missionary Society had had to move cautiously. Much of its effort, and indeed of the efforts of English and American missionaries in many parts of the Middle East, had been to convert Christians to Christianity (a statement that has less paradox in it than meets the eye). The C.M.S. reasoned that the best contact with Moslems was through medical missions, where the practising was more important than the preaching. It was the medical people who could move into the community and break down social fences between Moslem and Christian. It was the medical people who stood the best chance of establishing bonds of friendship with their patients. Even so for any missionaries who like to count the heads of "the saved" the ground was discouragingly sterile. In 1938 an Anglican Arab doctor who had worked in the Gaza hospital for 16 years was asked: "Do you know of any Moslem in Gaza who was converted and baptized and stood openly to confess his faith?" The answer was instructive. "No." He then softened it. "I heard of one who said he wanted to be Christian but never really came through."

By 1951 there had been little change in the score but it had not been for lack of effort on the part of Dr. Alfred Ridley Hargreaves, McClure's surgical predecessor.

*There have been changes since then. Today the penalty is more likely to be ostracism and/or harassment.

Hargreaves was a doctor of deep faith and strong convictions who, as his years of service had progressed, had become obsessed with the urge to propagate the gospel. The "infidels" were everywhere and he did not hesitate to identify them to their face. He found it almost impossible to participate in conversations with medical colleagues without launching into a theological dissertation. At least one Moslem medical student developed the ploy of saying, "Oh, but I've been a Christian for years", in order to move the conversation along to matters medical. Today Arabs delight to paint a verbal picture of Dr. Hargreaves arriving in the fields, his arms laden with copies of the Bible, calling out like some prophet of old as he distributed the Word to plough-men and planters. Some say that such was his absolute faith that he would operate on cases that were surgically hopeless, leaving it all in the hands of the Lord. Too often it turned out that God, although a mighty healer, was not adept at surgery. If the picture is remotely accurate it was the devout doctor's good fortune that his evangelical tactics made no open converts. His health was also preserved by the simple fact that the Arabs considered him to be bordering on insanity.

McClure arrived in Gaza knowing very little about his surgical predecessor. He had the distinct impression that the C.M.S. intended it should be that way. Now the administrative duties were in the hands of a young British doctor, an Edinburgh graduate, Oscar Barry. Barry was a tall, round-faced, gentle medical man with a compassionate heart and a retiring nature. Dr. Barry was to continue as Administrator. McClure was to be Chief of Surgery.

The hospital compound sat on one corner of a major square in the city of Gaza. The square had a bazaar-like atmosphere, its sides lined with open vendors' stalls, its centre constantly alive with the movement of people, donkeys, bicycles, camels, carts and trucks. Arab men strode by wearing hooded burnous or white flowing *galabia,* followed by Arab women wearing black robes, their features hidden by dark veils.

The compound itself was hidden behind high walls. The gateway that opened toward the city square was large and generous. Three small postern gates gave onto a back alley. One was so discreetly hidden that many hospital employees did not know of its existence. When the out-patient department was open and during visiting hours the main gates would stand wide and inviting. During off hours one would state one's business to the gatekeeper before receiving grudging admission. The gates and walls indicated no unusual inhospitality or insecurity on the part of the mission. Even private homes had gates and walls. They were indigenous to the East.

Inside the main gate the vista was unexpectedly expansive. To the left of the gate stood a large, square, two-storey house with a two-storey verandah supported on colonnades. This was the doctor's house and was set aside for McClure. In the centre of the compound, patients on their way to O.P.D.* or to Admissions walked past a flower garden bordering a pond. Fish swam in the pond. In the far corner of the compound stood a large, two-storey building that housed the 95 beds of the wards. This building had been strangely located with its back almost toward the entrance so that it was only as one circled the building to the other side that the arches of a pillared verandah came to view. Here, embraced by the verandah on one side and by a corner of the compound wall on two other sides, was a quiet courtyard where relatives and friends could await news from the O.R. On the fourth side of this courtyard was a building housing the O.R. itself, the doctors' examination rooms, and the Anglican chapel. This building, too, had a private courtyard where O.P.D. patients could sit and wait. Alone and incongruous in the centre of this courtyard stood two battered Greek columns. To the uninitiated those two columns were merely a sign that some missionary had yielded to a burst of misdirected archeological fervour. To those who knew history they were a constant reminder of Greek influence. They were also, in a way, a symbol of Gaza's resilience. Gaza had been destroyed by Assyrians, Babylonians, Macedonians and Israelites. Always it had sprung back. By the early 6th century A.D., when the Roman Empire had disintegrated and Europe was reverting to tribal barbarism, Gaza had become a prominent centre of Greek culture and of Christian learning. In that period the Western world's great centres of higher learning were Athens, Alexandria, Constantinople, and Gaza.

Just over the back wall of the compound was an ancient Greek Orthodox Church. It was so old that the floor of the nave

---

* As in Vol. 1, "O.P.D." means the "out-patient department", and "O.R." means the "operating room".

and chancel was now twelve feet below street level. It was said to have been built about 400 A.D. and to have been in constant service ever since. If that were true, its congregations bridged the gulf of the centuries and had survived the Moslem conquest and outlived both the Mameluke and Ottoman empires. It was just possible the Moslems were not the only tough-minded folk around.

McClure felt completely at home.

5

From Catastrophe to McClure

In Gaza they had a name for the partition of Palestine. They referred to it as "The Catastrophe". After any catastrophe whether it is brought about by flood, fire or war there is a period of chaos when food, clothing, shelter and medical supplies are badly needed. Governments move to fulfil these needs but governments move slowly. Even the Red Cross, as McClure had discovered in China, could get trapped by government red tape. The relief groups that appeared to be able to move the most swiftly were church-related agencies. One with a truly enviable record was the Quaker relief organization known as the American Friends Service Committee. In 1949, after "The Catastrophe", it was the Quakers who were the first to come to the relief of the displaced Arabs in the Gaza Strip. It was the Quakers who led the way in providing food, clothing, and tents and helped organize "temporary" communities. There were two hospitals in Gaza City itself. One was a civil hospital, large but poorly equipped and understaffed. The other was the C.M.S. mission hospital. It was smaller, reasonably well equipped and better staffed but without the financial resources to cope with a sudden surge of destitute cases. The Quakers helped the C.M.S. underwrite the costs of the hospital so it could rise to the current challenge. It was a Quaker who wrote to Bob McClure and told him he was needed in Gaza.

The Quakers were followed quickly by the International Red Cross and other volunteer agencies giving time for the United Nations to set up UNRWA (The United Nations Relief and Works Agency for Palestine Refugees). UNRWA took over as the major relief agency and by the time McClure arrived in March of 1951 the C.M.S. hospital was in many respects an arm of UNRWA. Of the hospital's 95 beds 85 were designated for refugee use. The civil hospital referred all surgical and complicated obstetrical cases to the C.M.S. hospital. Because the civil hospital had unreliable X-ray equipment and no laboratory facilities it also tended to refer its most serious medical cases to the C.M.S. people. UNRWA subsidized both hospitals so that all medical and surgical treatment for refugees could be free. Because the original inhabitants of the Strip were now inundated more than two to one by refugees, and because they were all trapped in a tiny area that was not economically viable, no one at the C.M.S. hospital or at UNRWA quibbled over the definition of a refugee. McClure had finally landed in the midst of what amounted to a missionary surgeon's dream: great need for his services, reasonable facilities and, for the patients, free treatment.

It was an unusual situation. The Church Missionary Society was still responsible for the administration of the hospital. The C.M.S. provided four senior staff who were missionaries and were paid missionary salaries. One of these four was McClure. Everyone else on staff, although under C.M.S. supervision, was an UNRWA employee and was paid according to more generous UNRWA scales. The resident surgical intern was being paid more than the Chief Surgeon but was very decent and made a habit of taking his Chief out for coffee.

Of the four career missionaries only two were of C.M.S. background. McClure was on loan from The United Church of Canada and Dr. Oscar Barry had until recently been serving in a faith mission in Ethiopia. The two C.M.S. missionaries were Miss Julie Dawber and Miss Beatrice Coggan. Miss Dawber was a nurse of wide experience who had served many years in Harmel Hospital in Cairo. Miss Coggan was a nurse and an evangelist. Two characteristics that the British missionaries had in common were inbred meekness and English accents. Both acted as subliminal irritants on the irascible Canadian. Moreover, Miss Coggan had such strong ecclesiastical leanings* that she tended to be more evangelist than nurse, a tendency that was not only a cardinal sin in McClure's professional book

*Her brother eventually became Archbishop of Canterbury.

but one that he feared could jeopardize the hospital's relationship with UNRWA which was not in the business of propagating the gospel. Miss Coggan also had a tendency to keep a close eye on the staff in the interests of maintaining a somewhat puritanical atmosphere. In China, McClure had dubbed her type "salvation sisters" and he objected to the gloom that accompanied the theology. A dispassionate assessment of the four missionaries, however, suggests that the three British carried a larger cross in the one Canadian than the Canadian carried in the three of them combined.

Miss Coggan may have had good reason to fear that the hospital staff might not at all times preserve the decorum she would like to see associated with an Anglican institution. Medical people are not noted for their inhibitions and the rank and file of this C.M.S. hospital were a lively crew. The ward sisters, the student nurses, the maintenance men, the admission clerks, the pharmacy staff and several junior doctors were all Arabs and one of the Arab doctors told McClure that if you saw an Arab sitting lost in quiet contemplation you could be sure he was thinking about Allah or sex, but if an Arab woman was sitting contemplating it was unlikely she was thinking about Allah.

The arrival of McClure in missionary circles where he was not known usually had an unsettling effect. He did not conform to any pattern except his own. He smoked, ate roasted watermelon seeds, rode a bicycle, and wore shorts on any and every occasion, just as he had done in China. The fact that he had weaned himself from cigars to a pipe merely changed the profile, not the atmosphere. No old China hand, seeing McClure in Gaza, would have given his appearance a second thought but a quarter of a century after his departure Arabs would still describe in detail the pipe, shorts, seeds and bicycle. To evangelical missionaries McClure looked dangerously like a bad influence. He was a paradox and the more pious the missionaries the more confusing they found the paradox. McClure would come out of O.R. clad in the familiar shorts, an underwear vest, blood spattered apron and rubber boots, his hair tousled and glasses askew like a wrestler fresh from the ring, and if cold tea was not instantly available he could be heard all over the compound bellowing for it. The same man in the chapel on Sunday could deliver a most challenging and inspirational address. He could tolerate the most outrageous language and put up with quite unorthodox behaviour from anyone who was competent in their work. A nurse could be scorched one minute in the flames of his wrath only to be bathed an hour later in the warmth of his personality. McClure disliked Bible-thumpers but was becoming more and more convinced that his reason for being in the Third World was not because he was a surgeon but because he was a Christian surgeon. In China he had once outraged members of a fundamentalist mission hospital, who had prayed overly enthusiastically in the O.R. before an operation, by announcing: "I may not be good but there is no need to call on the Almighty before I even start." Now, in Gaza, he instituted regular morning prayer in the O.R. before the first operation of the day. With the first patient already on the table, the nurses, the orderlies, and McClure would stand for a moment with bowed heads and pray to Allah to guide them in the footsteps of Christ the healer.

In a society where everything stopped five times a day for Moslem devotions, including public transportation, that little prayer in an operating room seemed like a small and almost insignificant affirmation of Christian motivation. The operating room, however, was at the absolute centre of McClure's professional world.

It was in the operating room that he put into practice in Gaza a philosophy that had motivated him for many years. He had been long convinced that good staff morale hinged on everyone, no matter how humble, having upward mobility. He was convinced that most members of the human race were happiest when they were training to improve their capabilities. It was not a matter of attaining affluence, security or even status. It had to do with inner satisfaction.

McClure's attention fell upon three somewhat unusual Arab orderlies, Mahmoud Lkotub, Mohammed Elabaddsi and Ahmed Hammo. Mahmoud and Mohammed were tall and rather gentle. Ahmed was short, broad, enormously strong and very excitable. None of the three had had much formal education but they had all been in the British Army during World War II serving as orderlies in the Royal Army Medical Corps. They had learned most of their English, complete with accent and curses, from Australian soldiers on the deserts of North Africa. Their unmissionary contribution to hospital conversations could cause pain to someone like Miss Coggan but could induce an almost mellow nostalgia in McClure. They reminded him of the sturdy group of Chinese medical assistants in Hwaiking who had been through the tempering fires of World War I and had then weathered the Warlord Era with him in North China.

McClure felt that Mahmoud, Mohammed and Ahmed, although excellent orderlies, were capable of branching out. The operating room was large. It contained two operating tables, separated by a low screen. With two surgeons at work, along with the efficient O.R. nursing staff, the facility was capable of handling twenty-five operations a day with as many as a dozen being major. The need was certainly there. When McClure arrived in Gaza there was a three month waiting list on hernia operations alone. It was a list he was determined to shorten. But there was one bottle-neck in the O.R. and it was the administration of anaesthetics.

McClure set about training the three Arab orderlies as anaesthetists.

The general anaesthetic most frequently used was pentathol, injected into the veins. Open ether, poured onto a face mask, was still in use. In hot, tropical countries, particularly during the dry season, ether evaporated quickly and it was sometimes difficult to put a patient under, so pentathol was used to put them under and ether kept them there. The students were taught to be properly cautious. Unlike North Americans, many Arabs preferred not to be rendered unconscious and would elect for surgery under a local anaesthetic or a spinal. Even in these cases, however, it was desirable to have an anaesthetist constantly at the head of the table to watch the patient, to take blood pressure readings at five-minute intervals, to chat to him to maintain his confidence, and to warn the doctor of any signs that the effects of the operation were moving outside the bounds of the anaesthetized area.

Mohammed and Mahmoud took to their training with alacrity but McClure decided that effervescent Ahmed would be better suited as an O.R. sterilizer and cleanup nurse. The day came, however, when muscular Ahmed won his medals as an anaesthetist.

The operation was a hernia. McClure was the surgeon. The patient was a young Arab man of powerful physique. McClure was impressed by the way so many of the men, even from the camps, were keeping themselves in excellent physical shape by constant exercise. They went in for weight-lifting, workouts on the horizontal bar, wrestling, and soccer. It was obvious that this patient was one of the physical culture enthusiasts.

The patient had had a pre-operative narcotic and was drowsy. He had been shaved, sterilized, draped, and strapped to the table. McClure made the injection of local anaesthetic and after a few moments tested the area for sensation. The patient claimed he felt acute pain. McClure signalled the anaesthetist who applied the face mask and began to pour ether. After a few minutes the combined effect of narcotic, local, and ether had the desired effect and the patient drifted off into apparently deep sleep. The team closed in, the anaesthetist by the patient's head, McClure by the patient's side and the scrub nurse by McClure's elbow. Only Ahmed, sterilizer and cleanup man, stood well off to one side.

McClure extended one gloved hand. A scalpel was slapped into it. He made a bold incision.

The patient uttered one tremendous yell and sat bolt upright, snapping the restraining bands the way Samson had snapped the Philistine ropes. He twisted around, seized the anaesthetist in a mighty grip, and rolled off the table.

On the floor there was a brief flurry of sheets, blood, and wrestling O.R. gowns, while the surgeon, scalpel in hand, stood above the melee like an astonished referee. It was at this point that Ahmed hurled himself into the fray. He executed a manoeuvre that turned the patient on his back on the floor. With his left arm Ahmed transferred swiftly to a wrestler's headlock and with his right hand he swept the face mask and ether down from the head of the table. "By Allah!", said Ahmed, administering a most liberal amount of ether accompanied by Australian unprintables, "You're going under!"

The patient subsided peacefully into deep slumber. Soon, with everything re-sterilized, the operation was completed.

McClure quietly congratulated himself on having had the foresight to train Ahmed who was obviously, like himself, a man of action.

6
Rabbits

On his days off McClure liked to go for long bicycle rides, occasionally with friends, more often by himself. Sometimes he would drop into one of the crowded, sprawling, tent cities that were refugee camps. He met an UNRWA engineer from Istanbul, Vart Korlu, who was building permanent houses and installing water and sanitation systems. Engineering projects that improved public health fascinated McClure just as they had in his youth. He and Korlu struck up a friendship.

Sometimes McClure would ignore the camps and cycle peacefully down the main road that ran like a spine the length of the Strip. At first, to his Canadian eyes, the countryside looked severe and desolate. There were signs of acute poverty and of wartime desolation. The earth was brown. Grass was sparse and coarse. This strange sandy soil was not like the loam of Ontario that covered itself with rich green grass. He learned not to look at the ground but to look at the growth; the shrubs, the vines, the trees. Each time he pedalled that road the Strip looked greener, more fertile, more lush. His eyes were adapting.

The road took him past grape orchards with their gnarled vines hanging low to the ground, past miles of citrus groves laced with irrigation ditches fed with water lifted by Diesel-driven pumps, past small almond orchards whose petite trees would bloom pink in the spring or stand daintily leafless in fall and "winter". The road took him past Bedouin camps with strange fences of wattle and brambles and dark people in dark robes looking withdrawn and remote as they tended grazing camels and herds of goats. UNRWA reported that 30,000

Bedouins had left the nomadic life of the Negev Desert and had taken sanctuary on the Strip where many of them still remained aloof from the camps and roamed restlessly to and fro in what was both prison and oasis.

The road was flat, paved, and almost straight; a cyclist's delight. For long stretches at a time it took him beneath the tunnel-like arches formed by acacia trees that flanked the highway, their branches almost touching overhead. It took him past Khan Yunis Town and Khan Yunis Camp; Khan Yunis, where the whale was supposed to have disgorged Jonah. It took him to Rafah Village and to the border of Egypt where barbed wire, gun emplacements and armed Egyptian sentries marked a very definite end of the line.

Often, as he returned in the twilight, he would see shadowy figures moving off through the citrus groves toward the not-too-distant Israeli frontier. One could hear no sounds other than the steady beat of the irrigation Diesels. He had seen silent shadowy figures like them before—guerrillas moving out in the Chinese twilight as the Japanese withdrew into cities for the night. And now, as then, he knew that the next morning there would be new patients in emergency; men suffering from injuries that they and their friends would try to pass off as agricultural accidents but which looked all too familiar to the surgeon from Honan. He knew that sometimes the raids were made in desperation to plunder parts from Diesels that the raiders had themselves once owned. He also knew that equally often the raids were efforts to create terror among the Israelis.

He had always felt that the shadowy figures of North China had been venturing forth under the shield of justice and right. Here, among the Palestinian refugees, he knew it was not that simple. Both sides were right and both sides were wrong. The political complications were truly mind-boggling. The wounds, both physical and spiritual, were hideous. He was learning that the Arabs were proud, emotional, and totally unwilling to deviate from what they considered to be a right action. He was also learning that "right action" could be barbaric beyond imagination or civilized beyond belief.

One day McClure, a young Arab student doctor named Antone Tarazi,* the hospital pharmacist and the lab technician

* Now a leading neurosurgeon in Jerusalem.

were cycling south towards Khan Yunis. They had a swim on their minds and picnic lunches on their handle-bars. En route they stopped to admire a small farm that belonged to the Tarazi family but was being tended by a hired man. The Moslem farmer, hardly more than a youth, was courteous and friendly and pleased to see his master's son. He showed them a new orchard of citrus trees and date palms. The planting had been done a few years ago, and the irrigation ditches had been dug and the pumps installed. For several years now there would be a latent period when he would have to tend to the trees and the irrigation without seeing any signs of fruit. In the meantime he had managed to save enough money to go into the wool business for himself. He showed them, with great pride, two fluffy angora rabbits. He was also starting a poultry business on the side. In a small pen he had three miserable looking chickens. The young farmer was working, gratefully, for the Tarazis, but his personal long-range hopes were pinned on the two rabbits and the three chickens.

The visitors returned to the house where a large skin bag containing camel and goat's milk hung from a sheltering tree branch. Each man in turn gave it a dutiful punch as he passed by, thereby helping to churn the family's butter. The farmer's wife was on hand to greet them. She was even younger than her husband and in her arms she carried a two-month-old baby. When she saw McClure she showed great excitement and pleasure and announced to her husband that this was the *hakim**** who had delivered their child.

The young couple's pleasure was not only obvious it was embarrassing. The husband explained that he had wanted to thank the *hakim* but had not as yet had the opportunity. The *hakim* had seen to it that he was presented with a fine son. The *hakim* and all his friends were to stay for lunch.

McClure, Tarazi and the others explained courteously but firmly that they were carrying lunch and were headed for the seaside. They appreciated the invitation but tendered a firm refusal.

The young man insisted that there could be no refusal, but to no avail. The hospital party went on its way.

They had their lunch and their swim and by mid-afternoon

*Doctor

were on their way back toward Gaza. As they neared the farm they saw the young farmer standing patiently beside the road. He ceremoniously waved them in through the gateway. They had no choice but to enter. They were shown to seats on a small outdoor patio in the shade of a tree and there they were served the meal they thought they had politely refused.

The meal began with some simple delicacies and home-made pickles. Then the young wife proudly brought out the main course. It was served in a dish that was more the size of a tub than a bowl. The dish was lined with a type of thin pancake and was filled with a mixture of boiled rice and tender cooked meats. McClure could see the rabbit pen and the chicken coop. Both were empty. The tender meat in the great bowl was that of two angora rabbits and three chickens. McClure ate with tears in his eyes and a restriction in his chest. Truly this was hospital-ity carried to the point of insanity. It was very Arabian.

It was no secret that the Arabs were proud, stubborn, and emotional; qualities that seemed to be evenly distributed among the various Arab nationalities of the Middle East. That same autumn, 1951, even playboy King Farouk of Egypt gave vent to some feelings of pride. When Britain proposed a new Middle East defence alliance under a joint command the King took a look at the proposed members of the alliance. There were the disliked Turks (they had dominated Egypt for almost three centuries); there were the hated French (they were still clinging to Algeria, Morocco and Tunisia by force of arms); there were the pampered Iraqis (whose leaders considered Russia to be the principal threat and not Israel); there were the meddling Ameri-cans (who had delivered, if not fathered, Israel); and there were the British (who were finding it increasingly difficult to do anything for or to anybody without being resented). Farouk not only rejected the British proposals but tore up an Anglo-Egyptian treaty of 1936 and proclaimed himself King of the Sudan. Fedayeen terrorists attacked British installations in the Canal Zone. Egyptian workers withdrew from British bases. From there on the political pot went into a slow simmer.

In the meantime Gaza was reminding McClure more and more of North Honan. "Lots of gunshot wounds..." he wrote to the Board Secretary, "we have just had three in a row, two of rifle bullets and one of Mills bomb wounds of the abdomen with all sorts of tearing to pieces inside the patients, and all three have made good recovery in the past ten days." These injuries had nothing to do with Canal Zone tensions. They were just part of the general atmosphere. Farouk's surge of national pride and the resulting flare-ups did not even disrupt train service to Gaza and the Egyptian postal service continued to function with amazing efficiency. But an Islamic festival shut Gaza down for two full days; days which were followed immediately by the Moslem Sabbath. During these religious observances there was an Israeli raid. "There were 8 wounded brought in," McClure reported, "and we worked most of the night in the operating room. One bloke lost his leg at the knee. The rest all look good . . . The people injured in these things are never the ones directly responsible for anything. It puts up our average for this month to well above 'one good deed a day' in the gunshot line."

Against this background it was not particularly surprising one day to hear the sound of a gunshot not far from the hospital compound. McClure heard the shot through the clinic window which opened out onto the central lawn and fishpond and gave a view toward the main gates, which at the moment were opened for clinic hours. He recognized the sound as that of a heavy handgun but since there was only one shot he conjectured that it heralded neither an Israeli raid nor the beginning of a war down in Egypt. He reasoned that if the gun had been fired to any purpose he would soon know about it. He was not kept waiting.

No more than a few minutes elapsed before a group of men hurried through the compound gate. They were carrying a long shutter-type door that had been hastily removed from a shop front. These doors, with their lift-off French hinges, were Gaza's emergency stretchers. The victim on this one was a man wearing the Arab's traditional long, white, flowing *galabia*.

The bearers burst directly into the midst of McClure's clinic (it was a gynaecological morning) and deposited their burden in front of him.

The victim was Arab, male, very tall, and probably very handsome with a large handle-bar moustache. At the moment he was a ghastly grey colour and in deep shock. In addition to the long white *galabia* he was wearing a very military-looking Sam Browne belt and on his left chest was a display of war ribbons. On the right side of his chest the clothing was torn and covered with blood. Blood was still pumping out into the folds of the *galabia* and soaking down onto the floor.

McClure could find no pulse. Blood-flecked foam was forming around the man's lips. He was breathing at extended intervals with a long heavy heave of the chest, but with each heave there was a loud sucking noise at the wound. He was a "whistler".

A swift inspection showed powder burns on the back of the *galabia* and a small hole. McClure, thanks to Chinese warlords, assorted bandits, Japanese invaders, and this post-graduate course in Gaza, had become a connoisseur of wounds. This looked like the work of a 9 mm Luger. The man had been shot in the back from close range and the bullet, on exit, had removed a section of the lower right chest leaving a hole large enough to insert a drinking tumbler. It had also removed a portion of the right lung. The whistling sound was the air rushing into the punctured chest cavity.

With a whistler rule number one is to stop the whistling. McClure, and the surgical resident who had arrived on the run, hastily and firmly applied a large field dressing. They administered a double hypo of morphine and started plasma running. McClure knew it was a lost cause and that the man had very little time left. They took him into a ward and installed him in what the staff called a "bed of honour". In a twenty-four bed ward it was one of two fully screened beds just inside the doorway. Those beds were easily accessible and bodies could be removed without upsetting the other patients.

There was not much more to be done. McClure put the resident in charge, with instructions to administer plenty of morphine and to keep the plasma running. He was to call McClure before the Arab died so that McClure could be at the bedside. In the event of legal complications McClure did not want the resident to be held responsible. McClure then returned to the women waiting patiently in the clinic. It was a little after mid-morning.

At 12:30 noon the resident and the ward nurse reported that the patient was now breathing steadily, the whistling had stopped and his pulse had become strong enough that it could, occasionally, be detected.

At 4:30 the patient was mumbling a few words. His pulse was now regular, although weak. Relatives were standing by the bedside.

By 7:00 p.m. the intravenous had been stopped. The patient had been able to talk, briefly, to selected visitors who by now had departed. One of them, however, had left a pistol under the patient's pillow.

The weapon had been detected by an alert nurse who immediately reported it to McClure. Knowing that the relationship between an Arab and his gun could be very special she had been sensitive enough not to touch the weapon or even to let on that she knew about its presence. The diplomatic problem of confiscating it was all McClure's.

At 10:00 McClure went on his nightly rounds intending to pay special attention to the Arab's pillow. McClure had been through this exercise many years ago, but with a difference. At that time he had been supported by his scrub nurse, Loving Lotus, who carried a Colt .45. Loving Lotus had been somewhat unique among mission hospital nurses and the object of their attention at that time had been a Chinese bandit who was willing to show humility in front of a six-gun. The present circumstances called for a more refined approach.

McClure found the patient awake and in amazingly good condition. He was an even bigger man than had at first been apparent. On a six-foot bed his feet were sticking out a good four inches. McClure pulled a stool to the bedside and sat down for a chat. The man spoke quite good English. His name was Mustapha.

Mustapha's war ribbons were British. He had been an armoured car pilot with the Long Range Desert Patrol, a unit that worked behind Rommel's lines during the North African Campaign of World War II. The shooting this morning had had nothing to do with the politics of the Middle East but was merely the result of a private feud. McClure had heard about Arab tenacity in carrying out vendettas and was interested in Mustapha's story. He was also interested in the old style Mauser automatic that he, McClure, was gently working out from beneath Mustapha's pillow while the latter talked.

As soon as he had a firm grip on the weapon McClure explained that since the hospital was a Christian mission hospital it was, in some ways, very conservative and did not approve of guns in the wards. He assured Mustapha that he was not confiscating the weapon but merely putting it in safe keeping and that it would eventually be returned. He admired the handgun and promised that even if Mustapha should not recover from his wound the heirloom would be handed over to Mustapha's son. McClure, a foreigner, had no intention of intruding into the cultural traditions of an Arab family. On the other hand, he explained, it would be unfortunate if Mustapha, in delirium, were to shoot up the ward.

Mustapha seemed to find this argument quite reasonable.

McClure then explained that in the morning they would be bringing a portable X-ray to the bedside in order to make certain there was no stray lead still inside Mustapha's chest. Judicious use of the X-ray would also tell them if Mustapha had tried to hide any extra ammunition. He might as well hand it over now.

Mustapha voluntarily surrendered two extra clips of Mauser ammunition.

Within a few days Mustapha was able to vacate the "bed of honour". By the end of three weeks he had made a miraculous recovery. One Monday morning while making routine rounds McClure told Mustapha that he was ready for discharge.

Arabs say "no" by means of a strange click of the tongue and the word *lah*. Mustapha tossed his head now and uttered the most emphatic click and *lah* that McClure had ever heard.

It was not unusual to have a patient resist discharge. The beds were comfortable. The service was good. The food was wholesome. Everything was free and the patient's family in the camp was drawing full rations from UNRWA. There was something about Mustapha's click, however, that indicated more than the usual reluctance. McClure told the matron he was keeping Mustapha another day for observation.

An hour later, having completed his rounds, McClure returned to Mustapha's bedside.

"Mustapha, I think we'd better have a little talk."

"Yes, *Hakim*. I agree. Might we walk in the garden?"

The male ward opened onto the pillared porch. The porch gave onto the quiet courtyard that ran the length of the building. It was a pleasant place for a stroll.

McClure was surprised when Mustapha, instead of explaining why he did not want to be discharged, launched into a war story.

"With the Desert Patrol, *Hakim,* we were often many days far away from base. Sometimes we would run out of food, but there are rabbits on the desert. Did the *hakim* know there are rabbits on the desert?"

"I have heard so."

"You can find their holes. Many holes in clusters. We would back an armoured car to one hole and put a pipe down from the exhaust. We would then stand at the other holes with Sten guns." He shrugged and waved his hands expressively. The picture was not too difficult to understand.

"*Hakim,* do you think that was sporting?"

"No. But efficient."

"Oh, very efficient. But *Hakim,* Mustapha is now the rabbit. For many days there have been three men waiting by the main gate. I am told they change, but there are always three. I am also told they are armed."

"What can I do about it?"

"If you announce in a loud voice in the ward that Mustapha is to be discharged then you might as well shoot me yourself. But if you say 'Mustapha, you are not ready' and then let me out quietly at night, all will be well."

"But you say they are there all the time."

"The compound has three small back gates that are always locked. One is very private."

"You know a great deal."

"Allah has shown me much mercy. Will you?"

"Yes."

"I will go tonight, *Hakim.* And remember, bring my gun. It is, as you know, a family heirloom."

That evening McClure made his ten o'clock rounds. Mustapha was sitting on the porch enjoying the cool night air.

"Care for a walk before you turn in?"

"Thank you, *Hakim.* I am honoured."

The two men strolled for a quarter of an hour back and forth in the courtyard. Mustapha took the opportunity to unburden himself.

"*Hakim,* I have been watching and thinking much these last weeks. You and your people have been very good to me. You are all very good to everybody. I watch the other patients in the ward. The nurses show much love to everyone. I have been thinking that if this is the Jesus way it is a good way."

"Well, it has advantages over blood feuds."

"Our feuds are insane." Mustapha sounded quietly angry. "The head of one family kills another. The victim's son kills the killer. His son kills in return. It goes on for years. Blood, death and vengeance without meaning. No one can even remember how it all started." He walked for awhile without speaking. *"Hakim,* I prefer the Jesus way."

McClure made no comment but the thought crossed his mind that they had made a convert. Converts in Moslem territory were hard come by.

Their nocturnal stroll finally carried them out of the ward courtyard and into the O.P.D. courtyard. This courtyard, nestled even farther into the back of the compound and away from the wards, was totally deserted this time of night. They strolled past the ghostly sentinels of the Greek pillars, disappeared quietly into deep shadows and in a few moments came to a small postern gateway closed by a solid door. McClure unlocked the door. He gave Mustapha the "heirloom". For a brief moment the two men stood in the dark shadows of the back alley.

"May your Jesus guide you and may Allah protect you," said Mustapha, and he was gone. McClure stepped back inside. He locked the door behind him and re-crossed the courtyard. He walked briskly through the central gardens to his own quarters. He had a warm evangelical missionary feeling inside and it should have warned him. The few times he had had it before it had always been a prelude to disaster. He was going up the steps of the front porch when he heard three loud shots from the street beyond the main gate.

McClure called for help, opened the main gate, and hurried out into the street. There were three Arabs there, each lying in a pool of blood. All three were armed. With help from other members of the staff he got them into the hospital. They had been thoroughly shot by an old Mauser, but were not dead.

It required great effort and an all night session in the O.R. but the men lived. During the weary hours of early morning an exhausted McClure found himself wondering if it was all really worth the effort. He thought of the young farmer's determination to show gratitude and now of Mustapha's determination for vengeance. He was beginning to get the distinct impression that Arabs gave vent to their emotions on a somewhat excessive scale.

7

Beginnings

McClure took every opportunity to visit refugee camps even though all those needs that would once have been the concern of missions—camp clinics, public health, nutrition, schooling—were being handled by UNRWA. He walked the sandy streets of the tent cities and talked to anyone who spoke a little English. He became good friends with Vart Korlu, the engineer, and got to know other members of the UNRWA staff. There was a nurse from Holland, Johanna Boender, who was setting up the UNRWA public health clinics and who came to the hospital to teach public health to the student nurses. Johanna liked to play cards and would regale McClure and the nurses with stories of midwife sorties out into the desert. Many people, even Arabs, considered Bedouins to be dangerous and untrustworthy but Johanna had made solitary pilgrimages into their mysterious camps and had been treated with great courtesy. The Canadian Red Cross was sending beautiful layettes and Johanna gave these to Bedouin mothers. One family reciprocated. They came quietly into town, a small delegation bent upon repaying a debt in kind, and tried to give Sister Johanna the baby.

By the very nature of his work McClure was more locked into the confines of an institution than he ever had been in China but through the eyes of his UNRWA friends he expanded his impressions of the refugee world around him. To McClure, the observer, it seemed that the great mass of refugees, who had undoubtedly suffered terribly, were now actually receiving better health care and better schooling than they would have received in their former conditions. But they were trapped in the Gaza Strip. Simply being healthy and educated was no passport to another country, another life. The refugees could not enter other countries, even Arab countries, unless they had a skill those countries needed. But what skills were needed? And how could the mission help? McClure could have been content doing surgery but he asked himself these questions and having asked them he looked for answers.

There was one area where the mission was doing a great deal. It was running a school of nursing. All the students were refugees. Some of them were from Gaza camps but many had received permission to come from camps in Lebanon and Jordan to train at the C.M.S. Gaza hospital. At the moment most of these girls were Christians. (The Moslems still believed in the segregation of the sexes and did not take kindly to the idea of a Moslem girl working on the body of a man.) Once a refugee girl had graduated as a nurse the immigration doors were miraculously opened into many countries. A nursing diploma was a good visa. There seemed to be no equivalent for young men.

McClure thought about what he had seen in Cairo, looked around him in Gaza, and asked questions of visiting doctors and nurses. He came to the conclusion that the hospitals of the Middle East had a pressing need for well trained laboratory and X-ray technicians. The mission hospital in Gaza, even though it had a modest laboratory, had had no lab technician when McClure arrived. He had immediately recruited the assistant pharmacist, Salama Shahin, a twenty-one-year-old Palestinian who was intelligent and keen. McClure became Shahin's private instructor and for many months spent an hour and a half out of every working day closeted with Shahin in the lab teaching him the mysteries of making cultures, cutting sections, preparing slides and interpreting the amazing world that lay beneath the lens of the microscope. By September of his first year, with Salama Shahin as his right-hand man, McClure enrolled ten refugee youths in a laboratory course. It was a small beginning but an important one. Lab work violated no traditions and could be taught to both Christians and Moslems.

Before long Salama Shahin was able to shoulder much of the teaching and McClure branched out and established an X-ray course. The laboratory, however, exerted a tremendous pull on McClure. He could not keep away from the microscope.

He had a meticulous desire to verify the findings of his fledgling technicians but it was more than that. He was teaching a medical science but more and more when he himself looked through the microscope he found himself pondering philosophy. Philosophy can be defined as "the study of the truths underlying all knowledge" and the older McClure grew the more truth he saw through the high-powered lens and it embraced order and intelligence and mystery beyond mind. That truth was as large as the universe and could be mounted on a tiny piece of glass. Even the voluble McClure could not articulate his feelings. With his students he stuck to science but for himself religion, philosophy and science met at the point of focus beneath the lens of the microscope. He was a surgeon, but the operating room was a mere repair shop; the laboratory was a chapel.

McClure's one-year term was almost ended when the Chief Medical Officer of UNRWA seized the initiative and with hearty approval from the C.M.S. asked the United Church to extend McClure's leave of absence by another year. The United Church gave in, but reluctantly.

It was significant that the initiative had come from UNRWA. In McClure's opinion the C.M.S. was getting tired. Like many missions it found itself in the post-war world weary and over-extended. The weariness concerning Gaza may have been caused in part by Gaza having been a singularly poor place for evangelism. Whatever the reason, McClure found himself writing to England to ask the C.M.S. why they did not sell the hospital to a mission that might be more interested in the area. Much to his surprise a friendly answer came back telling him it was a good idea and to investigate the possibilities! He started sending letters to Canada and the States trying to interest some church, any church, in the fact that a fully-equipped, well-staffed, UNRWA-financed mission hospital in a Moslem country was up for sale: "Here is a mission field 'going begging' that is a very nice little project for an all-round Christian attack... combining medical, educational and evangelistic work... It would be particularly ideal for Anglicans... I wonder if it would interest the Canadian Church Mission?"

He wrote to The United Church of Canada: "I should like to see our Board... taking on Gaza as a mission effort. I think we could do well to have one Canadian mission in Moslem territory."

He cast a lure toward the Quakers: "The Quakers did marvelous relief work when they were here and today there is not an eye that would not sparkle among the refugees if you mention the work the Quakers did here. They all ask, 'Can't those Quakers come back again?' "

There were no takers. Everybody seemed to be overextended already. His own United Church was still desperately trying to get doctors and other personnel for the field in India. It had already gone the second mile by extending McClure's stay in Gaza. Now he wanted them to take over the whole show!

McClure could understand the reluctance of the United Church. He felt the vacuum should really be filled by Canadian Anglicans or American Episcopalians. The traditions of the Gaza mission were all Anglican. In the meantime, he had more pressing projects than selling a hospital. He had to sell lab technicians.

July, 1952, found McClure taking a salesman's holiday and travelling by slow train and bus westward along the African coast toward Libya. Back in Gaza he had ten graduate lab technicians. In order to find them employment he had decided to make some personal contacts and the newly independent Kingdom of Libya seemed like a good place to begin.

He passed through places with names that had become world famous during World War II; Mersa Matruh, Tobruk, Dherna. The war in Africa had come to an end nine years ago, but the desert was still littered with the wrecks of armoured cars and tanks. It seemed that every small harbour along the coast had one or two wrecked warships as local landmarks. In Tobruk, McClure deviated from his main purpose long enough to go snorkelling in the harbour. In Benghazi he made his salesman's contact.

By the time McClure returned from Libya he had found jobs for all members of the first graduating class of lab technicians.

"If I do little else with my life," McClure reported, "this job will have been very worthwhile."

He had no way of knowing it, but "very worthwhile" was an understatement. Within the next few decades graduates of the lab courses begun by McClure would gravitate to hospitals and clinics all over the Arab world. There would be a proliferation of well-equipped, well-staffed labs in the little Gaza Strip itself—a large central lab for UNRWA, four labs at UNRWA clinics, two labs at government hospitals, and the original lab at the mission hospital. In several Arab countries the men supervising the labs would be from McClure's original group and would still consider themselves "McClure boys". In Gaza the Superintendent of the central UNRWA lab would be student number one, Salama Shahin, and UNRWA would be training lab technicians, many of them girls. But in 1952 all McClure knew was that he had made a good beginning.

In the third week of July, McClure passed through Egypt on his return to Gaza. He was lucky. A few days later and he would have been in the middle of the Egyptian Revolution.

On July 23rd, General Mohammed Neguib and Major Gamal Abdel Nasser ordered King Farouk to abdicate. It was a request that was backed by the Egyptian army. Farouk stalled for two days, waiting for the British army to rescue him. It was a game that did not interest the British. On July 26th King Farouk left Egypt aboard his royal yacht. Film of his departure was shown in the newsreel cinemas of the world and millions of people marvelled at the restraint of the revolutionaries who had permitted the king to depart, not only with his life but with his wealth. Egypt was now a republic.* One more country was affirming its nationhood in the chaos of the Fifties and was attempting to evolve through revolution.

*Not officially proclaimed as such until June, 1953.

8

Behind the Veil

McClure was intrigued by the whole Moslem society but to him the role of women in that society was particularly puzzling. As a doctor he had an enduring interest in gynaecology, obstetrics and family planning but he found that Arab women were very reluctant to come to a male doctor. He countered that by quietly opening a sterility clinic. Soon word of mouth passed the news around. Childless women began attending in great numbers to discover the reasons for their sterility. The clinic had considerable success and the barriers began to crumble. Through his patients and through social contact with Moslem associates McClure began to glean a variety of impressions.

In McClure's opinion Arab family life was, in general, of a very high order. It was also full of paradox. The more McClure saw the more conflict he found with his own preconceptions founded on Western and Christian culture. Many Moslem men had several wives and often their polygamous marriages were *happy!* Divorce could be incredibly easy but divorce statistics were very low compared to the soaring statistics of Christian North America. Arabs often married while very young and most marriages were arranged, but participation by both families, together with a well-drawn marriage contract, gave great support to the new couple. The more McClure saw the more he was impressed.

It was a social system in which the only ones guaranteed to be losers were the unwed mothers. That was a guaranty McClure hoped to break. One day he had his chance. It was presented to him during an afternoon O.P.D. clinic when an

Arab woman, who had been holding back to the end of the line, turned out to be both single and pregnant. She was about twenty-one. Her name was Fatimah*.

"Hakim," she said, "I do not wish to die."

"You are in good health. We'll try to see you have a healthy baby."

"Hakim, I do not wish to die."

McClure remembered the description of the trip across the Nile. He wondered what the Gaza equivalent might be. The only other person in the room with them was Sister Alice, a Christian nurse from Syria. He could see that she, too, was worried.

"We can do an abortion here in the hospital," he said, "but it will be difficult to keep it secret. It could ruin your reputation."

"Hakim, I do not—"

"Yes, I know."

The young woman was showing no signs of panic but McClure could hear both the nervousness and the determination in her voice. It was obvious that the Gaza punishment, however performed, was as ruthless as that of Egypt.

"There is something we can do. Every month I have a few patients that I refer to Cairo for special medical attention. We send them by train. There is nothing unusual about it." He went on to explain that in her case there would be one variation in procedure. Her ultimate destination would not be a Cairo hospital but a certain Catholic convent. McClure knew the Mother Superior and knew she would help. At that convent Fatimah would have her baby. She could leave it there for adoption. She would return to Gaza cured of her "medical ailment".

"Hakim, how many people will know?"

"Here, only Sister Alice and myself."

Fatimah agreed to the arrangement.

As it turned out it was not an easy conspiracy to control. McClure soon realized that he had to circumvent the censorship authorities. Most letters leaving the Strip were censored by four separate intelligence groups—military, police, civil, and postal. Some people never sealed their letters, hoping that way to preserve the envelope and gambling on the final censor having the courtesy to stick the flap down. A member of the office staff

---

* A pseudonym.

said he was trying to invent an envelope with a zipper. One thing was certain, a letter to the Mother Superior concerning Fatimah would be the equivalent of making an announcement over the rooftops of Gaza from a minaret.

McClure paid a visit to the local Roman Catholic priest and put a hypothetical case to him concerning the discreet transfer to Egypt of an unwed mother and correspondence concerning the same. The priest, a Syrian like Sister Alice, was equal to the challenge. He was in the habit of sending a courier to the Bishop in Cairo twice a month carrying money and correspondence of a financial nature. The priest explained that if he were involved in this hypothetical case and were wanting to send information to the Bishop to relay to the Mother Superior he would not write it in English or in Arabic, but in Latin. McClure's Latin was adequate for prescriptions but not suitable for clandestine ecclesiastical correspondence so he took the priest into his confidence and they composed the missive.

Within ten days a reply came back from the Mother Superior. It, too, was in Latin. In order to keep correspondence to a minimum she gave detailed plans which were to hold unless McClure cancelled them. The next Thursday Fatimah would board the train at Gaza at 7:30 a.m. That train was an express. It would pick up passengers in Gaza and across the Sinai Desert but once across the Suez Canal it would make no stops until it pulled into Platform No. 2 at Cairo Central Station at 4:00 p.m. Two European Catholic nuns would be walking up and down Platform No. 2. They would be conspicuous because of their incredibly wide Dutch hats. Fatimah, who would be totally unidentifiable because of the heavy veil that all Arab women wore in Gaza, would simply fall in behind the two nuns and follow them. As soon as the nuns realized they were being followed they would go to a taxi. Fatimah was to follow them into the taxi. From there on everything would be completely under control. It was all very clear.

McClure sent Sister Alice to give Fatimah the news and to give her one additional set of instructions.

Late Wednesday evening, following her instructions to the letter, Fatimah arrived at the C.M.S. hospital in Gaza City. She was feigning severe abdominal pains. The nursing sister on duty in the women's ward was Sister Alice. The doctor on emergency call was Dr. McClure. There was only one problem.

McClure had been side-tracked by a genuine emergency and an enthusiastic Arab intern reached Fatimah first. Fatimah's acting was so good that before McClure appeared the intern had her scheduled for an abdominal operation. The Chief Surgeon had some smooth explaining to do concerning this particular abdominal crisis. He drew upon his many years of vast experience and convinced the intern that *this* crisis was of a nature that should be put under observation for a few hours. He consigned the patient to Sister Alice in the ward.

The next morning McClure drove Fatimah to the station himself and gave her a train ticket. He saw her to the door of a train compartment segregated for women only. In those days, in that part of the Moslem world, not even a husband would have dared step across the threshold *into* the compartment. Fatimah departed for Egypt and McClure returned to the hospital, feeling saintly.

A few days later he received a terse message from the Mother Superior. All it said was, "When is your woman coming?"

McClure could never decide where the weak link had been in the carefully crafted chain of communication. He had absolute faith in Sister Alice, the local priest, and the Mother Superior. Was one of the intelligence agencies actually sophisticated enough to censor the Bishop's courier service? In Latin? Or had the young Arab intern been too astute for his Chief? All that seemed certain was that even Fatimah had not made it across the Nile.

Fatimah's fate was already past history when McClure returned from his salesman's jaunt to Libya. He had barely settled back to work when he was confronted with a surgical challenge that was totally new to him. The challenge was presented by a Bedouin father from the camp at Jabalia who brought his daughter to McClure and said that his daughter was meant to be a boy. He had heard that the *hakim* performed miracles. How about turning his daughter into a son?

McClure examined the girl. Certainly she had many masculine characteristics. McClure sent father and daughter away saying that he had some thinking to do. Part of the thinking involved the fact that the Bedouin father was now quite elderly and although he had had many wives he had only the one offspring. In that part of the world the offspring being a girl was a cultural tragedy for both father and daughter. It was worth thinking about and so were the surgical problems. McClure began to read. For several days his spare time was devoted to studying all the literature he could find that dealt with sexual anomalies and the corrective surgery.

He called father and daughter to another consultation. A series of operations would be required but corrective surgery could indeed be done. It seemed best for all concerned that such a personal operation be done quietly with little fanfare.

In 1952 a "sex-change" operation was not part of the normal repertoire for any surgeon let alone a missionary surgeon. That was the year that the news of Christine Jorgenson's remarkable surgical conversion set the Western world buzzing with a sensationalism that would not have appealed to the Church Missionary Society or to The United Church of Canada. The operation McClure was contemplating was one that most missionary surgeons would have side-stepped.

McClure went ahead. The operations were a success.

The moment the Bedouin father strode, rejoicing, out of the compound accompanied by his new son proudly wearing the robes of an Arab male McClure realized there would be no suppression of their tidings. Soon all of Gaza knew that the *hakim* had performed a most culturally acceptable miracle. He had turned a girl into a boy.*

---

*This case was unusual in more ways than one. In later years the details seemed to occupy little or no place in McClure's memory. The author was told of it independently by two ex-Gaza nurses, one now living in Toronto and one in New Zealand. Their information was corroborated and elaborated upon by several Arabs who are still employees of the Gaza hospital as well as by two Arab doctors and one Arab pharmacist. McClure had probably found that the problem was the very rare "male pseudohermaphroditism" in which external genitalia appear to be feminine but there are intra-abdominal testes. With the advent of adolescence the male characteristics begin to dominate. Although rare, male pseudohermaphroditism is familial and Gaza sources claim that McClure performed the operation at least once more, again upon a youth from Jabalia.

9

In the Name of God Almighty!

During the Thirties in China, McClure had carried on a full scale war against tuberculosis. Even during the chaos of World War II he and his associates of the China Convoy of the Friends Ambulance Unit had tried whenever possible to use their X-ray equipment for civilian chest screenings. Now, in Gaza, McClure instinctively rejoined the ongoing TB battle. The UNRWA engineers, like Vart Korlu, were working feverishly to improve the camp conditions but in the meantime the overcrowded, squalid tent cities were natural breeding grounds for the little killer known as Tuberculosis Bacilli.

UNRWA already had a TB hospital not far from Gaza City. It occupied an old air force base. The hangars had been turned into wards. To begin with it had no X-ray machine and its patients were sent to the mission hospital for screening. Then a powerful but ancient machine was sent in from Egypt. It looked like something from a Jules Verne novel and the Egyptian doctors called McClure in to unravel its mysteries. The man who had once set up one of the biggest X-rays in China in a hillside cave was equal to the task. McClure then supervised a clerk-turned-technician as he ran his first tests and developed his first film. The technician, a young Palestinian with the euphonious name of Shahin Shahin, trembled with nervousness but more than a quarter of a century later he still recalled the pride he felt upon passing his test under the eye of a "wonderful person who was clever in everything you could imagine".

The TB hospital was not a luxurious institution but it was efficient and did good work. Whenever the mission hospital detected an active TB case there would be an ambulance at the main gate within half an hour, an impressive achievement compared to the three month time lag said to be the normal situation in Canada. On the other hand, there was as yet no comprehensive survey underway to detect early TB.

In the meantime McClure was upgrading the mission hospital's technical facilities. Thanks to UNRWA and Vart Korlu the Diesel power plant was enlarged. McClure used funds received from private donors in Canada and acquired portable X-ray equipment suitable for TB chest screenings. He then persuaded Oxfam to finance a TB survey of 5,000 high school students.

By the fall of 1952 McClure had the TB survey underway. It was run as a clinic in the mission hospital. Every day, for weeks, batches of 50 students at a time were paraded before the X-ray. The task of operating an X-ray, even a small one, for prolonged periods was not one that many doctors liked. The younger doctors were afraid that constant exposure might affect their fertility and so McClure found himself functioning as chief X-ray operator in addition to his surgical functions. It was one day while he was fully occupied with the TB clinic that he met the Sheik of Majdal.

The sheik had been a prominent leader in the religious and political life of the Palestinian town of Majdal. It was an ancient community, noted for its beautiful women, one of whom had been Mary Magdalene, the friend of Jesus. The sheik, like so many of his people, was now a refugee but was still a man of great influence. Unlike the Hollywood image the sheiks were not ravagers of women but were more like defenders of the faith. Many of them presided over religious courts which had the power to settle disputes over marriage and property. Many of the sheiks of Egypt and Gaza were trained for their responsibilities at Al Hazar University in Cairo. When one saw an Arab wearing a white band around the lower edge of his fez one knew he was in the presence of a sheik.

The Sheik of Majdal had been aware of McClure long before McClure became aware of him. The middle-aged doctor, wearing khaki shorts, smoking a pipe and pedalling a bicycle, was highly visible on the highways and byways of Gaza. He could be seen and heard on a Sunday afternoon shouting his way into the breakers on Gaza's Mediterranean beach and returning, wet and happy, to flop into the shade of a crude beach hut where he

ate watermelon seeds, smoked, and yarned with the hut's owners, Jalal Ayyad, Salama Shahin, and other young men from the
hospital technical staff. It was apparent that he had no concept
of the dignity that should attend a Chief Surgeon. He would
amble off on a Saturday night to play cards in the homes of his
Palestinian friends. It was common knowledge that he once
argued openly in the hospital grounds with quiet Dr. Barry over
an ornamental gate that the Administrator liked to keep locked
but which impeded McClure's movements to the X-ray Department *and* to lunch. McClure had solved the administrative im-
passe by unlocking the gate and throwing the key away. To the
Sheik of Majdal McClure represented almost everything that
was bad about Western man. He was too loud, too energetic, too
aggressively sure of himself. The sheik did not care for Dr.
Robert Baird McClure and prayed to Allah that he and all other
Westerners would go away and leave the Moslem world alone.

It was the sheik's misfortune that one morning he fell down
a flight of stairs and seriously injured his right knee-cap. It
was obviously a job for a surgeon but he went first to the civil
hospital. There he was X-rayed, was given the film, and was told
to go to the mission hospital. Although he had injured himself
about 10:00 a.m. he managed to procrastinate until 3:00 p.m.
before finally, and very reluctantly, approaching the hated
mission doctor.

The sheik was assisted into the clinic area by two younger
men who also wore the white band around the fez. McClure saw
them enter but was busy putting a batch of high school students
through the chest X-ray. He committed the unpardonable error
of making the sheik wait. The latter was eased onto a bench,
where he sat and fumed.

When McClure finally did come to him the sheik was annoyed that the doctor would not settle for a look at the X-ray film
but insisted on lifting the skirt of his *galabia* to look at the knee
itself. Not only that, he insisted on inspecting both knees and
asking apparently idiotic questions about how the injury had
happened.

As for McClure, he saw no need whatsoever for the X-ray
film. The right knee-cap was so completely broken one could
almost put a finger in the groove between the halves. He asked
the sheik why he had been messing around for more than

four hours when it was so obvious he needed a surgeon. An operation was necessary and it would be done first thing next morning.

The answer was abrupt and hostile. A loud click of the tongue, and *lah!* "No!"

The chest clinic line-up was lengthening and McClure was needed. He was just as direct.

"Well, it's up to you, sir. It's 3:30 now. We admit patients up until 4:00 p.m. You have thirty minutes to think about it." He returned to the TB survey.

The Sheik of Majdal, supported by his fellow sheiks, limped out of the building. In the courtyard they were met by more men. All gathered around and engaged in heated and excited debate. After a few minutes one of the sheiks returned to the chest clinic.

"*Hakim,*" he said, "is there any medicine that would avoid an operation?"

"No," said the doctor.

McClure also pointed out that in twenty minutes time admissions would be closed to all except emergencies. The sheik could hardly say "no" now and claim later to be an emergency. The man conveyed that message to his friends clustered beside a Greek pillar. After more discussion he again sought McClure.

"*Hakim,* is there no injection that might make it possible to avoid an operation?"

"There is not." McClure glanced significantly at his watch and went on with the X-ray screenings.

It was a few minutes to 4:00 when the Sheik of Majdal had himself admitted to the Gaza mission hospital. He was angry and tense and not in a pleasant frame of mind. His worst fears were being verified far too rapidly. He had fallen into the hands of the uncouth and there seemed no way to escape.

Knee operations are among the "cleanest" of all surgical procedures. A long elastic bandage is wound around the leg beginning at the foot and working upward past the knee, thus forcing the blood into the upper leg. A temporary tourniquet is applied above the knee and the operation proceeds. If the operation can be completed before the tourniquet has to be loosened it can be done without spilling more than a drop or two of blood. It was normal procedure to begin each O.R. day with the clean operations. Thus it was that the next morning the Sheik of Majdal was the first patient on the table.

The sheik's hostility had been somewhat suppressed by a heavy dose of pre-operative narcotic but he was still tense and was praying inwardly to Allah for protection.

Much to the sheik's amazement the doctor came over to his side, bowed his head, and also prayed, first in English and then in Arabic: "Allah, grant us your blessing while we do our work this day and grant that we may try to do our work in the spirit in which Jesus Christ healed people in his time."

It was as though the surgeon, before even using his scalpel, had made an incision in the patient's soul and removed the hostility. The sheik felt a sudden surge of comfort. No man, he thought, could pray to Allah in such a manner and then intentionally do wrong. He fell asleep, his mind tranquil.

Several weeks later, when McClure was cutting the cast and removing it, the sheik told him how that one prayer in the operating room had helped soothe his apprehensions and dispel his hostilities. He was very frank. He also had a question.

"*Hakim*, the nurses told me you pray each morning as you begin the day's work?"

"Yes."

"But McClure, my friend, that is not enough. All patients are frightened. Raise your hand and promise that from now on you will pray before *every* operation."

McClure promised. He was to keep that promise for the remainder of his surgical career.

For McClure the introduction of regular O.R. prayers was to have a surprising side effect. The day came when he developed a pain in a tooth and took himself off to a local dentist. There were two dentists in Gaza working under UNRWA contracts, one Moslem and one Christian. McClure went to the Christian dentist without realizing that the O.R. prayers were beginning to earn him, McClure, a reputation as a "devout" Christian. Nor did he realize that that reputation was a challenge to the dentist, who also had a Christian reputation to uphold.

The dentist inspected the McClure tooth, sterilized his instruments, and prepared a large hypodermic needle. When all was ready he cradled McClure's head in the crook of his left arm and with his left hand bared the McClure gums. He took the formidable hypodermic in his right hand and for one dramatic moment held it poised aloft. He raised his eyes heavenward and suddenly bellowed, "In the name of God Almighty!", and struck.

McClure would have bellowed "God Almighty!" too, had it not been for the hammerlock on his head and the fist and syringe in his mouth.

10

Crisis at Home

It was almost two years since McClure had left home apparently on his way to India via Gaza. For Amy, those two years had not been uneventful. Norah had married David Busby and they were living in Toronto while David was doing postgraduate theological studies at Toronto's Trinity College, but they were not living at 108 Strathallan. Neither were the other two girls. Patricia was down on the Niagara Peninsula at St. Catharines, training as a nurse. Josephine was attending the University of Western Ontario in London, taking Physical Education. Doug was still living at home but had graduated from Arts and was working in the machine tool trade. The big house on Strathallan was beginning to echo.

Amy's major responsibility was looking after Grandpa McClure. The old gentleman was in his mid-nineties. He was becoming more feeble but was not bedridden and was mentally very alert. He was still reading daily extracts from the Encyclopaedia Britannica in order to improve his mind and was still following the daily stock market reports. He was still taking a keen interest in the mission work of the church and was actively assisting in re-directing investment money from the China field, which was closing down, to the field in India, which was expanding. He was still happy to see visitors and took great pleasure in regular visits from an old friend, Rev. Arthur Lochead, whom he had known in China as far back as 1904. In fact, old Dr. McClure was so well that Amy had decided to take a holiday and to join her husband for a few months in Gaza.

Amy's plans had already been made. She had arranged for

a friend of the family, the widow of a missionary, to come and keep house for Doug and Grandpa McClure. Towards the end of October, 1952, Amy was all packed and ready to go.

And then she had a hemorrhage of the bowel.

The McClures had close friends on a neighbouring street, Bob and Kay Laird. Bob Laird was a surgeon. Amy called Dr. Laird now and he was around at the Strathallan house in a matter of minutes. Amy was amazed, and frightened, at the speed with which he dispatched her to Toronto Western Hospital. There she underwent a thorough examination and was sent home with orders to stay in bed until the reports were all in. Norah and David hurriedly shifted quarters to 108 Strathallan.

Amy was almost certain she knew what the problem was. She had had nursing training herself. She had been married for more than twenty-five years to a surgeon who had always taken a special interest in cancer. She was convinced she had cancer and wondered what she would do if it were diagnosed as being serious, perhaps terminal. She thought she might continue with her trip and join Bob. Perhaps they could meet in London. Surely they could have a final few good weeks together. These were more than just thoughts. They were almost plans and she let Norah and David know what she had in mind.

Dr. Laird came with his report. He confirmed that her worries were not fantasies.

"Amy, I have some of the worst news I could possibly bring."

She appreciated his directness and his honesty. Having prepared herself she would have been annoyed by any evasion.

"You have cancer of the bowel and it is very serious. An operation is one hundred per cent necessary and I can't make any promises about its effectiveness."

"When should it be done?"

"The sooner the better."

"Where?"

"We can send you to England. I'll wire Bob and he can meet you there. I know a very good Harley Street man. Top surgeon."

Amy had been thinking of London as a place for a final holiday with her husband, not as a place for a do-or-die operation. She was not impressed by the idea. "There are only two persons I'd let do that operation on me. One can't because he's my husband. The other is sitting right here in this room."

Dr. Laird sat a moment without answering, then nodded his head. "I'll cable Bob," he said.

When Bob McClure received Bob Laird's cable he was in the O.R. closing up after an operation. A nurse brought the cable into the O.R. and handed it to him after he sewed the last stitch.

There was a UN 'plane leaving Gaza early next morning for Beirut but McClure had no travel permit. He also had no ready money for trans-Atlantic airfare and the world was not yet into the Age of the Universal Credit Card. It was now past banking hours in Gaza. The next day was Friday, the Moslem Sabbath, and the banks would not be open. He left anyway. The Egyptian officer who commanded the Gaza garrison re-opened his office after hours to stamp the *hakim's* exit papers. In Beirut the Air France people accepted a promissory note and put McClure on a flight to Paris. He made it to London. It was now Saturday and the banks were still closed. The British accepted a promissory note for the Montreal flight. They also loaned him a few pounds sterling in cash.

It was Sunday when McClure arrived at Montreal Dorval airport. He caught a train to Toronto.

McClure did not know it at the time but his youngest daughter was on that same train. Jo had been in Montreal for a McGill-Western football game and was now returning to London, Ontario. She was still unaware of a family crisis and remained so until a message a day or so later told her to come home to Toronto on Friday. Pat came from St. Catharines.

It was Friday, October 31st, that Amy went into surgery.

The operation was, and is, almost as formidable as its name—"Abdomino-Perineal Radical Resection of the Rectum with permanent colostomy". It involves the removal of a large portion of the colon, the lower bowel. The remaining portion of the bowel is re-routed. Instead of journeying to the rectum it is carried to a spot in the lower left abdomen, not far below the navel. Here the end of the bowel is brought through an opening made in the skin and is neatly sewn in place, open. It is a permanent opening. A kind of seal, or gasket, is glued in place around the opening. A flat, removable, plastic bag fastens to this seal and this bag accepts the body wastes. The whole thing is one of those so-called "miracles of modern surgery". Usually the body adapts to the new system more easily than does the mind.

Amy made up *her* mind that she was going to adapt. She was determined to follow all the instructions to the letter. Both Bob and Dr. Laird assured her that it was quite possible to lead an active and absolutely normal life while wearing a colostomy bag. She was determined she would do so. Amy and Bob also discussed how much to say about an operation that some people would consider "intimate". They decided to be frank. There was to be no mystery about why Amy McClure was suddenly swept into hospital. There would be no need for the ladies of Bloor Street United Church to speculate over coffee concerning the nature of Amy's operation. She had had cancer and had had a generous portion of the large intestine removed and that was that. Or at least everyone would pray that that was that. The malignancy had been quite advanced. The "cure" record at that time was not encouraging. Amy would be fortunate to live another five years.

Amy was at the half century mark and preferred not to think about the speeding years, numbered or not. She preferred to think in terms of a speedy recovery and a long life. One thing she found it difficult not to brood about, however, was that she had just missed a holiday on the shores of the Mediterranean. Instead, she was faced with recuperating through the long dreary months of another Toronto winter. Thinking about that was enough to put one into relapse.

In the meantime McClure had received two urgent and interesting letters from the C.M.S. people in London, England, and had been downtown for long conversations with the United Church administrators. They, too, had had letters from London.

Dr. Barry was leaving the Gaza mission hospital. The C.M.S. wanted Dr. McClure to take on the job of Administrator as well as Chief Surgeon.

One week after Amy had had her operation she was out of bed and sitting in a chair in her hospital room. McClure considered her progress to be quite astonishing; so astonishing that he was able to sit down and write a precise answer to the C.M.S. request.

"I enjoy very much the work in Gaza," he wrote, "and in spite of certain short-comings it is one of the best medical mission jobs of work I have ever been allowed to do. I like it. I should like to be able to spend the rest of my working life there, in fact. My wife shares this wish."

(This was not the first time McClure had buoyantly announced he was doing his "best job of work". He had felt the same way about North China in the Thirties and about the Friends Ambulance Unit in the Forties. Upon consideration one is struck not so much by the pride of the recurring announcement as by the fact that his enthusiasm was apparently indestructible from decade to decade.)

After stating his enthusiasm for the work he pointed out that his own services were promised to India and that anyway he did not think doctors made very good hospital administrators. He was convinced by experience that laymen performed the job much better. By this stage in his letter the C.M.S. people could have been excused for assuming that they had been denied their request. It was not so. The United Church, having already gone the second mile was ready, reluctantly, to go a third mile. "The C.M.S.," McClure continued, "can count on my services being available to Gaza until December, 1953. If I could be released before then my mission would appreciate it... I shall do the (administrative) work if it is necessary to do so. On the other hand if anyone else can be found to do it I shall very willingly confine my efforts to the clinical and the teaching work... When the surgical work in Gaza has been planned for I should be free to move on to India. The sooner the better."

That was settled.

McClure then announced that he was taking Amy to Gaza where she could spend a few months recuperating in the sun. He would book them both on a ship out of Montreal. They would be in Gaza for Christmas.

Their friends were aghast.

Everyone knew that Amy's operation was one that required at least six weeks of recuperation before one gingerly ventured around at home. McClure thought that was nonsense. It was negative thinking. Dr. Laird found it difficult to disagree. Amy raised no opposition. She knew her time might be limited and was determined to spend as much of that time as possible with her husband. The friend who had been intending to keep house for Grandpa McClure was quite willing to extend her stay. So why not go to Gaza? They left four weeks after the operation.

Amy was in a wheelchair when she and Bob boarded the train at Toronto to catch a ship at Montreal. Their acquaintances were still shaking their heads in disbelief at what some of them considered to be the overwhelming egotistical self-confidence of

Amy's husband. Those who knew McClure best, however, were beginning to realize that his tremendous assurance was rooted in a consuming belief that life is governed by positive forces, and that if one tries to do the right thing at the right time with the right intentions then all will be well.

McClure's confidence was not misplaced. By the time the ship reached Naples Amy was ready to go ashore to make a brief trip to Pompeii. There she and Bob walked among the Roman ruins.

The exertion of the Pompeii visit was enough for Amy but McClure managed a one day visit to Rome. The Eternal City did not disappoint him. He visited St. Peter's and felt the same sense of awe as had been felt by every tourist throughout the centuries upon first walking into the vast magnificence of St. Peter's Square. But the most overwhelming impression of awe came to him in the Sistine Chapel while he stood with his head thrown back and gazed upwards at Michelangelo's incredible painting. It forced one's mind to contemplate God the Creator and Man the Creator and to ponder the meaning of immortality.

Bob and Amy arrived in Gaza just in time to settle in before Christmas. It was Amy's first Christmas in a non-Christian land since 1937. She missed her children and there were few of the familiar trappings of a Canadian Christmas. The cold weather, however, was gloriously absent and she soon discovered that friends were abundant. She had expected the hospital staff to be friendly but was quite unprepared for the show of cordiality from the outside community. During Christmas and Boxing Day she and McClure received calls from 144 casual visitors, both Moslem and Christian, who dropped in to have a coffee, a chat, and to wish the *hakim* and his wife all of Allah's blessings.

On the evening of December 27th, 1952, while Amy rested, McClure sat down to write a letter home. Outside the house the hospital compound was alive with the voices of children. A party for Moslem orphans had been running non-stop since early afternoon and was showing no signs of ending. Now, with Christmas in his heart and the sounds of childhood in his ears, McClure must surely have thought back over the last few weeks and pondered the amazing texture of life. Only a few weeks ago in Canada his wife had gone through the trauma of radical surgery. Since then they had walked side by side through Pompeii, a city where one moment of time had hung suspended for two thousand years. He had seen the paintings of Michelangelo and had glimpsed another's immortality. In the last few days he had been overwhelmed by the demonstration of human warmth from people of another race, another culture, another religion.

He slipped paper into his typewriter and wrote: "Gaza is, as I have said so often before, one of the most cordial and hospitable places that I know of on the face of the missionary earth."

11

Allah is Great

In Gaza City some of the UNRWA personnel lived in a communal house that was like a university co-op, only more international. Its residents represented France, England, Turkey, the U.S.A. and Holland. Two of the residents were Vart Korlu and Johanna Boender. Amy was introduced into this little United Nations gathering. Johanna, the trained nurse, could hardly believe that the composed, serene woman who moved with such apparent and unassuming ease into new surroundings was still in the early stages of adapting to radical surgical alterations. No casual observer would have known that Amy McClure was undergoing anything more than a period of normal recuperation from a normal illness.

The UNRWA people had established a beach house where they liked to relax at the end of an afternoon. Amy found it a quiet, pleasant place to sit in the Mediterranean sunshine through the winter months of January and February, and a good base from which to go on walks along the beach. She and Bob played bridge with Vart and Johanna and their friends in the evenings and were invited into Arab homes on the weekends.

The ninth lunar month of the Mohammedan calendar came in March that year and brought with it the greatest of all Moslem annual festivals, the fast of Ramadan. The time of fasting was also, paradoxically, a time of feasting.

The guidelines for Ramadan were set down in the Koran and the orthodox Moslems of the Gaza Strip followed it with great faithfulness.

"O believers! A Fast is prescribed to you as it was prescribed to those before you, that ye may fear God, for certain days."

The days set aside to "fear God" were the days of the month of Ramadan. It was during this ninth lunar month that the Koran was said to have been sent down to Mohammed. Now, fourteen hundred years later, the faithful were following the injunctions of the Koran to the letter.

"As soon as any one of you observeth the moon, let him set about the fast."

In order that there would be no errors the beginning of the fasting month was announced by official observers in Egypt. The time for daily observances was announced locally, again following the Koran. *". . . eat and drink until ye can discern a white thread from a black thread by the daybreak: then fast strictly till night . . ."*

Not far from the hospital was the principal Gaza mosque. High on his minaret the *muezzin* stood, morning and evening, and held a white thread and black thread side by side in front of him at arm's length. In the morning, as the light increased, he would wait until he could just distinguish between the white and the black and then his call would echo out across the roof-tops. The fast had begun. No orthodox Moslem would touch food or water from then until dusk. The non-orthodox, and even visitors, indulged their cravings, whether for food, cigarettes, or a drink, in private. McClure heard many stories of people actually dying of dehydration when the fast fell during hot months. The hospital was Christian, but many of the staff were Moslem. Some were orthodox and some were not. Some refused to touch a drop of water during the day while others, like Ahmed the wrestler, sweating like a bull, would make copious use of the water jug. For the patients there was no problem. For them, the Koran had compassion.

"He who is sick, or upon a journey, shall fast a like number of other days. God wisheth you ease, but wisheth not your discomfort . . ."

McClure thought there was something pleasantly reassuring about the fact that God "wisheth not your discomfort" and it was a statement that the Moslems of Gaza took to heart. In most homes a feast, however humble, would be spread out in preparation for the day to end. Families would gather at the entrance to the dining rooms, their way barred by the head of the household. Crowds in the streets would stand quietly awaiting the crucial moment of dusk. High on his minaret the *muezzin* would stand, the two threads poised. Eventually he would sing out. A large green flag bearing a golden crescent and a star would be waved and half a mile away on the outskirts of town an old man standing beside an equally elderly Turkish army 75 mm gun would shout "Allah is Great above All!" and would fire the gun. The sound of voices would rise above the streets of Gaza, "Allah is Great," and inside the homes fathers and families would cry, "Allah is Great", and would descend upon the feast within. Thus every day was a day of extreme fast, so extreme that some would not even swallow their own saliva. And yet every evening was an evening of feasting; except, that is, for the destitute and the dispossessed. They could fast but for them the feast was a state of mind.

Bob and Amy walked to the park at sunset and watched the elderly gunner perform his ritual. They stood in Moslem homes with Moslem families waiting for the cry that "Allah is Great" and with those same families they enjoyed the feasts of Ramadan. It was a Moslem festival but an Arab who might angrily take a cigar from an infidel's mouth during the daytime would welcome that same infidel to the family feast in the evening.

Fasting was one of the five pillars of the Islamic faith. Another pillar was prayer. McClure had already had some instruction in that from the Sheik of Majdal. The other three pillars concerned Belief, Almsgiving, and Pilgrimage. Moslem belief hinged on one simple affirmation: "There is no God but Allah, and Mohammed is his prophet." There was no complicated doctrine of the Trinity in the Moslem faith. *"He is God alone,"* said the Koran, *"God the eternal! He begetteth not, and He is not begotten; and there is none like unto Him."* There was something very Old Testament about it all, and for that matter the Koran recognized the Old Testament prophets. It also recognized Jesus as a prophet. But Mohammed was *the* prophet. Some of the Koran, as scholars liked to point out, was based on Judaism. Racially, Arabs and Jews were both Semitic peoples. McClure found it difficult to rationalize this past with the present that had Arabs and Jews poised at each other's throats. Or was it simply an illustration of the old adage that there is no hatred to equal that of estranged brothers?

While McClure was studying the Moslems the Moslems

were assessing him. One in particular was a medical student named Kheiry Abu Ramadan. While Kheiry was studying in Cairo his father was dying in Gaza of cancer, with McClure easing him through the terminal stages. During frequent trips home the young Abu Ramadan found himself watching the mission doctor with a discerning eye with the result that he continued his studies almost obsessed by the urge to be like McClure. Many years later he sat in a Gaza garden and discussed the Canadian doctor. Dr. Abu Ramadan was now the Director of Public Health for Gaza, a forthright, cheerful man, uninhibited in speech. It was twilight and a gentle breeze was beginning to stir the red flowers of the jacaranda trees. Blue and white morning glory were softly folding their petals for the night. The scent of oleander drifted across the garden. From three nearby minarets the *muezzins* were calling the faithful to prayer, their voices intertwining on the evening air like verbal vines. On a vacant lot next door a Bedouin family, who had paused to let their goats forage on tough grass and shrubs, knelt towards Mecca. Abu Ramadan, deep in conversation with Westerners, ran Moslem prayer beads through sensitive fingers and hazarded an opinion concerning the secret of McClure's success in Gaza. "He had," said the Moslem doctor, "an excellent relationship with God."

12

Old Jerusalem

The Bible had been taking on new life for McClure ever since he had come into the Middle East. In April of 1953 it became even more alive when he, Amy, Vart Korlu and Johanna Boender visited the Holy Land.

Because they were living in Arab territory it was not possible for them to cross into Israeli territory. Neither side would recognize passports that had been stamped by the opposition. Old Jerusalem, however, was in the area of Palestine that had been annexed by Jordan.

They flew to Jordan, acquired a car and went on tour.

They visited Jacob's well where Jesus had talked to the woman of Samaria. They saw the ruins of Herod's palace. They visited the dungeon where John the Baptist was said to have been held prisoner while Salome danced for his head.

Their prime destination, however, was the city of Old Jerusalem.

Jerusalem lay in spectacular country. The city could be seen from far off. It appeared to grow from the hills themselves as though their limestone hearts had grown a limestone city. It gleamed grey-white in the Mediterranean sunlight.

A large portion of the city of Jerusalem lay in Israeli hands but a significant portion was under Jordanian control. The Arab-held section contained the Old City and the Old City contained some of the most sacred shrines in the world; sacred to Jews, Christians and Moslems. Since 1948 the Jews in Israel could visit King David's tomb which lay outside the Old City walls but they could not reach the city itself. They could almost

touch the western wall of the city and the Jaffa Gate but could
not pass through that gateway. They could look with nostalgia
at the tall shaft of David's Tower rising above the forbidding
fortress walls but only their memories could reassure them that
deep within the Old City lay the "Wailing Wall" which had been
part of the foundation of the ancient Temple.

The McClures and their companions were more fortunate.
The Old City was open to anyone from Arab territory.

Old Jerusalem was a snare for the mind. It looked so ancient, snuggled within its great walls, that one instinctively felt
it had not changed since the days of Christ, but in 70 A.D. the
legions of Emperor Titus had levelled Jerusalem to the ground.
Jerusalem had been "ploughed under", so it was said, although
if Jerusalem and the ground on which it sat had been made of
the same stuff then as now the Romans must have been sturdy
ploughmen. The city had been rebuilt but with considerable
variations from the ancient pattern. Most of the great city wall
that the McClures and their friends admired had been built by
the Turks in the 1500s. Somehow or other it did not really
matter. It was the atmosphere that was important. In the alley-
ways and doorways and small restaurants of the Arab Quarter
groups of robed men puffed on communal *hookas,* and mingled
with the scent of the smoke was the aroma of history.

On the edge of the Jewish Quarter the travellers followed a
path that led upward, rising to the heights above the Wailing
Wall. The great stone blocks of the sacred wall still seemed to
retain the hillside just as once they had supported the holy
Temple of Jerusalem which had been at its peak of architectural
beauty during the time of Christ. In those far-off days the white
marble temple had gleamed above the city like snow on a sacred
mountain. Its grounds had embraced the rock said to be the very
place where father Abraham had prepared to sacrifice his son,
Isaac. Inside the temple had been the holy of holies containing
the Ark of the Covenant. But the Romans had destroyed the
past. Today only the Wailing Wall remained and another temple
now rose in austere splendour from the same rock. It was the
Mosque of Omar, the "Dome of the Rock", next to Mecca itself
the most holy place in the Moslem world.

Orthodox Jews would not walk the grounds of the Mosque
of Omar for fear they might inadvertently tread the ground that
had born the Ark but the restriction was of their own making.

The McClure party walked across the great paved courtyard that rose in gentle tiers to the mosque itself. The Mosque of Omar had been built in the seventh century. Since then its great golden dome had dominated Jerusalem, rising high above the city walls. Inside, one moved quietly on shoeless feet. This mosque, like all mosques, housed what was essentially open space for worship. Here were no furnishings; no pews, benches, communion tables, pulpits, altars, baptismal fonts or lecterns; no candles, statues, scrolls, flags or relics. On the floor were prayer rugs where five times a day the faithful knelt to worship Allah. In only one respect was this mosque essentially different to any other mosque. In its centre, directly under the great dome, several hundred square feet of natural rock surfaced in a gentle swell. This was said to be the rock of Abraham but it was also said to be the very place from where Mohammed and his horse had ascended to heaven.*

The sacred rock was protected by a low wooden wall that extended around its entire perimeter. On the far side of this wall, in the women's section of the mosque, there was a small, simple door. Even now, although it was not an official prayer time, worshippers knelt in front of this door. It was said to be the doorway to Paradise. Here, on the last day of the world, the faithful would pass through to Heaven.

Down from the holy hill, in the Arab Quarter of the Old City, the travellers found the Via Dolorosa, the Street of Sorrows, said to be the very street that Jesus and the crowds had taken on that terrible day when he carried the cross to the hill of Golgotha, the place of the skull. The four tourists paused at the various "Stations of the Cross" each of which was identified in Latin on a plaque by the doorway of chapel, convent, or monastery. Here Christ fell, here he met his mother, here Simon of Cyrene took the cross, here Veronica wiped the blood and sweat from Christ's face, here he fell again, here he turned to speak to the women of Jerusalem. It was highly improbable that any place marked was in reality *the* place of the action described in legend and sacred writings but a liberal Christian could accept the markings of the "stations" as being a suitable narrative device without worrying about historical distortion or archaeolo-

*For the credulous there were four great prints in the rock, said to have been made by the hooves of Mohammed's horse.

gical truth. The Street of Sorrows was a living street with living atmosphere. Christ could not have walked this identical street but it must surely have been a street very like this, with its steep incline, its open gutters, its slippery cobbles, its sudden turns, the forbidding walls leaning so close on either side that over- head arches of stone held them apart as though trying to keep history itself from falling inward on the tourist beneath.

The Street of Sorrows led to the Church of the Holy Sepulchre.

The church itself was interesting. It had been built by the crusaders on foundations that had been laid in the days of the Emperor Constantine. It surrounded an upthrusting of rock that was said to be Golgotha, the place of execution. It housed what was said to be the very tomb in which Christ's body had been laid. The church was large, solid, and massively austere.

Whatever sense of history the old crusader church might have once enshrined had been smothered during the centuries.

If Golgotha was actually here all that could be seen of it was a few square feet of vertical rock viewed through an opening in a wall beneath a staircase. There was a horizontal split in the rock said to have been caused at the moment of Christ's death when *"the earth did quake, and the rocks rent"*. One climbed the staircase, seventeen steps in all, and found oneself supposedly on top of Golgotha but all the eye could see was a chapel—iconed, gilded, painted, candled and ornamented to the point of hideousness. Behind the altar stood three ornate golden crosses. The central one was said to stand on the very spot where *the* cross had stood. One could crawl beneath the altar and reach down through a brass-ringed hole in the floor and touch the rock beneath. One could also make cash offerings and, for a price, burn candles for departed souls.

Back down the steps again (a vertical descent of some eleven or twelve feet) and about twenty paces away from the base of the cross, lay a large rectangular slab of rock said to be the rock on which Christ's body had been laid for wrapping in its burial sheet. Another thirty paces beyond the slab stood what was said to be the tomb itself.

The exterior of the tomb, somewhat dimly lit in the great interior cavern of the crusaders' church, appeared to be made of polished red marble. It was large, and square, and solid. If the tomb within it had ever been carved into a hillside the hillside had vanished but never mind; here was *the* tomb. On one side was a low entrance that led into an outer chamber. From this small chamber an even lower doorway led into the tomb itself. Beyond that doorway was a cave-like room about six feet square. Along one wall was a rock-hewn ledge said to be where Christ's body had lain. Here the imagination could almost bridge the centuries. One could almost smell the scent of spice and see the empty winding sheet. One could almost imagine the angel clothed in a long white garment sitting casually on the ledge saying quietly, *"He is risen; he is not here; behold the place where they laid him"*. Almost. Not quite. Where the angel should have been stood a grey-bearded grubby priest in a long grey robe soliciting money for the church.

Outside the northern wall of the Old City, half a block up the Nablus Road that ran from the ancient Damascus gate, there was a narrow laneway between two high stone walls. The lane curved out of sight, inviting the travellers to explore its depths. At the elbow of the curve a narrow gateway extended an equally inviting invitation to pass through the flanking stone wall. The gateway was unmarked and was blocked by a simple wooden door with a latch that yielded easily to a visitor's touch. Inside the door and beyond the wall lay a garden.

The garden occupied an acre or so of land. It was a place of pathways and flowering shrubs and fruit trees. Beneath one portion of the garden lay an ancient cistern with a capacity for 200,000 gallons of water, enough to carry this garden through the eight-month dry season. Archaeologists said the cistern had been built about the time of Christ. Beside a path lay the shallow two-level pit of an in-ground wine press. On the higher level the wine had been trampled until the juice flowed down a rocky gutter to the lower end. The wine press, too, was said to date from the time of Christ. It was quite possible that here the archaeologists and gardeners of modern times had recreated a garden that had once bloomed two thousand years ago.

The garden skirted the base of a low hill and when the McClure party followed the path to the southern end they found themselves looking up at the highest point of that hill, which here was more like a cliff. It was rough, rugged and stony. On top were gnarled trees and a Moslem cemetery. Of more interest were the gouges of time-worn caves part way up the cliffside. Even now one could imagine that their dark openings were the cavernous holes in a skull. The whole front of the hill was like a skull. The Bible spoke of Golgotha as the place of the skull. Little more than a stone's-throw away to the south rose the wall of Old Jerusalem.

At the far northern end of the garden, almost around to the back of the hill, was another cliff. This one was man-made. The hillside had been carved away leaving a wall of rock. At the base of the cliff a doorway had been hewn into the rock. In front of the doorway, and parallel to the cliff front, a great groove had been carved in the ground as though to guide a huge rolling millwheel of a door. Inside the doorway lay a large vault; another tomb.

This tomb had not been discovered until 1867 but archaeologists said it dated from the same era as the cistern and the wine press. Many Christians, particularly Protestants, felt that this tomb fulfilled the requirements for Christ's tomb, as described in the New Testament, more fully than did any other tomb in the area.* For McClure the archaeological truth of it was not nearly as important as the atmosphere. Here was a place that helped the imagination complete the momentous journey begun on the Street of Sorrows.

McClure returned quietly to the garden several times. Here were no ornaments, no priests, no hucksters and sometimes even no tourists. He sat quietly on a bench beneath a fruit tree and looked at the entrance to the Tomb. It must have been a place very like this where the compassionate carpenter of Nazareth had been buried. It must have been a place like this that was the setting for what Christian theologians maintained was the most significant single event in the history of mankind, the resurrection of Jesus.

"He is not here; he is risen."

McClure thought of himself as a Christian. He had worked most of his adult life as a Christian missionary. But he was also a doctor who saw Truth through a microscope. He was a surgeon and knew about flesh, blood, bones, death and decay.

He pondered the Resurrection.

The four tourists were back in Gaza by the third week of

---

*Even today the custodians of the Garden Tomb refrain from making categorical claims. They use words such as "could have been", "possibly", "a likely place" and "one wonders if".

April. They had had a marvellous trip. Amy had regained her health. The trauma of last October seemed far away. For the McClures the trip had been like a second honeymoon. Or was it the third, the fourth, or the fifth? The one good thing that could be said on behalf of the long separations over the years was that the times together again were always so renewing. Each reunion was a new beginning.

Vart Korlu and Johanna Boender also had thoughts about a new beginning. On the 29th of May they were married in the little C.M.S. chapel next to the hospital O.P.D. The wedding reminded Amy and Bob of their own wedding twenty-seven years earlier in far-off China.

A few days after the Korlu-Boender wedding Amy took ship for home. She was returning to resume charge of family headquarters and of the family patriarch, old Dr. McClure. For Dr. McClure the younger, the halcyon days of his wife's visit had been the respite before the storm. For almost a year now he and the C.M.S. had been trying to peddle the Gaza hospital to another mission; any mission. So far there had been no takers and time was running out.

13

Rebel in a Foxhole

The mission hospital in Gaza was working at full capacity. It was functioning smoothly and efficiently and its facilities were being steadily improved. Shortly after returning from the trip to Jerusalem McClure, almost in a state of euphoria, wrote to the Board Secretary: "We shall have the finest power house in any mission hospital and the finest operating room in any that I know of too... We usually run about 40 (operations) per day. The tools are good, the nursing is good and the work is needed, so one's own steam and the bed capacity are the only limitation."

There was one other limitation pending. The C.M.S. had decided they had to pull out by the end of 1953 whether another mission could take over or not.

McClure had already tried to talk the United Church into taking on the Gaza work and had failed. As usual he had been thinking in terms broader than just medical work.

"In agricultural work," he had written, "no mission work effort has been made whatever, but the appointment of one agricultural man could make a great change to the livelihood of the people in the realms of desert agriculture, use of mechanization on a progressive scale and citrus fruit culture. Such things as a fishery co-operative, cold storage plant for both fish and fruit, are things that come naturally to a Canadian mind but which never occur to the English mind as having anything to do with 'mission'. Altogether the new look is wanted and Canadians or Americans are the ones who can give it."

The United Church may not have shared McClure's optimism about Canadian expertise in either desert agriculture or citrus farming. At any rate, it had India to worry about.

McClure had then tried his sales pitch on the Americans, through the Christian Medical Council of Overseas Work, New York: "For years, even during the British Mandate, this hospital has been *the* hospital for the people of Gaza when they were sick. They are very loyal to it and the reputation is excellent indeed. In any Moslem country the Christian work has to be more in the form of 'witness' work rather than direct evangelism anyway. As an instrument in such a policy this hospital is a well-developed tool for that work."

It appeared that no American mission was interested in accepting a ready-made foothold in the Moslem world.

As soon as Amy was back home in Toronto she had a quiet conversation with the Board Secretary in an attempt to convey the depth of McClure's feelings for the Gaza mission. Her lobbying was met with sympathy, but no more.

It was all very frustrating. Then the American Southern Baptists began to show an interest in the Gaza hospital. McClure was schizophrenic about the Southern Baptists. He had had dealings with them in China. He did not care for their theology. They were far too fundamentalist for him, with their strict and literal interpretation of the Bible. They prayed and preached too much. They could be intolerant to the point of bigotry. They had no sense of humour. His list of personal antipathies was rather long but could instantly be outweighed when he thought of individual Southern Baptists like Dr. Ayers of Chengchow. And McClure would take his hat off any time, any place, to the Southern Baptists' ability to organize; to their ability to raise money; to their determination; to their perseverance in raising their children in their own faith.

The Baptists looked, for awhile, as though they would provide the rescue for which McClure was praying but by the autumn of 1953 even that hope seemed forlorn. It appeared to him that medical mission work in Gaza would end at the same time as his own already twice-extended term.

McClure wrote one of the most pessimistic letters of his career to the Board Secretary: "The truth is that Southern Baptists have been waiting for a written invitation from the Government of Egypt to welcome them to Gaza for evangelistic work. With the state religion of Egypt being Islam and with the present enthusiastic nationalistic feelings I don't think they will get it... Imagine where we should be today had all early missionaries or their Boards waited for written invitations and welcomes from governments of the lands concerned. This sort of thing to me goes to show the decadence of the Christian missionary movement from the top right down. Since there is no chance of their getting such an invitation as they want I assume that the Southern Baptists will not be coming. The C.M.S. policy is to retreat from Gaza and hold on to the work in Cairo. I shall wait two weeks therefore for a reply from Southern Baptists and then give notice to UNRWA that the hospital will close down in 3 months time as per our contract with them. I have to give notice to all our employees too on the same lines."

One is tempted to ask whether the letter was not merely an attempt to bluff the United Church into some last minute action but it had few earmarks of a McClure political ploy. His emotion was running high. The tirade against missions in general and the use of words like "decadence" and "retreat" were not characteristic of McClure. Strange contradictions rage through that letter. He was fully aware of the history of imperialism that was finally driving countries to take nationalistic stands. He understood and was sympathetic. But for one brief moment he sounded like a missionary of the Old School who thought it preposterous that the heathen should have any say as to who entered within their borders. Or perhaps it was simply that he had been feeling pursued ever since the Japanese invaded the North Honan mission territory away back in 1937. He had had little peace since then; had never, until now, really been able to get on with the "work". In North Honan his own hospital and the mission station around it had been literally razed to the ground. His Chinese medical trainees and nurses had been killed, dispersed, or forced into useless anonymity.

The problem was that McClure, in his own words, was a "foxhole Christian", and circumstances kept turfing him out of his foxhole. He spelled it out in that same blazing letter: "It seems that my job has been to hold the line as long as possible then make a retreat. Sometimes the word 'orderly' is placed in front of the word retreat. Such action tends to be demoralizing on the troops involved," (one can still hear the sarcasm and the anger, followed by an attempt to soften it) "though in the overall picture of the job to be done it is probably quite correct."

He did not think it was at all correct, and went on to say so: "With nearly all missionaries out of Iran and with the lands closing around us it seems positively fantastic to see Christian missions giving up such an excellent toehold as Gaza. Here is a hospital with 72 years of history behind it that has become a community hospital. It has become the community hospital in a way that I have never seen any other mission hospital in the world except perhaps Kukong in Kwangtung, or Kwangsi Province in South China. Yet here we have all the missions with their displaced money, personnel and energy displaced from China and yet not able to adapt themselves to keep open a valuable beach-head on the shores of Islam. Why do nations hang on to places like Gibraltar and Malta in times of trouble? Why not drop them and win them back later? Because later it cannot be done. The strategy of Christian missions has, I feel, been sacrificed to the conditions of the moment."

The letter was vibrant with anger but it was equally alive with frustration: "I have looked forward to going to India. I still do. I dream at night of the various things I'd like to do there. Most of them are things that I've done in Gaza and been able to establish here—pathology sections, reliable and cheap X-ray facilities, blood bank and blood chemistry in the laboratory—all these things. But I do not feel happy at all if by going to India I have to close down a hospital such as Gaza. I am prejudiced. I am here on the spot. I cannot see the wood for the trees. But still I just don't feel right about it, and when I have done things that I don't feel quite right about at the time I have discovered that I still do not feel quite right about them five or ten years afterwards, either."

And then, discipline took over: "Anyway, I'm going to India..."

The Board Secretary, on the receiving end of that letter, no doubt heaved a sigh of relief by the time he reached the final line. The United Church's hot-blooded, peripatetic surgeon was still willing to obey commands.

But the crisis was not over. McClure had said he would give the Southern Baptists two more weeks before he gave the orders to shut down.

The two weeks ran out.

McClure had been spending more time than usual walking of an evening in the courtyard; more time than usual sitting in his office lost in thought; more time than usual sitting quietly in his room deep in silent prayer.

Twenty-eight years earlier McClure had had a "moment of truth" when he was forced to assess the reasons for his presence in China. He had been a young, untried doctor then, number three in a hospital hierarchy. Now he was mature, incredibly experienced, and Administrator and Chief Surgeon. Once again he was approaching another moment of truth. This time it had nothing to do with why he was here but with why he was leaving.

Where, at this moment of crisis, did his loyalty really rest?

With the United Church? His mission had other missionaries, other doctors. He could name several who had been in China and were now in Canada. Why were they not going to India?

Were his loyalties to the Gaza hospital as an institution? The institution would probably survive. UNRWA would finance it and the Arabs would run it.

Were his loyalties to the people of Gaza? That was a difficult question. He had to be careful not to be too subjective. A year ago when his extended term was approaching its expiration there had been a great outcry from the populace. The editor of the local paper had gathered a petition with upwards of 5,000 names on it calling for McClure to remain in Gaza. There had been some confusion as to who was threatening to take him away. Blame tended to centre on a nebulous "government". Many people did not know McClure was from Canada and most had never heard of the United Church. But there had been no confusion in their determination to keep him, and lobbying had been done by community leaders and even by private medical practitioners. It was difficult now for McClure to erase the memory of that spontaneous and emotional outburst.

The people of Gaza would still have a hospital. But would they have *this* hospital? *This* hospital was not just brick and mortar and a well-equipped O.R. *He* was this hospital, and so were all the Christians working within its walls. This was a *Christian* hospital and *in* this hospital and reaching *out* from this hospital he and the others were able to witness for the faith they believed in.

That was the answer.

McClure was a foxhole Christian and this time they were going to have to flood the foxhole to get him out.

Bob McClure decided to resign from The United Church of Canada mission and to remain in Gaza. Whoever owned the hospital, however it was financed, at least there would be a Christian doctor running it. "To think that it would never again come into Christian hands," he wrote later. "It was too much for me."

His decision never had to be put into effect. McClure had misjudged the Egyptians. The Southern Baptists were given the permission they sought. Suddenly everything began to happen swiftly and with great efficiency. The Baptists provided two young American doctors and three American nurses. All five arrived speaking fluent Arabic. More personnel was on the way. McClure found himself involved in one of the most efficient command change-overs it had ever been his pleasure to witness. He was filled with admiration.

The people of Gaza knew little or nothing of the drama that had been going on behind the scenes of the Gaza mission hospital. They knew that a new mission was now taking over. They also knew that the *hakim* McClure was leaving. Farewell parties were numerous and emotional.

An Arab staff member of the hospital composed and read a speech that put the finger on the essence of Bob McClure:

"Dr. McClure will live long in the memory of many of the people of Gaza as a great surgeon and a brilliant physician. But by some of us who, as far as our bodies are concerned, have had the good chance not to need to prostrate ourselves under the mercy of his sharp knife, his name will always be remembered for happier experiences than herniotomies, appendicectomies, gastroenterotomies, cholecystectomies, haemorrhoidectomies and all the rest of the breed of the 'tommies'.

"No matter to what measure he excelled as a surgeon, we feel that his most precious and amiable talents were exercised outside the operating theatre. His frankness, his humility, his sincere respect of every individual without exception, his generous ear towards all those who sought his advice or assistance, his inspiring enthusiasm and genial and original suggestions when trying to help those who stood in need of encouragement or guidance, all these charming traits will ever mark him out as one of the most if not the most popular and loved physician that has come to Gaza.

". . . Most missionaries lead what seems to us a reserved, retiring unsociable life when they come to work among Arabs.

They appear to be also living somewhere in the uncongenial climate of lonely social self-sufficience, but Dr. McClure is quite unique in his openness and frankness and naturalness ... It is not surprising then to see that he has so many friends, and that many hearts harbour deep regret at the thought of the departure from Gaza of this good man, in spite of the fact that he has succeeded in placing the future of this hospital in such good and strong hands as the Baptist Mission . . . "

The day McClure left there was a crowd at the little Gaza airstrip to see him off. From the hospital, fifteen taxis went out loaded with staff and students. Locals came by car, foot, cart and camel. The airstrip ran close to Israeli territory and was always under surveillance. So many people gathered for the farewell that the Israelis feared an invasion and sent two scout 'planes up to keep an eye on events.

McClure shook hands with the hospital staff, trying all the time to maintain his professional dignity. He came to Ahmed, the wrestling anaesthetist, and suddenly found himself enwrapped in a bearhug. He managed to break away and boarded the UN Dakota. The 'plane took off, climbed and banked in a wide turn across the airport. Below him, for just a few moments, McClure could see his Gaza friends, faces upraised, hands waving. Some were waving handkerchiefs. The 'plane levelled off. All McClure could see below was the Gaza Strip, a green emerald washed up on the edge of a desert of sand. The emerald was clasped in a setting of barbed wire and blue sea.

The new Baptist superintendent* of the Gaza mission hospital returned to the compound and wrote a letter to the Board Secretary of The United Church of Canada. The subject was McClure: "I have never seen a person in love with a place more than he loved Gaza. I have certainly never seen any group of people who loved their chief more than did the hospital staff, the patients and the people in the city of Gaza."

McClure was on his way to India. He was only three years late.

*Dr. J. T. McRae.

14

India

One fantasy had persistently tantalized Bob McClure. It was the fantasy of making a long sea voyage in a small sailboat. At one time he had seen himself sailing to Canada from Hong Kong but World War II intruded into those dreams. While in Gaza he imagined himself sailing single-handed to India and even selected the boat for the voyage. The pressure of time and commitments again destroyed the delectable daydream.

McClure flew to India, not only missing the realization of a dream but also missing the scenic sea approach to Bombay, the traditional gateway to India. The beautiful natural harbour, laced by a network of islands, backed in the distance by the hills of the mainland, had borne the commerce and the pageantry of empire. When new British Viceroys were sent to India they always came via Bombay and were met on the quayside by the outgoing Viceroy. So strong was the symbolism of Bombay as the gateway to India that the British actually built a gateway, large and monumental, dominating the Bombay harbourfront. Steps led up from the water to the shelter of the massive arches where Viceroys shook hands and transferred, from one to the other, the white man's burden.

To arrive at Bombay by air was like coming in the back door. To McClure it was one of those small sacrifices that had to be made in the interests of getting on with the job.

On this first passing he gleaned the merest impressions of Bombay; wide streets, boulevards, fine public buildings, gardens and people, people, people; handsome men, beautiful

women, beggars, cripples, and poverty; flowering trees, bloom-
ing shrubs, the scent of blossoms and the reek of urine; fine
hotels, beautiful homes, hovels, and families sleeping in the
streets. He would come to think of Bombay as India in microcosm; a microcosm that escaped the extremes of the well-
planned unreality of New Delhi and the abject depression of
Calcutta.

He left Bombay by train from a station that looked as though
the British had picked it out of the heart of London and dropped
it in Asia and, shades of Kipling and of romance and adventure,
the train was called the *Frontier Mail* and was headed north eight
hundred miles to Delhi and beyond to Kashmir and the far
frontier. Half way to Delhi it would come to a major rail junction
at the small town of Ratlam. To most Indians Ratlam was just
that, a junction on the railroad. To Bob McClure it was his
destination and his future.

It was already dark when the train pulled out of Churchgate
Station, passed through the city, crossed the causeway that
linked the island city to the mainland, and struck north-east into
the interior of the great sub-continent. Beyond the windows
there was blackness, relieved occasionally by the warm glow
from the cooking fires of village homes.

McClure had been to India before. The first time had been in
1938. Always he had been in transit to or from war-torn China.
Then he had thought of India mainly as an extension of the
British Empire, a place where a Canadian could pass "without
let or hindrance" in compliance with the regal admonition in his
passport. Most people of the Western world had been thinking
of India as a part of the British Empire for almost two hundred
years—long enough to give the illusion that British and Indian
destinies were intertwined. It had also been long enough to
establish the mythology that Europe had conferred the blessings
of civilization upon a backward and stagnant culture.

It was true that in the 1700s, when the British began to
establish control through their East India Company, India was at
a low ebb as its own great Mogul Empire crumbled and decayed,
but that empire had held sway for three centuries. A good case
could be made to support the contention that the East India
Company in fact contributed to the chaos and anarchy from
which the British Crown then "rescued" India when it took over
the Company's assets and obligations.

Indian nationalists saw the British regime in India as a temporary aberration in an otherwise long and illustrious history reaching back more than five thousand years. There had been waves of invasions by Aryans, Dravidians, Iranians, Greeks, Parthians, Bactrians, Scythians, Huns and Turks. The most successful invaders had turned into settlers and had become part of the indigenous life of the sub-continent. The conquerors were conquered by assimilation. (The less successful, like the mighty Alexander, were turned back almost at the borders.) Only the British had imposed a rule from the outside.

China was the only other country in the world that had had such an unbroken continuity of culture. India had had longer periods of uninterrupted peace than Europe had ever enjoyed. India had its own great literature, poetry, art, music, and architecture. It had been no stranger to the world's religions. Christianity had been introduced into India in the second century. Jews had migrated to India and so had Zoroastrians* and Moslems. (The rulers of the Mogul Empire had been Moslem.) Guatama Buddha had been born in India and here he had founded Buddhism. Hinduism had evolved here, a religion so mystical, so complex, so non-doctrinaire that even its own intelligentsia could not explain it.†

While Europe was moving into the barbaric twilight of the Dark Ages, Indian authors wrote books on medicine and surgery. Sophisticated surgical instruments were described and instructions given for amputations, abdominal and Caesarean sections, and removal of cataracts. The scholars of Greece and Alexandria led the way in geometry but the scholars of India led the way in algebra and mathematics. Out of India came the decimal system, the minus sign, and the use of letters of the alphabet for unknown quantities. Out of India came the *zero*, a creation of the elastic Hindu mind that was able to conceive of both a name and a place for *nothing*.

European mythology liked to credit the British with bringing democracy and with showing the Indians how to create a civil service, but Indian nationalists could look back to the Mogul Empire and see an elaborate, functional and efficient civil service. They could also look about them and see an ancient

*Parsees

†And for that reason the author of this book makes no attempt to do so.

democratic tradition at grass-roots village level that rivalled even the touted Athenian model. And they could look back and see palaces, kingdoms, and rulers as magnificent as any Europe had produced.

Indian nationalists, looking back from the vantage point of the twentieth century, found it quite easy to convince themselves that their country would have been able to rescue itself from temporary anarchy and chaos without the intervention of the British. It appeared to them that the wealth of India had been siphoned off to finance the British Empire. They could make a fascinating case to show that the plunder of Bengal had provided the capital which made possible the Industrial Revolution in England. Ironically, India did not benefit from the same Industrial Revolution. Even during the twentieth century when most countries were moving from rural to urban economies, colonial policy was forcing India from an urban to a rural economy.

Even the most ardent nationalists would admit that modern India was facing horrendous problems—over-population, appalling poverty, famine, the caste system—but the caste system was the only major affliction they would accept as being entirely of Indian origin.

There had been many rebels against caste. They had often gathered many followers. But such was the strange power of the system that the rebel and his followers usually ended up being the nucleus of a new caste. Even Christianity had developed into a caste. In a strange way, so had the civil service. Among the vigorous opponents of caste in the twentieth century were two leading nationalists, Mahatma Gandhi and Jawaharlal Nehru. Nehru blamed caste for the decline of India. "Along with the growth of rigidity of the caste system grew rigidity of mind," wrote Nehru, "and the creative energy of the race faded away." Nehru saw caste as "a very prison for the mind".

When Britain declared war on Germany on September 3rd, 1939, it took the independent self-governing Dominion of Canada a full week to ponder the implications (and to preserve its self-respect) before its parliament declared war. India's millions were hurled into war by the autocratic declaration of a single man, the Viceroy, an Englishman representing the King. In 1941, while Europe was still in the doldrums of its "phony war" the nationalists, under Gandhi, staged a massive civil disobedience. Gandhi's major weapon was the philosophy of non-violence, a philosophy almost incomprehensible to the European mind. Gandhi himself and about thirty thousand of his followers wound up in prison.

Gandhi and Nehru and many others like them did not consider everything British to be wrong. Far from it. In 1941, while thousands languished in British prisons, Tagore, a renowned Indian poet and humanist who, along with Gandhi, dominated Indian cultural life in the first half of the century, summed up his feelings for the English in a moving speech on his eightieth birthday. "It was mainly through their mighty literature," he said, speaking for several generations of educated Indians, "that we formed our ideas with regards to these new-comers to our Indian shores . . .discussions centred upon Shakespeare's drama and Byron's poetry and above all upon the large-hearted liberalism of the nineteenth century English politics." He spoke of "the generosity of the English race", of their "unreserved welcome" for political martyrs and of their "liberal humanity", all of which led him "to set them on the pedestal of my highest respect."

Countries that had become independent within the empire, like Canada and Australia, were stimulated by the war. Their industries flourished and they gained an increased sense of self-identity. India, still a colony, stagnated industrially and chafed at its subservience while millions died of famine in Bengal. There were riots, demonstrations, and incidents of varying importance.

Somehow, amazingly, miraculously, the Indians seldom lost their perspective. Perhaps, as Tagore implied, they managed to balance the thoughts of Shakespeare, Milton, Burke, and Bright against exploitive colonialism and garrison troops and found that the legacy of English liberal humanity outweighed all the rest. Even writing from his cell in a British prison Nehru was able to say: "I do not know of any other nationalist movement which has been so free from hatred." In the truth of that statement lay the *real* glory and the strength of both India and Britain.

The British genius for reconciliation was never more evident than in 1947 when a new Viceroy, Lord Louis Mountbatten, managed to so personalize the best attributes of the British peoples that he strengthened India's emotional ties with Britain while surrendering forever all pretence to political domination. India became an independent self-governing Dominion within the Commonwealth.

The final birth pangs, however, had not been without trauma. Two states had been born. They were not identical twins but were squawling siblings.

In the huge Indian sub-continent all minorities were traditionally religious minorities. The largest of these minorities was Moslem. The Moslems feared immersion in a Hindu majority. Prior to independence there had been riots almost verging on civil war. The British had been caught in between as referees, a situation that undoubtedly contributed to Britain's reluctance to withdraw too quickly. The solution involved the creation of a separate Moslem country. The same day that India was given her independence the new country of Pakistan was formed. India was predominantly Hindu; Pakistan, Moslem. Pakistan was in two parts, east and west, built around the old territories known as the Punjabs and East Bengal.

In India the president of the Congress Party* became the new Prime Minister. He was Jawaharlal Nehru. Nehru did not think of himself as a Hindu and was dedicated to the proposition (set forth in the constitution) that India was a secular state, not a religious one.

The independence celebrations had barely ended before religious civil war broke out in Pakistan. In the East Punjab, Sikhs and Hindus fell on the Moslems with guns, swords and knives. In the West Punjab, Moslems fell upon the Sikhs and Hindus with equal ferocity. Tremendous two-way migrations began; Hindus into India and Moslems into Pakistan. Thousands of Hindu refugees surged into Delhi and anti-Moslem emotion ran high in India's capital. Mahatma Gandhi, a little man in a white dhoti who by now was regarded by much of the world as a saint, came to Delhi to soothe his people and was assassinated by a Hindu fanatic.

After the trauma of partition Prime Minister Nehru and his government still faced a formidable task. India was not completely united. There were about five hundred independent principalities within her borders that had been British protecto-

---

* The major Indian nationalist party.

rates rather than subject states. Britain released the rulers from any obligations to the Crown and recommended that they join India but it was now up to each maharajah and his little kingdom to decide for themselves. By use of a statesman-like combination of sound argument, financial inducement, and armed blackmail Nehru managed to turn the independent principalities into Indian provinces. India, with approximately four hundred million people was now a democracy with the world's largest electorate. The majority of that electorate was illiterate.

In 1949 the world was presented with an astounding paradox. India proclaimed herself to be a *republic* but remained within the British Commonwealth, an organization that had as its symbol of unity the British Crown and as its figure-head George the Sixth of England (soon to be followed by Elizabeth the Second). To many observers that very paradox held great hope for the future. Obviously the world contained many minds capable of great flexibility.

It was into the heart of this new India that the *Frontier Mail* hurled its way through the dark hours of that March night in 1954. On a bunk in a second-class sleeper Bob McClure dozed fitfully and thought of the challenge ahead. It was an exciting challenge. In China he and three generations of Protestant missionaries had helped move China into one of history's most significant revolutions but had been barred from participation in the rebuilding. Here, in India, the new country was still in its formative stages and he was being permitted to participate. He knew in his heart that the measure of success would lie in the speed with which he and his Western associates could pass on their knowledge, skills and motivation and then withdraw.

The train skirted the edge of the great Deccan Plateau, that covered most of southern India, and pulled its swaying cars through hills that led onto the Malwa Plateau. Here lay the Province of Madhya Pradesh. Before independence it was a region belonging to princely kingdoms. Now it was one of the largest states in the republic and had a population of almost 30,000,000 people. All but one of The United Church of Canada's seven hospitals lay in Madhya Pradesh. All were on the Malwa Plateau. By the time the *Frontier Mail* approached Ratlam it had travelled 400 miles and had steamed its way some 1600 feet above mean sea level. It had entered into desolate country where the impression of "hills" came not so much from the heights of land as from the depths of eroded valleys.

It was dawn now and the villagers were moving out into the fields. Lithe women in brightly coloured saris were carrying headloads to nearby markets. Men with shovels were being lowered into semi-dry community wells where they would try to coax more water from the depths of the dry season soil. Small boys were herding cattle in quest of pasture. McClure saw none of it. At sometime well on into the night he had gone soundly to sleep dreaming the sweet missionary dream of becoming obsolete. Nor did he see the outskirts of the town of Ratlam, or the mission compound sliding by almost within a stone's throw of the railway, or the station itself, bustling with the traffic of a mainline junction. Nor did he see the welcoming committee waiting to greet him on the platform.

The informal committee was led by Dr. Walter Anderson, the Canadian doctor at Ratlam who had been patiently postponing his furlough until Bob McClure could break free of Gaza. With Dr. Anderson were other Canadian missionaries and a sizable delegation of Indian friends.

McClure woke up just as the train came to a stop. Looking through the unshuttered windows he suddenly realized where he was. He knew there would be a delegation to meet him and that it would be undignified to be ejected onto the platform in a state of undress. All at once the railway car with its uncovered windows and open cubicles seemed like a goldfish bowl. He dressed with remarkable speed becoming acutely aware as he did so that he had been identified by the onlookers on the platform. With clothes still askew he followed the porter onto the platform.

Handsome dark-eyed strangers hung garlands of fresh flowers around his neck. English and Hindi words flowed together in lyrical verbal welcome. Heads bowed over hands clasped together (as though in prayer) in the *pranam,* the gracious Indian greeting. McClure had arrived in the heart of "backward" India and, dishevelled and unshaven, he felt awkwardly uncouth.

15
Whirlwind in Ratlam

The Westerner, particularly a Canadian or American, always has difficulty assessing the size of an Asiatic community. The geographical spread is often small while the population is large. McClure was not a typical Canadian but even for him the Ratlam of 1954 was not easily assimilated. By Canadian standards it had the acreage of a town and the population of a city. By Indian standards it was a small town on both counts. Its population stood at about forty-five thousand people.

At the railway station the newcomer saw a spread of tracks, multiple platforms, overhead walkways, and a station building that would have done credit to any medium-size city in England. One section of town that had been the railroad cantonment in British days still sported solid homes and wide lawns and was *the* place to live for well-to-do Indians, particularly those in retirement. There was a palace in Ratlam which had been the home of the late Maharajah Sajjan Singh and was at the moment the home of his son who was still referred to as "His Highness" although the power and the pomp had vanished. In the centre of town there was a fine statue of the old maharajah looking very pukka mounted on a prancing horse, which was fitting for a ruler who had been a polo pal of the man who once reigned as King Edward the Eighth of England.

The streets of Ratlam were thick with dust and thick with people. Shops and vendors sold everything from jewellery to cigarettes. There were a few cars, several trucks and many bicycles. Great-horned bullocks pulled heavy two-wheeled carts down the major thoroughfares and horses trotted in the

shafts of brightly coloured two-wheeled *tongas,* the taxis of
Ratlam. Pedestrians shared the street with buffaloes, goats and
sacred cows. Animal dung and human urine mixed with the
dust of the unpaved roads. Ratlam was not a pretty town, but it
was not without colour. The mills of Madhya Pradesh were
renowned for the brilliant hues of their cloth and the women of
Ratlam wore those colours as daily wear. And even now in the
dry season Ratlam was ablaze with the blossoms of the flowering tree so aptly named "Flame of the Forest" and was softened
by the gentle white flowers of the chandni, the "Tree of Moonlight".

On the outskirts of town there was a cotton mill and some
light industry. In town there were the streets of the artisans—
the basket weavers, the brassworkers, the pottery makers, the
tailors—a list that read like the guilds of mediaeval Europe. On
the brassworkers' street the ear was engulfed by the sound of a
hundred hammers ringing out a syncopated symphony. In the
treed areas of Ratlam songbirds sang, parrots screamed and
monkeys chattered.

McClure was engulfed by the sights, sounds and smells
of Ratlam. He was also engulfed by the people. There were
Hindus, Sikhs, Jains, Moslems, Christians, Parsees and even
Rotarians. Most sent representatives to greet him on the station
platform. The Moslem community had already received a letter
from a Gaza sheik telling them to treat McClure as a brother. By
the end of his first day in Ratlam McClure was being entertained
by a cross-section of Ratlam society in the home of Gustad
Anklesaria, a gracious Parsee businessman. "Gracious" was
indeed the word for the town fathers of Ratlam and for their
wives. To a Westerner it seemed strange that they could be the
heads of a community of forty-five thousand people that had
neither a town water supply nor sewage disposal.

The Christian compound was on the outskirts of town. It
was a sprawling complex that covered more than eighty acres
of land. Along the front, or street side, it was sheltered by a
masonry wall. On the sides opening toward the countryside
there were simple wire fences. Unlike the compounds of China
and Gaza there was little feeling of the Christians being behind
fortifications. There was a large boarding school here for both
boys and girls, open to Christian and to non-Christian. There
were large two-storey houses and sprawling bungalows, small

staff homes and a nurses' residence. There was a church for Hindi-speaking Christians and an accompanying home for the pastor. Inside the large compound was another compound. This contained the Ratlam Christian Hospital.

The hospital wards, the O.R., and the administrative offices were built to face into an open square. The hospital had grown beyond the square and had acquired appendages such as a special procedures room, an X-ray room and a Bohra ward.* It had also acquired trees, shrubs, flower beds and a giant sacred banyan tree that loomed massively behind the O.R., its strange roots wandering up and down from its lower branches like scaffolding supporting a botanical failure.

This was a hundred-bed hospital and, as soon as Walter Anderson handed over, it would be McClure's domain.

For forty-seven-year-old Dr. Walter Anderson the hand-over of Ratlam Mission Hospital was, in a way, the end of an era. He had been born in Ratlam, of Canadian missionary parents. Ratlam had been his home until he had gone to Canada to attend university. He had returned to Ratlam as the mission doctor in 1938. Almost immediately the Second World War had created an interruption. Dr. Anderson had joined the Indian Army Medical Corps and had been posted to Singapore in time to be taken prisoner by the Japanese. He then spent the duration of the war in the infamous workcamps of the famous River Kwai where the prisoners were building their legendary bamboo bridges for the railroad. After the war, and a brief furlough, he had again returned to Ratlam and to the Ratlam Mission Hospital. Now, in 1954, it was again furlough time but the doctor who was reliev-ing him was not simply an interim replacement. He was Bob McClure, and McClure had come to stay.

To the casual observer it was a somewhat ruthless business this, in which the church could tell a doctor to hand over his institution to another. Each medical chief invariably left his personal stamp on a mission hospital. The type of service the hospital provided depended not only upon the ailments of the community and the facilities of the hospital but to a certain extent upon the medical interests of the doctor in charge. Dr. Anderson's interests were broad, embracing both medicine and

---

*The Bohras were a Hindi-speaking Moslem sect who years before had been helped by the hospital after a disastrous fire. They had been so impressed they had built a ward for themselves. It was open to all, but Bohras had priority for its use.

general surgery, but there was no doubt in anyone's mind that under McClure the Ratlam hospital would be given an impetus toward surgical specialization. A year before McClure's eventual arrival Anderson had helped prepare an extensive report to the Board detailing the areas in which it was felt McClure would want to expand and improve the facilities. It was neither a warning to the Board nor a roadblock to McClure but a preparing of the way for both.

Other people had been preparing the way as well. McClure's father, who still had trusteeship of some modest funds originally destined for his own work in China, had already requested the Board to divert that money to India to buy equipment for the Ratlam hospital. He had added $3,000 from his personal savings. The Board not only made the requested diversion but responded to the old doctor's generosity by adding to the sum being transferred so that it matched his personal gift. News of this arrived from Canada one week after McClure arrived from Gaza. The timing was psychologically perfect. He needed all the moral support he could get.

A hospital is a community in miniature, complete with its own official and unofficial hierarchy, its political intrigues, its devoted servants and its self-seekers, its traditions and its habits. For any new doctor taking over as Administrator it is a little like the mayor of a small Canadian town having to take over in another town where he or she is known only by reputation. McClure was not only a stranger in town, but a stranger to the culture. Normally he would have overlapped with Anderson long enough to receive several months of indoctrination. As it was he was three years late and Anderson was already long overdue a furlough. They overlapped by a few days. To McClure it seemed like a few hours.

Dr. Anderson was totally in tune with India. A quiet, soft-spoken man, he could gently surrender some of his authority in order to avoid head-on collisions with staff. An Indian associate considered Anderson to be "to all intents and purposes a Hindu." One of the attributes of a good Hindu was the ability never to go through an obstacle one could go around.

The day came when Anderson caught the train for Bombay. As he and McClure stood on the platform he gently warned McClure that there were certain individuals on staff who should be watched, perhaps even fired. McClure wondered why Anderson had not cleaned house himself, but McClure was not culturally attuned.

To begin with, however, McClure's eye was on the physical plant itself.

The Ratlam Mission Hospital left something to be desired. There had been very little new equipment added for at least twenty years, which was not surprising since those had been years of depression followed by World War II and then the general upheaval leading to Independence. During those years it had been difficult for colonial India to modernize extensively in any field. Understandably, a philosophy had developed among the missionaries that one should simply muddle on and "make do". Walter Anderson, back from prison camp, had done more than muddle on. In recent years he had managed to build the out-patient clinic to such a size that the hospital was practically self-supporting. The hospital had a nurses' training programme that was excellent. The O.R. and laboratory, however, were so poorly equipped as to be primitive. There was a large X-ray machine but it was broken and had not functioned for more than seven years. There were no developing tanks, refrigerated or otherwise. The wards were, in McClure's own words, "not very nice". Even ten years later a newly arrived Canadian doctor described the ward area as being "a large square courtyard bounded on each side by a row of ruins". The wards suffered from an over-abundance of visiting relatives. Because of the caste system, that dictated what foods could be eaten and that also prevented a patient eating food cooked by a member of a lower caste, the relatives prepared food over open fires behind the wards. The accompanying confusion reminded McClure of his old pre-revolutionary hospital in China, without the warlords and bandits.

Most of the buildings in the compound were made of large clay bricks stuccoed over and painted with a light yellow wash. The roofs were tile or corrugated iron. All buildings in India suffered from the climate that went from the extremes of dry heat to sodden heat. In the monsoon rains everything tended to streak, grow moss and crumble. In the dry season heat, walls dried out and cracked. The parched soil could break open and shatter foundations the way frost heaves attacked Canadian homes. It was a constant battle to keep premises looking proudly neat. A newcomer had to be careful of first impressions and McClure struggled to be charitable.

General maintenance had been poor, and no wonder. This was the first hundred-bed hospital McClure had ever seen that had no carpenter shop, workshop, or paint shop. There was no hospital washing machine. Some of the laundry was done by hand in large tubs but most of it was taken six miles out of town on the back of a donkey to the shores of a lake where it was, so McClure reported, "literally smashed against the rocks in an effort to wash it". He was told that this season the local wells were still full and might remain so but that normally the wells ran dry and that before the monsoons arrived the hospital would be buying its water in kerosene cans. He was upset to see that the mission homes were screened from flies and mosquitoes but that the wards were not, nor did the individual beds have mosquito netting.

All these deficiencies McClure set about remedying. He drew up a detailed budget for immediate requirements. It was more than double the estimated income from all sources. McClure had restrained himself. He had kept "future require-ments" for an addendum. That list included two "old-style" electric washing machines, a water softener, deep wells, a refrigerator for the lab and a future blood bank, a Diesel AC generator, a small Ford ambulance, and a modest budget for rural medical work. These requirements, too, totalled more than the estimated income from all sources.

As Administrator, McClure could not ignore Anderson's casual warning about certain members of the staff. He kept his eyes open. He also conferred with Miss Dulcie Ventham, a fellow Canadian missionary who had had some business train-ing and was overseeing the business end of the administration. She, too, had had her eyes open. Even before McClure had completed his budget he dispatched a letter to the Board Secre-tary that must have caused some trembles of trepidation among the Board hierarchy.

"When things are ready," wrote McClure, "we are going to have to let out some eight people or so who are known far and wide as unreliable and crooked and who have run the out-patient department in this hospital for years. Naturally 'trim-ming things up' to give us a loyal and reliable staff is not going to make for self-support this year. However, this is the time to do it. We cannot take new pupils into lab and X-ray and have them contaminated by this old gang that has run the hospital and its chief for so many years."

Before long "things" were apparently ready and a half dozen members of the Indian staff found their employment terminated. It was apparent that the new *doctor sahib* not only wielded a new broom but was willing to probe into all the corners.

There was another member of the staff who also wielded a broom and soon turned out to be just as stubborn as McClure. Her name was Mrs. Nagaji and she was a sweeper.

At some much earlier stage of her life Mrs. Nagaji had had one knee badly infected and arthritis had developed. The most comfortable position for her to sleep had been with the knee bent at right angles. She had begun to favour it in that position. Eventually the knee joint had become inflexible and she now had a permanent right angle bend in one leg. In some ways it was an occupational advantage. Not only did Indian custom decree that sweeper folk were outcaste it also decreed that they must use a broom with a very short handle. The grotesquely bent leg gave Mrs. Nagaji a list to one side that nicely accommodated the short broom. Nobody seemed to be concerned, least of all the woman herself, until McClure came along.

McClure, following a habit he had picked up many years ago of calling people by their afflictions rather than their names, dubbed her "Mrs. Limpy". McClure liked Mrs. Limpy but he did not like her disability. It offended his surgeon's pride. There was no need for a person to have a crooked leg like the one Mrs. Limpy flaunted around the hospital. It was like a beacon announcing that either the surgeon did not care or could not do anything about it. McClure cared and he knew he could do something about it. The leg would always be stiff but it could be straight.

He told Mrs. Limpy he was going to straighten her leg for her.

Mrs. Limpy informed the *doctor sahib* she was quite content the way she was.

McClure told her she was a bad advertisement for the hospital.

Mrs. Limpy merely kept out of his way. She came to work very early and tried to avoid him. For some weeks he was vaguely aware of a figure ducking in and out of cupboards and closets as he made his rounds. One day he spotted her trying to conceal herself behind a verandah post. The deformed leg made the task hopeless.

McClure informed her that, since she would not be helped, she could pick up her separation pay and leave the hospital's employ. He instructed the business manager to take the appropriate action.

Mrs. Limpy became emotional. She shed copious tears. The nurses took her side. They came to McClure and interceded. One of them shed more tears than did Mrs. Limpy.

McClure stood firm. It was obvious to all that he had a swinging brick for a heart.

Mrs. Limpy, faced with the prospect of unemployment, relented and went tearfully to surgery. The operation was not difficult. Some bone had to be removed from one place and inserted as wedges in another, but the leg was straightened and Mrs. Limpy came through it all in fine condition. It was the aftermath that was more difficult. She had to be in a body cast for three months to immobilize the entire leg.

It was then that Mrs. Limpy discovered the swinging brick had some soft spots. She found she was to be on full pay for the entire period of convalescence.

Mrs. Limpy was a bed patient but in excellent health. McClure would check on her about once a week during rounds. He never lifted the bedclothes of a female patient if it could be avoided. Indian women, even men, were terribly sensitive. With Mrs. Limpy there was no need anyway. He would talk to her, give the big cast a tap through the sheets, and continue on his way.

The day came when he tapped the cast and there was nothing there; nothing solid.

He tore the sheets off only to discover that the cast had all but vanished. The patient had picked it to pieces.

McClure was outraged. Mrs. Limpy tearfully protested that she must have done it in her sleep. It was an interesting excuse except that there was no loose plaster in her bed. She had obviously been at it for weeks, patiently picking away and just as patiently shipping the bits of debris off with relatives carrying out food plates. The surgeon was neither impressed nor amused. Mrs. Limpy, the staff, and assorted patients and onlookers witnessed a display of temper that made the old building shake. The patient found herself summarily discharged from hospital and sent home, again to the accompaniment of much lamentation from herself and the staff.

Fortunately the cure had taken effect. Before long Mrs. Limpy was back at work again and the terrifying surgeon flouted several thousand years of tradition by giving her a long-handled broom in keeping with the dignity of a straight, stiff leg.

It was a strange incident and one that almost defied analysis. One could debate, and they did, whether McClure was right or wrong to be so high-handed. It illustrated, however, two things about McClure. He could be very sure that he was right and, once convinced, it was almost impossible to move him. The other thing, and more important, was that in his eyes it was an offence against God for a person to be mis-shapen or to suffer if it could be corrected or prevented. Afflictions were not something sent by God to be endured for the good of one's soul. Most definitely Bob McClure was not in tune with the fatalistic philosophy of Hinduism that seemed to imply that the cycle of life must be endured whatever form it takes because each cycle leads to the next.

There was some concern that McClure was not in tune with anyone. The hospital staff were scrambling to adapt to his seemingly arbitrary demands, to his incredible energy and to his mercurial temperament. He was often in head-on collision with the Nursing Superintendent, Miss Margery Robson, a Canadian. When he detected incompetence in a nurse he said so and she invariably rushed loyally to side with the nurse. Even so, the operating room was soon functioning more busily than it had at probably any time in its previous history. McClure, in high spirits, was writing of it as "the little red workshop" and proudly reported his satisfaction with the O.R. team that coped efficiently one steaming Sunday afternoon in July with the unusual load of three emergency Caesarean sections.

McClure busily upgraded hospital equipment and service. By mid-summer he had obtained a rotary converter to change incoming Ratlam city power from DC to AC and had the X-ray department functioning with a new, small machine. The hospital was then rewired so that the X-ray machine could be wheeled to every bedside. He ordered refrigerated developing tanks for X-ray, having discovered that water normally came out of the mission water pipes, which had been laid above ground, at about 115°F. Soon the X-ray was in use almost every day of the week. All usable parts from the old machine had been salvaged.

McClure soon had the laboratory functioning to the point where it was able to do some blood analysis (sugar and proteins) and he was looking forward to being able to do pathological sections and cancer diagnosis. For McClure the next step after that would be the introduction of radium treatment. As each new lab service came into being McClure notified private practitioners in the area that these services were now available in Ratlam and at just a little over cost.

None of this was achieved without some trauma. Ever since McClure had fired some of the support staff letters had been flowing in from lawyers representing the dismissed employees. By late autumn all these complaints were reviewed by the members of the Medical Commission that represented the entire mission field and in every case McClure's action was felt to have been justified.

Fur had been flying in the O.R. as well. Here the conflicts had been with other doctors and were caused by the clash of personalities and of differing opinions concerning techniques. It was customary for the hospital to have several Indian doctors on staff. When McClure arrived there was a handful of male doctors and one woman doctor. Attrition soon set in among the younger men who found McClure too demanding and abrasive. The senior male doctor, however, was a Dr. Joshua Naku, a round-faced, genial man in his late thirties with a sound medical background. Naku was able to bend with the storm. He absorbed criticism of his slowness, of the way he handled the forceps and held the scalpel. As time went on he found his skills were improving, O.R. tensions were lessening, and he was actually becoming friends with the Chief Surgeon. Naku did not know it but at the same time McClure was reporting to the Board Secretary how pleased he was that Naku had had post-graduate work in both TB and eye. McClure admired Naku's cataract technique and learned it himself. He also gained useful pointers on tropical medicine. In McClure's eyes Dr. Joshua Naku rapidly became a colleague in the full sense of the word.

The woman doctor was not so fortunate. She was an obstetrician who was not noted for either energy or adaptability and McClure was not noted for being inhibited by chivalry when it came to medical matters. Nor as Chief Medical Officer and Administrator was he about to brook opposition from a staff doctor concerning hospital policy. He was turning Ratlam hospital into a surgical hospital as everyone had expected. He was also beginning to send poor patients to the government hospital, where service was free, and was accepting them back on referral. He was bringing in a sliding scale of fees which, he unabashedly claimed, would permit the rich to pay for the poor. He and the woman were at loggerheads on all of it.

McClure and the business manager, Dulcie Ventham, had a conference and then diplomatically suggested that the obstetrician would find work much more interesting at one of the other mission hospitals. The suggestion caused the disgruntled Indian doctor to write a letter to the Board Secretary that almost curled the paper with vitriol. The letter was written, so she said, in the spirit of "a true follower of Christ" and made some "revelations" about McClure: "Let it be candidly said that soon after his coming over here, he discharged innocent, faultless and sincere workers of the hospital and eventually rendered about six Indian Christian families practically without subsistence. What a curse it is to these poor people you can imagine. He calls all workers and his colleagues, lazy and inefficient." She was now getting down to the real complaints which, in her eyes indicated that McClure was neither a gentleman nor a true missionary. "He uselessly finds faults with us, and in his vanity of a top-rank surgeon—which has proved bogus here—he recklessly takes the instruments in his hands and growls at us in the operating theatre. Sometimes, he goes to the mean extent of using abuses, and though unprovoked as we stand—turning a deaf ear to his hysteric eruptions—we can only pity the man for his bad and low manners."

In spite of her "sacred duty to serve the Kingdom of Christ" the doctor threatened to leave the service of the mission unless something could be done about McClure.

The Board Secretary probably heaved a little sigh as he filed that letter away and did nothing about McClure. McClure had once been aptly described as a red-headed whirlwind and the members of the Board had known full well what they were doing when they sent the now grey-headed whirlwind to India. For awhile they would have to reap what they had sown.

16

The Canadian Connection

There were seven hospitals and numerous rural dispensaries in The United Church of Canada mission field in Malwa Presbytery. The hospitals were headed by Canadian doctors and Canadian nurses. Their numbers fluctuated but when the presbytery's medical sub-committee, the "Medical Commission", met it numbered some twenty-one members, most of them Canadians. By an unusual quirk of history, when Walter Anderson went on furlough McClure found himself the only *male* Canadian medical missionary among the lot. He was not only a newcomer but a minority of one and unfortunately when the newcomer surveyed the seven Canadian hospitals he did not like what he saw.

To put McClure's reaction into perspective it is necessary to understand something of the evolution of the church's work in Central India.

The Canadian mission field had been established in 1877 by Presbyterians. They had begun at the community of Indore. From there the work had fanned out and various missions had been opened. The one at Ratlam had been established in 1886. The area the Canadians had elected to work in was known as the Native States of Central India. It was an area that was very backward. A large proportion of its population was not only poor and illiterate but also outcaste. A sizable proportion of the outcastes belonged to a tribal group known as the Bhils.

There were, of course, other mission fields established in neighbouring areas of Central and North India by various North American and European churches and denominationalism was transplanted to India just as it had been to China. In 1924, however, many of the Indian Presbyterian churches and some Congregationalists united to form The United Church of Northern India (U.C.N.I.) and the various mission fields became presbyteries within the new church. From that time the various Irish, Scottish, English, Canadian and American parent mission churches became "partners" within the larger organization. From then on their missionaries worked in India by invitation of the U.C.N.I.* It was a similar evolution to the one McClure had witnessed in China, except that it happened earlier in India, a year earlier, in fact, than the formation of his own United Church of Canada. But in China the union had come about as a result of militant nationalism, the rise of Chiang Kai-shek and the military sweep of the Second Revolution during which missionaries fled the interior and the new church had to form or go under. Because of this totally different political scene, "devolution", the transfer of authority and responsibility from missionaries to indigenous leaders, was much more swift in China than in India.

In India devolution was something that was talked about with more passion than it was implemented. When McClure had returned to China four years after the formation of the Chinese church he found devolution already a fact. When he arrived in India some *thirty* years after the formation of The United Church of Northern India he found devolution, particularly with relation to medical work, still proceeding slowly on its way. To McClure, who had a tendency to reach swift conclusions based on even swifter survey of the facts, it was a shocking situation.

The entire medical work had evolved differently in India than it had in China. From the earliest days the missionaries had run into the problem of *purdah,* the ancient custom which kept women literally screened from male view either in curtained women's quarters, the *zenana,* or, in public, behind the veil. It had been almost impossible for male doctors and evangelists to have any contact at all with Indian women. It seemed evident that Indian women were in many ways more oppressed than were women in any other area of the world. They would not

*In 1970 after a further union with the Anglicans it became the C.N.I., the Church of North India.

even attend government-run "Civil Hospitals" because of lack of privacy. Since women missionaries could make contact where men could not and since the need seemed obvious, it had been quite logical for the Canadian church to send more women to the field than men and early mission hospitals had evolved essentially as women's hospitals. India, not being torn by constant war, revolution and anarchy as China had been, was a much more acceptable field for women workers. This combination of policy and circumstances had resulted in a somewhat unusual situation, particularly in the medical work, of total domination by women.

McClure had worked with many women doctors in China and had had great respect for them. He had had nothing but admiration for Dr. Stuart, his Chief at Harmel in Cairo. Now, when he reacted to his medical mission surroundings in India, it was not male ego that motivated him but professional pride.

McClure was not impressed by the quality of medical work being performed in the seven hospitals and, with more candour than diplomacy, he said so. He found the medical work to be, in his own words, "low in both quality and quantity".

Shortly before he had left Gaza McClure had received a letter from the Board Secretary that contained some pithy advice: "Always remember that ex-China missionaries . . . have to be a little careful in making suggestions to old India hands!"

The advice was ignored.

McClure not only made suggestions, he drew comparisons. He described one hospital as being "semi-conscious" and pointed out that it was not doing half as much work as had been done by any one of his eight country clinics in China under their "quack" doctors. He heaped Gaza upon China. He pointed out that the seven hospitals in Malwa Presbytery had one functioning X-ray amongst them and that a glance at the log book showed it had done as much work in all of 1953 as the Gaza X-ray would do in one afternoon of any week. (In Gaza he had sometimes chafed over their lack of efficiency.) He went further. He looked for some sign of medical mission policy and could find none. "What are our hospitals supposed to be doing?" he wrote in some bewilderment. "Where do they fit into the total picture of mission work? . . . We have bitten off considerably more than we can chew and today are over-expanded and without a policy." It never seemed to occur to him that there might be some relationship between what he was finding and the fact that the Canadian church had been reluctant to leave him in Gaza.

He blew off steam at the lethargy being shown among the Canadian medicals in the whole matter of devolution: "We have not gone far enough or fast enough in this. Our hospital staff members (Indian) do not feel that it is *their* hospital. They feel that they are all working for The United Church of Canada. It is not a healthy nor a modern outlook in this day and age. The difficulty in correcting it is twofold. First, one's own Canadian staff are not keen on the change. They like the feeling of having supreme authority in matters."

The Canadian women could be forgiven if they viewed McClure in their midst with some dismay. During medical committee meetings it often seemed that McClure was on his feet suggesting solutions before anyone had had time to articulate the problem. He expressed himself with a vigour that was unsettling. He was impatient with doctors who let evangelical zeal get in the way of their practice of medicine. He himself would rather have full wards than a full chapel. He would rather do a vasectomy than emotionalize over a full nursery and he would rather preach family planning than salvation.

Some of his conflicts were with Dr. Catherine Whittier, one of two marvellous Canadian sisters who were both doctors and who both served on the India field. Dr. Catherine had been at university with McClure and had then gone to India. She was the "old India hand" personified. Canadian missionaries had absorbed some of the habits of former British days and tended to rule the mission as though wearing the mantle of the British *raj*.* McClure looked at the way Dr. Catherine controlled the dispensation of scholarships and other largesse and immediately called her "Queen Victoria". The saving grace was that both doctors always knew what the other thought. They were not given to talking behind backs. Dr. Catherine once received a critical letter from McClure which she read to other Canadian medical personnel at the dinner table. When Dr. Catherine was agitated she tended to overeat and this time her companions listened with interest to Whittier mutterings and watched in fascination while she unconsciously ate most of an entire chocolate cake.

*Government.

Many years later an Indian nurse said that she felt much of the friction between McClure and some of the other Canadian doctors was because the latter did not like to be forced into using new techniques. Certainly the acquisition of new techniques had been one of McClure's major priorities and he showed no intention of changing that priority. "Adopt and adapt" had been his slogan for a quarter of a century.

No place was the extent of the conflict more interestingly illustrated than in the matter of Caesarean sections. The traditional method had involved an incision quite high on the abdomen. The operation tended to weaken the wall of the uterus so that usually it was inadvisable for the woman to bear more children. McClure came along with the Marshall technique for "low segment Caesarean" that he had learned in Harmel Hospital in Cairo. This was a more difficult operation but the patient could continue to bear children. McClure was frustrated to the point of exasperation when some of his colleagues in India resisted learning the low segment technique. He was even more frustrated by the fact that the resisters were not only Canadians but women.

McClure was in conflict with the Medical Commission not only over techniques but over policy. When another Canadian doctor, Dr. Helen Huston, arrived on the field and was immediately thrown into hospital work virtually on her own McClure protested loudly. He recognized that there was a certain urgency for the Commission to want all doctors to "get on with the work" but he remembered his own early years on a mission field. He knew that he owed a great deal to having been able to work under two experienced doctors when first he went to China and his gratitude was unending to Dr. Gushue-Taylor for having ruthlessly knocked the rough edges off him in Taiwan. He assessed Dr. Huston as being not only a fine person but a conscientious and able doctor and he chafed all the more at the fact that she was not being permitted a good solid break-in period with another doctor. He voiced the opinion that to send new missionary doctors out on their own was to "start them on the downward path." It was, to McClure's mind, totally unfair.

McClure did not endear himself to anyone at a committee meeting in the city of Indore held soon after his arrival in India. He yielded to the temptation to extrapolate from skimpy observations in the Ratlam area (a very backward region) and applied his findings to all Malwa, including the much more advanced area of the city of Indore. He announced that "all Indian Christians have V.D." This brought an immediate challenge from Reuben Moses, a tall, imposingly handsome Indian gentleman with a Ph.D. and a wife who was not only a doctor but the secretary of the Medical Commission. Reuben Moses demanded an apology and offered to present himself and an impressive number of friends for immediate and thorough V.D. tests. McClure, who as usual had overstated his case to make a point, rephrased with more diplomacy. The V.D. remark was not an isolated verbal indiscretion. "I dislike what he says," said one Canadian missionary after another vibrant meeting, then added, charitably, "but I like the way he says it."

The people of Ratlam were being instructed by more than words. In the hospital they had McClure in action and what they were seeing was creating an indelible impression. No action was more revealing than that which took place in the O.R. during a total hysterectomy.

A total hysterectomy involved the removal of the entire uterus and both ovaries. The operation was a major one and could entail heavy loss of blood. In those days of poor refrigeration and consequent absence of blood banks McClure would not do a hysterectomy without a blood donor standing by. Unfortunately blood donors were every bit as reluctant as they had been in China. Superstition was involved and just plain fear. Many Indians were convinced that giving blood would kill the donor. On this particular day the patient was a woman whose hemoglobin count was 8 gms instead of a minimum 12 gms. For her a blood transfusion would be absolutely essential. The staff had convinced the patient's husband to be a volunteer. They had typed his blood and had him standing by in the O.R. anteroom. At the appropriate moment he would be taken into the O.R., placed on a table next to the operating table, and the transfusion would be made with no intervening steps. The only hitch in the system came when the assistants went to bring in the donor. He had fled. In the O.R. the patient's life hung by the proverbial thread and there was no time to go recruiting another volunteer. While the O.R. team stood by in amazement the surgeon himself climbed on the donor's table.

When the transfusion was completed McClure climbed off the table and calmly completed the operation. The word went around Ratlam that once you put your life in the hands of *McClure sahib* he would back your life with his own.

There was another blood donation, however, that McClure himself found far more impressive. One day the donor was a Hindu man who was *absolutely convinced* that giving blood would kill him. Even so he donated to his wife.

17

The Whole Man

The poorer villages in the Ratlam area were little more than a collection of adobe huts with tiled, thatched or corrugated iron roofs. Each house was usually joined to its neighbour with the result that each side of each dusty street was flanked by depressing rows of depressing human habitations. The layout inside was almost as uniformly simple and depressing as the exterior. Each house had three rooms. The front door led directly into a room where friends could sit and visit or where family could work at household crafts. Directly behind this room was the bedroom and immediately behind that was the kitchen. The latter was used for cooking mainly during the wet season. At other times the cooking fire burned in the small backyard. Light came through the front and back doorways. Windows were a luxury.

The floors of the three rooms were made of a mixture of mud compacted with cow dung. When the mixture was correctly applied it created a smooth surface that could be rubbed to a gloss and that could be renewed by rubbing on a fresh application of moist dung and mud.

The Bhils, who were the native tribal people, preferred a slightly different interior layout. Their homes often contained only two rooms, the front one being used for storage and as a place where visitors could sleep and cook. The second room was kitchen, bedroom and family room all in one. It also housed a few farm animals. There were no windows, but an open space at the top of the walls below the eaves permitted air to enter and smoke from the open cooking fire to leave.

Most Western doctors would not have thought of either

style of house as lending itself to the practice of medicine. McClure, however, saw the necessary requisites for X-ray clinics; rooms that could be made almost totally dark.

It became a familiar occurrence in the villages of the Ratlam area of the Malwa Plateau for a team to arrive from Ratlam hospital. They would bring with them a portable X-ray and a portable generator. They would descend upon the home of a volunteer and would drape the doorways with heavy cloth or cover the eave vents to block out light. *McClure sahib* himself would arrive by train, foot or bicycle. He would don a huge apron that appeared to be very heavy, and indeed it was for it was lined with lead. He would slip red goggles over his eyes and after a few minutes he would pull on heavy, rubber, lead-lined gloves that reached almost to his elbows and he would disappear inside the converted house.

The portable gasoline-driven generator would begin to thump away and all the village school children who had been brought together by their teachers and the hospital nurses would begin to file in and out of the suddenly mysterious house.

In the dark of the interior the children would find the *doctor sahib* sitting in front of the X-ray machine. Between him and the machine a fluoroscope screen hung suspended from the rafters by ropes that went over pulleys and were fastened to weights. The doctor could raise or lower the screen at will to adjust it to the patient's height. Pictures were not being taken on film. Film was too expensive and difficult to process under primitive conditions. McClure read the fluoroscope shadows and dictated his findings to a staff member.

To the smaller school children it was terribly mysterious and even frightening and sometimes the *doctor sahib*, no doubt irritated by the heat and pushed by the need to screen as many children as possible each day, would shout at them to hurry up, to hold their heads up, to hold their breath, not to hold their breath, to put their hands on their hips, to move on and not to hold the curtain open. On one occasion a small boy found it all so frightening that he completely lost control of his very full bladder.

"What's this? What's this?" shouted McClure, in the dark. "I'm all wet!"

"Doctor," said an Indian nurse, just as loudly, "if you

would not shout so and frighten them so this would not happen."

Outside, Nurse Robson heard the exchange and called out, "Good for you!"

No one knew whether she was complimenting the nurse for her courage or the boy for his aim.

For McClure, being urinated on in the dark was merely an occupational hazard that one faced when embarking on public health. That he should be involved in public health was as natural to him as the monsoons were to India but public health was not a subject in which Indians themselves showed much interest nor had it been very high on mission priorities. Most mission hospitals struggled to be self-supporting by charging fees for curative services. Money spent on preventative public health was money lost twice over. Nor was public health work attractive to doctors who found great satisfaction in being busy with curative medicine.

McClure had not been in India more than a few weeks before he was commenting on the lack of public health and of preventative medicine at the village level. He was also commenting on the fact that the rural Christian Church seemed to be strong, with "exceptionally fine" pastoral leadership. He saw that rural church as the foundation upon which to build good rural medicine and public health.

In McClure's opinion the medical profession had already missed too many good opportunities. He visited the agricultural school of Allahabad which had been established as a joint enterprise by several missions and while there he made a speech to the Christian Medical Association. He then told the Board Secretary what he had already said from the platform: "Allahabad is the biggest tragedy in rural medical work for there you have a marvelous agricultural institution—the most advanced of any mission field in the world doing a fine job of extension work in the villages and *all without a medical side to the program!** Seldom has mission medicine missed the bus so completely as it has in Allahabad."

When it came to getting involved in public health McClure had one unfailing asset; he always recognized an opportunity when he saw one. In India that opportunity had come at an early

*Author's italics.

stage in the form of a donation of 500 rupees given by a bereaved Rotarian to the club's service fund. McClure had suggested that an excellent community service project would be to conduct a TB survey of local school children under the age of 12. The Ratlam hospital would provide personnel and X-ray equipment free if Rotary covered the costs of material. (It worked out at about one rupee per child.) Other Rotarians had matched the initial donation.

During the initial survey twelve active cases of TB were detected. Madhya Pradesh State Health Service had a sanatorium at Indore under a Dr. Mukerji. McClure arranged for the young patients to be treated there at nominal charge. He raised $500 from Canadian well-wishers and the Ratlam Rotarians set about trying to match it.

Everything escalated.

It seemed obvious that Ratlam hospital itself should be more actively involved in the treatment of TB patients. The average mission hospital, however, with its relatively small bed capacity, had not been in the habit of treating TB patients. The cure was long and the presence of the disease endangered fellow patients and nurses-in-training. On the other hand, India had very few TB beds anywhere and none were within easy reach of Ratlam. Nor did the government offer free TB care. But there was a model TB centre being run in Delhi by "a very fine Indian doctor" working under the auspices of WHO and UNICEF. McClure made a trip to Delhi to observe and came back to Ratlam full of enthusiasm. He and Dr. Naku set up a system based on the Delhi model. It was a system of treatment requiring only a short stay in hospital. Early detection usually meant that the TB was present in only one lung. A small operation on the neck of the ailing side paralysed the diaphragm on that side and then air admitted into the chest collapsed the lung, giving it the rest required for healing. The operation cost $5.00 (Cdn). The patient would be in hospital about one month during which time he or she was given the newest drugs. The patient's diet was supplemented by milk powder donated by the World Council of Churches. While in hospital the patient was taught how to look after himself at home and after release from hospital would return every two weeks for an air refill of the chest cavity and for an X-ray and blood test. Within about three months of implementing this system Ratlam hospital had seventy-eight TB pa-

tients on active treatment and McClure was amazed at the results. He suspected that the antibiotics worked better than they
would have in Canada because in India the patients were not
already pre-doped on other medications. He also acknowledged
the curative powers of India's climate that provided almost eight
months of dry, sunny weather.

The cost of the TB treatment seemed modest by Canadian
standards but not by Indian standards. A hard working farm-
hand in the Ratlam area might make the equivalent of $6.00
(Cdn) a month, gross. The total cost for the treatment, which
lasted about a year, was $25.00, the majority of that being for
drugs, in particular, streptomycin. Streptomycin had to be im-
ported and a heavy import duty was charged. That kind of duty
always angered McClure. To him it was simply a case of a
government being willing to make money from its TB victims "at
a lusty rate". There were others willing to make money from TB
patients. A local farmer borrowed the money for his treatment
from a money-lender at an interest rate of 25 per cent *per month*.
It was the kind of usury that could put McClure into orbit. He
would become angry with everyone, including the patient.

In the meantime the TB screenings had been extended out
to the villages and McClure had managed to have a TB fund
established as part of his hospital budget. He was also using
funds from what was known by the Board as the "McClure
Project Funds". For years people at home had donated money
"for Bob McClure's work" and such money had been duly
administered by the Board as McClure called for it. It was quite
separate from any allocated budgets. This fund had been, and
always would be, used for a variety of purposes. It underwrote
worthy students, it rescued patients from the hands of money-
lenders, it bought equipment that McClure felt should not come
from the hospital budget. On occasion, it cut the Gordian
knot of bureaucratic delay by making it possible to initiate action
while the mission or the Board were still thinking about it so that
the decision makers were handed a *fait accompli* and could then
have the pleasure of refunding the money from proper channels
to the McClure Fund.

When McClure talked about some new scheme the Mission
Council had to listen with care. It was always possible he might
dip into the McClure Fund and launch it in spite of them.

After the Rotarians had given him a TB toe-hold in the area

of public health McClure was bursting with ideas. (He was always bursting with ideas and one cannot help but sympathize with mission committee members who had to sort the good from the bad and the rational from the irrational.) The four major medical problems in India appeared to be TB, syphilis, typhoid and malaria, all of which could be tracked down and fought at the village level. McClure wanted to train "quacks" as he had done in China, and send them out to run rural clinics. Training quacks was a good idea in the China of the Thirties but did not sound so good in the independent, post-British India of the Fifties. McClure wanted to train laboratory technicians to function in the villages in conjunction with public health nurses. He suggested training the mission driver-mechanics as lab technicians. They could drive the evangelists to their rural meetings and, while waiting, set up microscopes and get to work. It was all a bit much for the twenty-one women on the Medical Commission. They were singularly unimpressed by McClure's suggestions. As it turned out, however, since the Commission was only a sub-committee it could be overruled by its parent. It was.

In October of 1955 the Central India Mission Council appointed McClure as convener of a "Rural Pilot Project Committee". It was not surprising that before long that committee selected Ratlam area as the focal point for a Pilot Project and under its umbrella McClure was soon training young men as lab technicians for future village work.

The church already had an evangelical toe-hold at a village called Bamnia, a one-hour train journey from Ratlam. A mission house had been built in Bamnia in 1933 and there was an active Indian pastor there. A small clinic was established in charge of an Indian nurse under the guidance of a Canadian nurse who acted as an itinerant public health supervisor.

There was an outbreak of typhoid in Bamnia and two people died. McClure organized a vaccination campaign with enough vaccine to inoculate 2,000 people. Only 42 showed up. It was obvious that public health had a long path to travel.

The rural project at Bamnia was soon given an enormous boost by the appointment of a United Church of Canada agricultural evangelist, Rev. Norman Mackenzie, and his wife, Dorothy. Dorothy was a registered nurse with a special interest in public health. The Mackenzies took their three young children with them and set up home in a Bamnia house with a corrugated iron roof and a cow dung floor. Dorothy took some training at Ratlam as a lab technician and joined the Indian nurse at the clinic.

Norman Mackenzie put his energies into agricultural work with McClure always in the background ready with moral support, mechanical know-how, and ingenious ways to procure equipment and make financial ends meet. Many years later a resident of Bamnia would describe the impact of the Mackenzies in their midst as "a revival of life itself where before it was despair and hopelessness".

Although considerably younger than McClure both Norman and Dorothy had been born in the Weihwei compound in China where Bob had spent his childhood! Dorothy was a Lochead, the youngest sister of Marnie Copland whose path had crossed and recrossed that of the McClures for years.

At last there were others close by who shared McClure's concern for rural work and who felt as he did that mission work could not be compartmentalized. Evangelism, agriculture, medicine—it was all intertwined.

There was no doubt in McClure's mind of the importance of rural extension work whether it was in agriculture or medicine. Nor did he have any doubt but what that work, to be successful, had to be done by missionaries. He spelled it all out in an unusual letter to the minister of a Vancouver church:

"The need of the villager to change his ways is obvious to everyone—to everyone except the villager. Don't get the idea that he is thirsting for a change. He is not at all. To change he requires such a break from tradition that some very deeply rooted and fundamental change has to take place in his character before he will change some of the simplest of his farm methods. This fundamental and deeply rooted change is going to be brought about as the result of education. Teaching is the big thing then . . . Does he keep his religious superstitions but adopt new farm techniques? I doubt it very much. Until the shell of superstition in his character can be cracked and until a new viewpoint is had toward the world in general there will not be a change in his techniques. It is the mental block that is holding up progress, not merely a technical ignorance.

"... your agricultural people want to increase the food supply. Increased food supply means the farmer and his wife will produce more children to eat the food . . . If you take India as a whole the standard of living is going down slightly in the past

100 years due to this problem. Family planning is the answer . . . but in the village health scheme you find that people believe that anti-typhoid inoculations will make them sterile. So they won't take them. This is the complicated chain of events that one sees. *This is not theory** . . .

"It is the inability or unwillingness to make mental changes that make 'backward people' backward . . . What easier way to change the entire mental personality of a man than by religious conversion. Nobody would try to make him modern in chemistry and physics and leave him ancient in superstition. That's all modern missions are doing is to change the whole man."

"To change the whole man"; McClure, in his mid-fifties now, was finally beginning to verbalize his philosophy of mission. It was a philosophy he had been trying to put into action for years.

Toward the end of 1955 McClure received a letter from the Board Secretary telling him he should be thinking in terms of a short furlough. The letter reminded him that his father would soon celebrate an important birthday.

McClure needed no urging. He was becoming terribly lonesome for Amy. His first stint in India had been a long, hard haul. He could leave the hospital in the capable hands of Dr. Joshua Naku. By now McClure considered Naku to be one of the finest colleagues he had ever had.

McClure would be back. He had already written to a medical colleague in Toronto: "I am completely fallen in love with medical work in India and if I am spared for ten years to do this work it will be the height of my ambition."

If heredity was to play a hand the chances were very good that McClure would be "spared". His father's approaching birthday was number one hundred.

* Author's italics.

18

Dr. William McClure

Bob McClure arrived home by air near the end of March, 1956, in time to be an active participant in the final days of family activity leading up to his father's 100th birthday.

The old gentleman was in remarkably good health, considering his age. For a year or more now he had not been making regular journeys downstairs but he was still not completely bedridden. He preferred to sit, fully dressed, in an easy chair in his own room where he could read, doze, or talk to friends. His eyesight had failed badly but he used a large magnifying glass to help him through daily readings from his Bible and he was still forcing his mind to consume information from the Encyclopaedia Britannica. His hearing had deteriorated to the point that he had abandoned the telephone some time ago but until recently he had continued to negotiate on the 'phone with his stockbroker by the simple expedient of having his grandson, Doug, use the instrument for him and act as intermediary. Over the years a judicious use of stocks and bonds had been important to the old gentleman. He used the capitalist system to make money so he could indulge in private Christian socialism and give it away. It was only now, in the final months of his hundredth year, that his mind could no longer quite cope with the mathematical complexities of the stock market.

It was an augmented family that was preparing for Grandfather McClure's birthday. Norah and David Busby had been married in 1951. About the time McClure was transferring from Gaza to India, Josephine had married Bruce Taylor, a tall, quiet young man, who had known the family for years, having been a friend of Doug's since their early teens. He was working in the world of finance but Grandfather McClure, who was gaining a new perspective on the world from spending more and more time in bed, was more impressed by young Taylor's height than by his profession.

With the exception of Doug the grandchildren were not living at Strathallan but two newcomers were. Vart and Johanna Korlu had emigrated to Canada from Gaza and were living with Amy while they got established. They had decided to settle in Canada largely because of the salesmanship of Bob McClure. McClure was always urging friends from other countries to migrate to Canada. He would go to great lengths to write introductions for them, to sponsor them and, whenever necessary, to lend them money for the transition. It appeared to some that McClure's enthusiasm for Canada was bounded only by his own unwillingness to live there.

McClure found his father full of questions concerning the "work". The old gentleman was still interested in hearing about hospital details and about new equipment and techniques. He was even more interested in hearing whether any strides were being made in the general improvement of the human condition. He himself had never wavered in his faith that the human condition could indeed be bettered nor had he ever seemed to question the Christian imperative that one must try to better it. And yet he himself had never been driven by the imp of aggressive impatience that pursued his son. William McClure was one of those rare men in whom all parts had merged with harmony. He was, as his grandchildren would say, completely together. He was one of those fortunate people who, without any bombast or rhetoric, had faith in himself, in mankind, and in God with the result that even in his gentleness he had always had a certain aura. There was power in William McClure's presence. He emanated courage. Even now, as he approached the century mark, the aura was still there.

Television was of no interest to Dr. William McClure but he was of great interest to television. In those formative years of CBC-TV there was a programme called *Tabloid* that was popular with the Toronto-Ottawa-Montreal audience. The programme featured interviews with unusual and interesting people. The producer of *Tabloid* took his crew to 108 Strathallan and filmed an interview with Dr. William McClure. It was aired to coincide closely with the doctor's 100th birthday. The producer, using his imagination, had broken from format and had chosen an unusual interviewer. The interviewer was Dr. Bob McClure. For the family it was part of the general air of festivity to watch a TV programme featuring both father and grandfather. For the CBC it was something of a coup.*

On April 9th, the day of his 100th birthday, Dr. William McClure held court for a general gathering of the clans. On hand to pay homage were his son, daughter-in-law, eight grandchildren and three great grandchildren. Nieces and nephews came from afar. There were representatives of the Bairds, his wife's people from Pennsylvania. There were Rodgers from his mother's clan in Quebec. There were old China hands: members of the Menzies clan, whose illustrious forbear, Dr. James Menzies, had been murdered at Hwaiking; the Roulstons, now from the States, who had been foster parents to Norah and Doug at the boarding school in Weihwei; Dr. Mary Grant (now Atack), who had been born in Weihwei and who shared childhood memories with Bob and who had practised with him as a doctor in Hwaiking; with Dr. Mary came her parents, Rev. and Mrs. Harvey Grant, whose own memories of China, like Dr. Wm. McClure's, went back a decade before the Boxer Rebellion; there were Bruce and Marnie Copland and, unfailing now on the day of the birthday as he had been unfailing in regular visits for the past many years, came Marnie's father, Rev. Arthur Lochead. Others came, too numerous to name, all gathering to pay homage to the gentle patriarch.

After the birthday celebrations were over Bob McClure enjoyed a short furlough during which time he caught his breath, became acquainted with his grandchildren, raised money for India projects and viewed the Canadian scene. The latter activity became a spectator sport as the parliamentarians in Ottawa launched into the notorious Pipeline Debate. One of the players was a good friend and neighbour of the McClures', Donald Fleming, a Conservative M.P. Bob and Amy listened with fascination to the news accounts of Fleming defying the Speaker and being evicted from the House of Commons while behind him his empty desk was draped with the Union Jack to the accompaniment of Liberal derision and Conservative histrionics. On

*Unfortunately the programme was not preserved.

Strathallan street, Donald Fleming was the man of the hour.

In spite of the turmoil in Ottawa, Canada seemed to be as stable as ever. McClure's old acquaintance, Vincent Massey, was re-appointed to another term as Governor General. Quebec was still in the grip of the Union Nationale under Maurice Duplessis. Saskatchewan was in the process of returning to power the socialist C.C.F. government of Tommy Douglas. In Ottawa, once the pipeline dust settled, a joint committee of both Houses brought in a report concerning capital punishment. It recommended execution by gas or electrocution rather than hanging. Bay Street economists were debating the pros and cons of a recent rise in the Bank of Canada interest rate to 3 per cent, and, while the debate continued, it was raised to a record $3^1/4$ per cent. But for Dr. William McClure the time had finally come when bank rates, politics and even the human condition were of no further concern.

On July 16th, 1956, while his son was still home on furlough, Dr. William McClure died peacefully in his sleep.

The funeral was a quietly informal occasion in keeping with the life of William McClure. There was no sermon and no eulogy, but several people who were close to him and to the family rose and spoke the things that were in their hearts. One was Donald Fleming. Another was Arthur Lochead who, with the genius of a true clergyman, managed to turn a prayer into a reminiscence of his old friend's days in China.

For Bob McClure the quiet funeral brought forth many private memories of his boyhood in China and of the doctor who was his father; the man with the fiercely drooping moustache and the gentle eyes who drew a chalk-line across the doorsill and told his son he must not speak Chinese inside the threshold; the man who dispensed Bob's allowance every Saturday and let him scamper off with his Chinese playmates to the walled city of Weihwei to barter in Horsemarket Street; the man who understood rabid dogs and Chinese warlords and so taught his thirteen-year-old son to use a 30-30 Marlin rifle; the doctor whose depression after losing a tiny patient to hydrophobia had been the catalyst that made his son decide to be a doctor; the doctor who, at retirement age, had willingly handed over his hospital to younger men, had encouraged them to revitalize it, and had then taken himself off to Cheloo University to translate medical texts into Chinese and to spend two of the most productive decades of his life teaching a generation of Chinese doctors.

Bob and his father had never been "close"; not in the superficial sense in which father and son are "chums". They had been closer than that. They were tied by more than blood and were interlocked on another plane than that of mere physical association.

The day the men from the funeral home carried Dr. William McClure's body out of 108 Strathallan was the only time Amy had ever seen tears in her husband's eyes.

19

The Prisoner

In October of 1956 the world went into spasm. The Hungarians revolted against Russian domination and the Russians sent tanks into Budapest. In the Middle East the Israelis, apparently exasperated by terrorist attacks launched from the Gaza Strip and the Sinai desert, invaded both regions and struck towards the Suez Canal, enabling Britain and France to invade Egypt's canal zone in the name of "protection". At home, the Canadian government of Louis St. Laurent found itself angry at the Russians, the Israelis, the British and the French. In India, Prime Minister Nehru managed to confine his anger to Britain and France, thereby losing something of his reputation for impartiality.

In the meantime, however, Bob McClure had returned to India and Amy McClure was packing her bags in preparation to follow him. Amy was approaching a milepost she had almost despaired of reaching. For the first time since 1937 she was to join her husband permanently on the mission field. Her sister and brother-in-law, Janet and Dr. Stan Montgomery, were moving into 108 Strathallan as tenants.

In Ratlam, Bob McClure prepared the doctor's bungalow for his wife's arrival and read the international news with concerned interest. His beloved people of the Gaza Strip were now under Israeli military occupation rather than Egyptian. Only time would tell how it would all end.

McClure had returned to find the Ratlam mission hospital functioning well but not at full capacity. The empty beds illustrated a phenomenon that bothered him; patients tended to be attracted to a Western doctor rather than to a particular hospital. The Indian tendency to assume that their own people were second best was undoubtedly a legacy from colonial days. It was a phenomenon not unknown in Canada except that there the medical profession at least had shaken free of it. It was McClure's hope that at Ratlam he and his Indian colleagues could create a reputation that would cling to the hospital, not to its Chief. He now talked the Medical Commission into naming Dr. Naku "Deputy-Superintendent" of Ratlam Christian Hospital in an attempt to keep the devolution process going. "One of the greatest thrills of mission life," he wrote, "is to watch the devolution of a piece of work and the making of oneself dispensable."

In other directions everything seemed to be making good progress. The course designed to train lab technicians for rural work had drawn in students from as far away as the borders of Burma and Afghanistan. The Ratlam Christian community was trying to inaugurate a medical health insurance scheme. McClure attributed much of the impetus for this to the work the Mackenzies were doing at nearby Bamnia in planting the idea of co-operatives. In the hospital, electric washing machines were installed to take care of all surgical linens. The only person who objected was a Canadian who thought the old ways should not be tampered with. "If the Indian sun plays on the top of the missionary cranium too long," wrote McClure, "it produces changes in the thought patterns that are hard to reverse!"

Other facilities had been steadily improved. X-ray and lab equipment were such that now routine urine, stool and blood tests were made to detect syphilis and every in-patient had a routine chest X-ray for TB.

The programme for conducting TB screenings in rural areas was still underway, backed now by Canadian Rotarians as well as by the Rotary Club of Ratlam. And at last Bob McClure himself became a Rotarian. Over the years he had addressed more than three hundred Rotary Clubs in various corners of the globe but it was not until he was permanently established in Ratlam that he became a member. He could not have found a more unusual service club.

The only social institutions that seemed able to cut across all of India's religious groups were the international service clubs like Rotary and Lions. Ratlam seemed to be more free of religious frictions than were many other parts of the country and much to McClure's pleasure he found the Ratlam Rotary Club to be singularly unprejudiced. In his opinion its members gave ample proof of that by inviting him to join them.

In Ratlam Rotary there were Hindus, Moslems, Parsees, a few Sikhs and now one Christian. The Hindus, Moslems and Sikhs had strict regulations concerning what food they could eat and with whom it could be eaten. In addition, the Hindus, particularly the Jains, were strict vegetarians while the others were not. There was a potential for friction here that threatened to destroy the club until the members declared their club to be strictly vegetarian. From then on any visiting orthodox Hindu could visit the Ratlam Rotary Club of India without any fear of being defiled. (It was reported among Rotarians that another service club had debated going vegetarian but that the debate had ended when a member had growled, "Who ever heard of a vegetarian lion?")

Another diplomatic problem concerned not Hindu food but Christian prayer. It was the custom for the club president to open every meeting with a prayer that had been composed by St. Francis of Assisi. Each week, whether the president was Moslem or Hindu, Sikh or Parsee, the words of the Christian, St. Francis, were read: "Lord make me an instrument of Thy peace. Where there is hatred let me sow love; where there is injury, pardon; where there is doubt, faith; where there is despair, hope; where there is darkness, light; and where there is sadness, joy."

In those days of nationalism and growing pride of culture it was not unnatural that some members suggested that the words of St. Francis should be replaced by readings from the greatest of Hindu religious books, the *Bhagavad-Gita*. This suggestion was debated by the club members (while McClure kept to the sidelines) and it was laid to rest by a Hindu who was also a charter member of the club. He had been a member of the nationalist Congress Party and had spent, at intervals, seven years in prison under British rule for his radical nationalist activities. "Brothers," he asked, "is the music of Beethoven only for the Germans? Are the plays of Shakespeare only for the English?

Are the words of St. Francis only for the Christians?" The Ratlam Rotary Club made no change in its opening prayer.*

The Hindu Rotarian who made that short but moving speech was a banker named Manohar Nagpal. In the person of Manohar Nagpal, McClure met a man whom he truly admired. It was customary to hear that any nationalist who had been a political activist during the British regime had spent some time in British prisons, but every December this ex-prisoner, a Hindu, exchanged Christmas cards and friendly letters with the British judge who had sentenced him. The judge was now retired in England and was, in Nagpal's forgiving eyes, lonely and in need of personal contact.

Manohar Nagpal had been a devoted follower of Mahatma Ghandi and had been particularly dedicated to Ghandi's policy of non-violence. McClure was no stranger to pacificism and non-violence but he had never heard anything to equal pre-independence happenings in Ratlam. The more he learned about it the more his admiration grew.

After the end of World War II the nationalists had been more determined than ever to speed India to independence. There had been disturbances and riots in various parts of India. A state of emergency had been declared and by law it was an offence for more than five people to gather in public. In Ratlam, Manohar Nagpal and the other Congress Party organizers gathered two thousand people together and marched to the Collector's house.† There they shouted some slogans but were scrupulously non-violent. (In Nagpal's code one did not club police dogs, because they were doing their duty. One did not curse policemen because they,too, were doing their duty.)

The demonstration had the desired effect. The authorities could not ignore two thousand people when the law said there should be no more than five. The entire crowd was arrested. In reality, they arrested themselves since the only law enforcers were a half dozen policemen armed with old Lee Enfield rifles.

The two thousand went peaceably to the local gaol which held about 125 people. The authorities had a problem that they themselves could not solve. Only the two thousand could solve

*In 1978 the same prayer was in use, but in Hindi.

†Collector: the district administrator, appointed by the government.

it. They did. Next to the gaol was a large field. The prisoners found a supply of lime and with it they marked the outlines of imaginary cells of an imaginary prison. As far as possible they designed the prison to conform to the shade beneath handy banyan trees. The two thousand trooped into their cells, ten to a cell, and sat down.

There was no way the authorities could organize the feeding of a sudden influx of two thousand prisoners and so, still demonstrating that they themselves were the true custodians of civil order, the prisoners went home for their two daily meals and after eating returned to sit in their imaginary cells.

The next problem that faced the authorities was that of writing out two thousand charge sheets since no person arrested could be arraigned in a British court without one. It was obvious that the clerks would be several months in the process. Manohar Nagpal had had some legal training and he made out the charges for himself and about twenty others in adjoining cells. He took great care with the "whereases" and the "wherefores" and made certain he had the correct section of the code so that the authorities would know that even here the system was functioning correctly only by grace of the prisoners.

Thanks to his diligence he and his companions were the first ones arraigned in court. The judge complimented Nagpal on his skills as a legal clerk, apologized for having no alternative, and sentenced them to two years in prison. The sentence had to be served elsewhere, Ratlam's facilities being somewhat overcrowded.

While Manohar Nagpal was in prison India achieved independence. He was released from gaol and within hours was installed as the Mayor of Ratlam. He returned to the banking business.

The whole story fascinated McClure. He was also fascinated by the fact that, from the day of Independence, Nagpal had ceased to be an active member of the Congress Party. Nagpal continued to wear the white "Nehru" hat and the white homespun coat of the Congress Party but more as a badge of honour than as a partisan uniform. In his code the British were forgiven, the freedom struggle was over, and from there on the battle was between the politicians. He had been fighting for Independence, not for Power.

McClure and Manohar Nagpal served together on many

Rotary committees. Frequently they were in each other's homes. One evening, while eating vegetarian oatmeal cookies and avoiding non-vegetarian cake that had an egg in it, the ex-Congressman told of going to join Mahatma Ghandi in the nineteen thirties. His account of his first meeting with the little saint reminded McClure of the New Testament story of Jesus and the Rich Man. The banker from Ratlam was told to go to an ashram for two years to meditate, then to come back and join the Ghandi movement.

McClure laughed. How could anyone spend two years meditating!

"I'll tell you, Bob," said Manohar. "You must understand what the meditation was to accomplish. We had to learn how to hate the British government and how to love every individual Englishman." There was a twinkle in his eyes. "You cannot do that in under two years."

20

Amy

The year 1957 began most auspiciously for Bob McClure. Amy arrived in Calcutta on New Year's Day and he was on hand to greet her.

The journey from Calcutta to Ratlam was by train across the vast heart of India. They travelled in a first class compartment which was comfortable but not nearly as luxurious as the accommodation aboard the Green Express by which Amy had first travelled into China. Luxury was unimportant. For a period of three days they were alone, in transit.

There was a long-standing tradition on the mission field that new arrivals should stop over at any sister mission stations they passed through en route to their own areas. The route from Calcutta passed through Indore, the major community on the Canadian field. McClure had not announced that Amy was coming and now, en route to Ratlam, he ignored established protocol and went straight through. Twenty years later there were still people in Indore who remembered.

Amy had been well briefed and Ratlam held few surprises. If anything everything was better than she had expected.

Her initial view of the compound was inviting. They drove through the arched gateway with its sign announcing "Ratlam Christian Hospital". Ahead stretched a long laneway, flanked on one side by the low walls of the hospital. Near the gate the branches of the old banyan tree reached out over the hospital wall as though offering shelter to newcomers from the moment of arrival. On the other side of the lane the red flowers of a giant Bougainvillaea tree vied with the yellow flowers of an equally large gulmohar tree.

The McClure's destination lay far at the back of the compound, past the hospital, past the nurses' residence, along the
lane to the house that was to be home. It was the Administrator's
bungalow. It stood at the upper end of the lane and at the very
back of the compound. It was "bungalow" in name only. The
house stood, large, square, and two storeys high. The long lane
ended at a modest wire gate flanked by an evergreen hedge. The
gateway led onto a driveway that looped around in a full circle
and passed beneath a covered portico that sheltered the front
door.

There was a verandah along the front of the house and it,
too, was two storeys high. On the second storey the verandah
thrust out over the portico. From there one had the illusion of
being able to survey the entire compound.

Downstairs, the house was spacious, with a living room,
dining room, and a large study. The kitchen thrust out to the
back. Upstairs there were several bedrooms. There was running water and a flush toilet.

On close examination it was obvious that the house, although large and square, was not necessarily solid. Decay was
setting in and here and there a wall looked alarmingly ready to
crumble. The kitchen was primitive. Even so, the bungalow was
more comfortable and better appointed than Amy had dared
hope.

Basic furniture went with the house but McClure had been
scurrying around and had bought new wicker furniture for the
living room. Amy now added pleasantly textured window
drapes, a few colourful scatter cushions, some richly woven
Indian rugs for the floor and some pictures to brighten the walls.
Not since 1937 when the Sino-Japanese War had separated the
family in China had Bob McClure's mission home felt the benefit
of his wife's civilizing influence.

In a burst of domestic enthusiasm McClure ordered a new
double bed for the master bedroom. The church had a technical
training institute, at another station, in charge of David Eadie, a
Canadian. Eadie's students were doing excellent work in the
woodworking department and so McClure gave Eadie the order
for the bed. It was a commercial project and was paid for in hard
McClure cash.

The day the purchase was delivered McClure was extremely pleased. The bed was a truly splendid looking piece of

furniture. Several members of the hospital staff were taken on a guided tour to admire the new acquisition, no doubt so they could report abroad concerning the excellent work the students were doing.

Late in the evening of that same day McClure, still feeling domestically exuberant, charged from the bathroom into the master bedroom and leaped onto the splendid and expensive bed. It collapsed around him.

The night watchman at the hospital gate was surprised to see *McClure sahib* leaving the compound on his bicycle at a late hour and at a high rate of speed.

The night operator at the Ratlam telegraph office was equally surprised to have *McClure sahib* rouse him to send a "triple express" telegram to David Eadie. The message said, "Come at once, bring the truck."

Eadie, thinking a missionary must have died and that they needed the truck to take the body to Indore before the heat of the day set in, was on hand by 5 o'clock the next morning. The unfortunate Eadie was greeted in words that could be heard all the way down to the nurses' residence. The flaws in his students' handiwork were described with great vigour to the accompaniment of loud noises that sounded very much as though sections of a large bed were being thrown down the front stairs in the doctor's house.

Nurses claim to this day that Eadie went into a state of shock.

The occasional outburst notwithstanding, the members of the hospital staff were of the definite opinion that McClure was much easier to get along with after Amy arrived than he had been before. There might well have been truth to the claim because McClure himself had made a similar report to the Board Secretary after Amy's visit in Gaza. "They say I'm much harder to get along with without my wife," he had written. "My colleagues know more about this than I do."

There is no doubt that Amy could manage her husband at times when others feared to try. Nurses who felt oppressed or insulted would seek Amy and shed a few tears. When Dr. Naku thought his Chief was being too obdurate he would have a quiet chat with Amy. Invariably McClure would melt into sweet reasonableness. Amy knew the music that soothed the savage breast.

From the moment Amy McClure arrived in Ratlam she set

up her typewriter in the study and took over the job of private secretary. Keeping up with the McClure correspondence became a full-time task in itself. McClure would rise early in the morning and dictate letters that required his personal input. Amy would begin typing when he left for work, and during the day she would take finished correspondence down to the hospital for McClure's signature. Amy estimated that their correspondence averaged a thousand letters a year. It was a flood that kept flowing for many years.

On the days when McClure was making rounds Amy would expect him and the supervisors back for coffee and cookies by mid-morning. On O.R. days she would see that coffee and cookies were sent to the O.R. (She did her own baking from favourite recipes, some of which were adjusted to suit vegetarian requirements.) Westerners who found themselves in hospital often found that their meals were originating in the McClure kitchen under Amy's supervision.

Amy had brought a loom with her and thread was available from the local mills. She wove shawls and table mats. Her technique improved until she was able to weave a woollen suit length and have a local tailor make a suit for McClure. Soon she was giving lessons to some of the Indian ladies.

Amy also ran a guest house.

There was a great deal of to and fro travel on the mission field. Ratlam, being a rail junction, was particularly active. It was customary for travelling missionaries and visitors from Canada to be entertained either at the McClure house or at the big house occupied by the single lady missionaries. Occasionally Amy would become annoyed when it seemed that every committee on which her husband sat insisted on meeting in Ratlam. And sometimes McClure would suddenly bring Indian friends on a tour of the house. Such tours would embrace everything from the bathroom to the kitchen to the contents of the pantry. He would also spring overnight guests upon her unannounced. She always kept the guest room ready so visitors could move in without feeling they were causing an upset but occasionally guests could sense the autumn chill that indicated Amy McClure was human.

Sometimes McClure could feel it, too.

On one occasion, after a committee meeting had just disbanded, Amy commented to the Indian Superintendent of Nurses that she wished the committees would not always insist on meeting in Ratlam. The comment was made in McClure's presence.

"What?" said the astonished nurse. "But don't you know? It's all Doctor's fault. *He* tells everybody to come here. He doesn't want to take time to travel."

Amy looked at McClure. "Is that true?"

McClure looked at Amy. "Yes."

The nurse fled the house as the row started.

Such flare-ups by Amy were rare but her friends knew there was a point beyond which McClure should push only at his peril.

Everyone also knew there were points beyond which McClure should not be pushed by anything or anyone, other than Amy. Even animals were not immune to the McClure temper. Sometimes Amy would find the routine of office dictation suddenly disrupted as her husband would burst from the house and speed down the long lane to prevent goats from demolishing a hedge. Cows were sacred to the Hindus and wandered unimpeded through Ratlam but not through the McClure vegetable garden. More than one cow found itself unceremoniously ejected, propelled by McClure wielding a length of two-by-four. On such occasions Amy worried about her husband's blood pressure but had to acknowledge there was something suitably symbolic in the spectacle of McClure in pursuit of a sacred cow. Monkeys were also sacred. They were particularly active at night and liked to scamper across the rooftops and enjoyed tearing loose tiles off the McClure house. McClure could have tolerated the vandalism but the monkeys also disrupted his sleep and that, for the monkeys, was a point of no return. One morning McClure surged forth into the dawn twilight and shot a chronic offender. The hospital staff was horrified. Two of the men spirited the corpse out of town and discreetly buried it some twenty miles away. The monkeys, being fast learners, moved to the pastor's house.

For Amy it was all merely part of life with Bob McClure.

The McClures enjoyed a quiet social life. They had numerous friends in the Ratlam community. One couple with whom they became very close were the Anklesarias, the Parsee businessman and his wife whom McClure had met his first evening in Ratlam. They grew to know the *Takur sahib* of Bercha. Bercha was a village near Ratlam. "Takur sahib" was a title that belonged to the days of the princely kingdoms and denoted a line of Hindu nobles who had been advisors to the maharajahs. The *Takur sahib* of Bercha was the type of man who appealed to McClure. He was intelligent, open, self-disciplined, and devoted to India in spite of having been stripped of most of his former power and wealth. There were several other couples the McClures came to know well through the Rotary Club. Rotarian Sapat lived across the road from the hospital and the Sapats and the McClures passed many a pleasant evening playing Scrabble. The McClures, however, were addicted to bridge. Every Saturday night was bridge night at the McClure bungalow. Members of the hospital supervisory staff could be enraged with McClure on Friday and not be speaking to him on Monday but in the meantime they would play bridge together on Saturday with Amy unaware that she was in the calm centre, the eye of the storm.

Amy McClure was not, officially, a missionary. But she believed in the importance of her husband's work and she believed just as firmly that it was her function to support him. Nowhere was her devotion more evident than in her willingness to travel third class on the Indian railways.

First class was at least private. Third class had slatted hard wooden seats, open compartments, open windows, and seemed to carry half the population of India at a time. It was also incredibly cheap (to Westerners). The combination of inexpensive fare and the opportunity to mingle with real people was always too much for McClure. He avoided first class the way a Hindu avoided meat. He would erupt from the train at station stops to buy sticky Indian delicacies from the carts of platform vendors. He would be accosted by ex-patients wanting to unveil their scars for his inspection. Small crowds would gather to watch him inspect scarred stomachs and compliment the owners. For McClure third class travel was an adventure in fellowship.

For Amy, it was a nightmare.

Hard, hot, crowded, smelly and uncomfortable were all adjectives applicable to third class. In addition the toilet and washroom facilities were, to say the least, abominable—and Amy had her colostomy problem which called for fastidious cleanliness.

One day the Superintendent of Nurses asked Amy why she

let the doctor take her third class. The nurse knew that she herself and the Indian doctors would most certainly travel first class and be proud of it. Amy answered in a burst of rare confidentiality. "Because I love him," she said. The nurse thought she could detect a slight sigh.

The Indian climate was hot. Nine months of the year it was also dry to the point of aridity. Fortunately, Amy preferred heat to cold. She had never been a fan of the Canadian winter. It was well that she had such a tolerance for hot weather because McClure changed a tradition that had been part of the long-established cultural pattern for missionaries. He refused to head for the hills during the hot weather that preceded the monsoons of July and August. The hot season, when the temperature soared to 115 degrees Fahrenheit and the rivers dried up and farming was impossible, was an ideal time for the rural folk to travel. Then they could come to hospital for elective surgery and other treatment. So McClure stuck to his hospital and Amy stuck to the house. In the O.R. an air conditioner, a gift from a Canadian congregation, eventually eased the burden of oppressive heat but at the house the only relief came from the big blades of large ceiling fans. Amy seldom complained. She knew that out at Bamnia the young Mackenzies, too, were hanging on. (Dorothy claimed that in the house at mid-day it was best to stand in the arch of an interior doorway. There the top of one's head had some protection from the waves of heat pulsating down from the corrugated iron roof!)

Even in the hot season the yard around the McClure house was never permitted to turn into desert. On the contrary, with supervision and assistance from Amy and McClure, the gardener turned it into an oasis.

Amy could think in terms of the "dry" season or the "wet" season and both concepts were depressing. But she could think in terms of flower seasons and conjure up an intricate never-ending cycle of nature's miracles. Even in April, as the dry season intensified and the heat escalated, several big gulmohar trees that had been standing stark and bare suddenly began putting forth rich red and dark saffron coloured blossoms. They would bloom through until June and then, as the flowers faded, would put forth great frond-like leaves in time to welcome the monsoon rains. Before the rains came the gardener would be busily digging the flower beds and working-in rich manure. The smell of manure from the doctor's gardens pervaded the entire compound. In the midst of the rains a kamini shrub burst forth with lilac-like flowers and glorious perfume replaced the stench of manure. A gnarled woodapple tree produced the fruit that amply justified the tree's name but that made excellent jam. A little ragged robin tree that had stood like a dead stick for eight months produced pink flowers and then, magically, leaves.

In September, after the rains had finished, the gardener planted colourful zinnias, and mogra plants that bore pure white flowers. These were followed shortly by nasturtiums and phlox.

In October the sad little ragged robin tree lost its leaves but the kamini miraculously repeated its feat of flowering. Out in the front yard a bush-like Bougainvillaea bloomed white and beside the house another Bougainvillaea, pretending to be a vine, climbed upward and blossomed orange. At the same time a guava tree bore white flowers and then fruit.

By late November, as the "cold" weather was approaching, white roses bloomed around the orange Bougainvillaea and chrysanthemums flowered next to the roses. The roses and the chrysanthemums bloomed on into January, even after the fronds had begun to drop from the gulmohar trees. And then, possibly because McClure had managed to drain the water from the bathroom sink and shower into its flowerbed, the orange Bougainvillaea kept its blossoms until the big gulmohar trees flowered in April and the cycle was complete.

While the strange Indian seasons slid by the McClures always tried to make Sundays a time of rest. For McClure it was a day when he could read something other than medical journals without his conscience bothering him. They had subscriptions to the *National Geographic* and to *Life*. Over the years their reading list embraced such diverse titles as *The Agony and the Ecstasy*, *Honest to God* and *The Spy Who Came In From the Cold*. Sunday was also a day to write letters to family and close friends and to listen to some of the handful of recordings of light music that Amy had brought with her. The family in Canada sent more books and records. For awhile the strains of *Camelot* emanated from the big bungalow and Indians taking a Sunday stroll through the upper compound could hear King Arthur singing of "How to Handle a Woman" and Sir Lancelot's booming baritone announcing himself to be the paragon of all virtues.

On the Sundays that McClure was not on call he and Amy would go for long walks, often out into the country. They would walk the roads where the bullocks pulled two-wheeled carts loaded with sugar cane, where half-naked herdsmen shaded by black umbrellas moved dusty goats to pasture, where women in bright saris carried huge headloads to market walking with lithe grace beneath their burdens. If Amy was not feeling like a walk McClure would take his bicycle and it was not unusual for a Sunday ride to take him to the village of Bercha for a friendly chat with the *Takur sahib*. But walks and rides were mere side excursions between the two major events of the day; morning and evening church services.

The evening service was a strange phenomenon. There was a small English-speaking Anglican congregation in Ratlam that was visited only at intervals by an ordained pastor. McClure, who believed that people had the right to be able to participate regularly in public worship, took on the task of conducting Sunday evensong service. He forced his literal mind to accommodate itself to The Book of Common Prayer. He suppressed his heretical instincts and led in the declaration of the Nicene Creed. He delivered brief sermons of encouragement. It was a voluntary office that required time and effort but McClure enjoyed doing it because the congregation seemed to appreciate his leadership. He was suitably surprised one weekend when an ordained Anglican minister turned up and refused to let him participate. It was a gentle reminder that in every institution there was hierarchical territory where the uninitiated were not intended to tread.

There was a Sunday morning service in the little church in the mission compound. Here the congregation was Hindi-speaking and so was the pastor. The McClures attended that service with great faithfulness even though the hymns, sermons, and readings were all in Hindi. For McClure this church with its hard-slatted benches, its "I" beam pillars, its open-raftered roof and its cement floor was a little oasis within the oasis that was Sunday. The small rafters resonated to the majestic strains of *Old Hundredth* and *Nun Danket* and *Cwm Rhondda* but they also vibrated to the livelier notes of Indian melodies framing new hymns. One of the missionary ladies played a violin, and sang while she played. There was often an accordionist, usually a guitar player, and sometimes a drummer. One of the pastors composed anthems for the choir, and his music, both voice and instrumental, would undulate over the hearer like the warm waters of a southern ocean. There was a strange quality to that music, as though it spoke simultaneously of the optimism and joy of the Christian and of the fathomless sadness of the human condition. For McClure the Sunday morning service in the Hindi church was a weekly healing process that soothed his soul. He listened to the voice of the pastor speaking the vowel-filled rhythmical language and he wondered at the paradox that could make corporate worship all the more meaningful by being unintelligible.

21

Dada McClure

Patients who were fortunate enough to be mobile, or any members of their families who happened to be in the hospital courtyard at eight o'clock in the morning of any weekday, never had any problem telling the time. The most regular clock in Ratlam was Bob McClure himself. He would leave the house via the side door that opened out of the study, would pass beside the orange Bougainvillaea and the white roses and exit through the driveway gate. He would walk briskly down the long lane, past the nurses' residence and turn into the walkway that led past the O.R. and into the courtyard. When *McClure sahib* appeared inside the hospital grounds patients and staff knew that it was precisely eight a.m.

He would proceed first to the office of the business manager, Stephen Haider Ali (who succeeded Miss Ventham), and spend fifteen minutes discussing business matters after which, if it was a Monday morning, he would give orders for the Diesel engine that drove the emergency power generator to be started. In the meantime he would vanish into the X-ray department to see any film that had been processed overnight. If he could hear the Diesel's throaty rumble as he emerged from X-ray then all was well and grand rounds would begin.

There could be as many as four junior Indian doctors on the Ratlam staff and all would move along in the wake of their Chief. They would be accompanied by the Nursing Superintendent and at each ward would be joined by the ward nurse and her staff. (Ratlam was a teaching hospital and each ward usually had four or five student nurses on duty.) This medical entourage began its stately procession at the TB wards, progressed to the Bohra ward, continued past the O.R. (losing its leader for a few moments as he took a swift detour through the O.R. to make certain the lights and the refrigerator were functioning), then on to the maternity ward, to the female ward, the male ward and, eventually, to the private rooms.

No member of the staff dared relax during grand rounds, neither the most experienced doctor nor the most junior student nurse. At any moment, as they gathered by a patient's bedside or as they walked the outer corridor from ward to ward, the Chief might suddenly ask a question or give an instruction. If he gave an instruction that was not immediately written down the heavens themselves trembled. McClure's pockets were a reservoir of scrap paper and pencil stubs and anyone who did not have writing material with them would find paper and pencil thrust into their hands. Often the donation would be accompanied by the demand to calculate a medicinal dosage or to draw a picture of a particular germ. The Chief would then go on his way from bed to bed, apparently ignoring the pupil until the answer was forthcoming, but one eye was always alert and a blast would greet anyone who tried to whisper the answer.

McClure blithely called his stethoscope a "guessing tube" but if anyone was clumsy enough to knock the guessing tube while he was using it their own ears would tingle in return. If, in the middle of rounds, he came across an interesting case the whole entourage could find itself suddenly swept off to the lab to inspect a specimen through a microscope. Sometimes the Chief would stop suddenly in the middle of a ward to pass on information he had gleaned from constant reading of the latest medical journals and his own pencil would fly as he made elaborate drawings to illustrate his new-found knowledge. He would be suitably impressed if another doctor had been at the journals ahead of him. On rare occasions a recent graduate would point out that something McClure thought was new had been on the curriculum at medical school and the Chief would be seized by a momentarily pensive look, as though counting the passage of the years.

McClure had difficulty remembering names of patients and student nurses and when in doubt called them "Mrs. McGinty". A nurse would suddenly find herself addressed as "Mrs. Sajjan Singh", a use of the Maharajah's name that indicated McClure thought the nurse in question was getting too big for her sneakers. McClure talked English, which was understood by the staff but had to be translated to many of the patients. As time went by the nurse translating would often be corrected on a detail and the staff gradually realized that McClure sahib comprehended far more Hindi than he ever spoke.

Nothing was safe from McClure scrutiny. If a screen had a hole, if a hinge was loose, if a tap dripped in the service room, it would be observed and noted. If the Chief sat on a bedside stool and its legs wavered the offending furniture would be sent soaring through the air into the backyard from where the maintenance man would have to retrieve it. While McClure was reading a patient's chart his fingers would caress the edges of the metal chart board searching for dents and abrasions. If the board was found to be damaged it would leave the ward under McClure's arm and would be returned later after he himself had straightened it.

At the conclusion of rounds the Chief, the doctors and the ward supervisors would head for the McClure residence for coffee.

After rounds it was time for the out-patient department. The doctors all shared the burden of O.P.D. Because there were so many people in desperate need of medical help McClure was particularly short with those who asked for and then rejected treatment. If a patient returned for an appointment and McClure found his previous instructions had been ignored he would draw a red line through the case file which meant that patient had lost further access to Ratlam hospital. Once, before he had become culturally acclimatized, he strode into his office to find a man already on the examination table. Upon the doctor sahib's entrance the man leaped off the table and pranamed so vigorously McClure thought the greeting was a rejection and immediately drew the red line. The nurses protested, and explained, and the red line was obliterated. The nurses soon found that by using gentle reason they could get their terrible Chief to withdraw most red lines. They also found that many a consultation with an impoverished patient would be followed by McClure having a quiet chat with Stephen Haider Ali to consider ways to solve the patient's financial problems. The patient would learn the solution from Haider Ali and many never knew what role the brusque doctor sahib had played, even though money for their assistance often came from the McClure Fund and sometimes from the McClure private pocket.

McClure kept a list of other doctors pinned to the wall of his examination room. The criteria for being on the McClure list was a simple one; those doctors had earned his professional respect. When patients came from a distance McClure would check his list to see if he could refer them to a good doctor closer to home. He himself would often suggest the need for a second opinion and would refer patients to Indian specialists at Indore or Bombay. The patient would go armed with detailed notes from McClure. The Ratlam files still contain copies of letters of appreciation from McClure sent to other doctors to thank them for proving him wrong and thereby saving a patient from an unnecessary operation. There were flaws in the McClure character but professional jealousy was not one of them.

Indian women would submit unquestioningly to an operation by a male surgeon but many were reluctant to be examined by a male doctor. For McClure, who had always taken a great interest in gynaecology, it added one more strain to O.P.D. He consoled himself with the knowledge that at least there had been improvement since the days when the hospital's founder, Dr. James Waters, had had to treat high-caste women by reaching through curtains to take their pulse. Dr. Waters had treated the Maharanee for years without ever seeing her.

The women of Indian nobility were no longer in *purdah* but they had not lost their illusions of special status. One day McClure received a message from Her Highness the Maharanee of Indore requesting him to make a palace call. When necessary McClure would make house calls around Ratlam but Indore was sixty-five miles away. He sent a message to Her Highness pointing out that she could afford to hire many McClures but that the McClure of Ratlam belonged to the people of Ratlam. If she cared to come to the Ratlam O.P.D. he would be happy to see her.

In Ratlam the widow of Maharajah Sajjan Singh had the temerity one day to send for McClure to treat her dog. She was an elderly lady and frequently ill and McClure had an oriental's respect for the elderly. He sent a polite message saying he would be happy to treat the dog at O.P.D.

When other missionaries needed medical treatment or advice they, too, were given appointments during O.P.D. hours. On at least one occasion a missionary who arrived fifteen minutes late found his appointment cancelled and had to return another day. He was advised that missionaries were supposed to be able to tell the time.

The O.P.D. hours were not a good time for Westerners to pay social calls upon McClure. A nurse announcing that the local Roman Catholic Mother Superior was paying a visit was once astonished to be told to "Tell Mother Superior to go to hell". She rephrased the message. On the other hand, a drug salesman who overheard McClure protesting that he would not receive Queen Elizabeth herself that day loudly announced that it was General De Gaulle who was calling. He was immediately received with grace and good humour.

O.P.D. was open until 12:30 p.m. at which time the staff broke for lunch. It was customary, particularly during the hot season, for everyone in India to have a little siesta after lunch. In many walks of life the day did not get underway again until around four o'clock but McClure would usually be back on the premises by 1:30 and if nothing else demanded his attention he could be found in the lab with his technical trainees. McClure's love for the lab was a cross the lab staff had to bear. They owed their careers to his preoccupation with things technical but that same preoccupation spoiled their siestas.

The O.P.D. re-opened at 4:00 p.m. and between then and 6:00 McClure saw the patients who were being admitted for operations. After that he adjourned to the X-ray room, donned the lead apron and the red glasses, sat for the obligatory ten minutes while his eyes adjusted to the dark, and then did a fluoroscope chest screening of every patient who had been admitted that day. The routine screenings could be done by the other doctors but the younger men, as in Gaza, were not enthusiastic about absorbing radiation. Through the years the Chief bore the brunt of the X-ray burden, averaging close to ten thousand screenings a year.

Tuesdays, Wednesdays and Fridays were O.R. days. A day that had twelve or more operations scheduled, with an almost even split between majors and minors, was a day guaranteed to find McClure in a good mood. He and his team would begin their labours at 8:30 a.m. and work through, with one hour for lunch, until the schedule was completed.

A short schedule would invariably leave McClure restless and unhappy. He would prowl the hospital looking for hinges that needed repair or furniture that needed painting. It is said that he would cast speculative eyes upon the mature family men as though hoping for a vasectomy or two to fill in the time. Indeed, on one such day a member of the O.R. team, a family man who had been talking vasectomy for some time, suddenly found himself brusquely ordered to be in the O.R. within fifteen minutes. Twenty-five minutes later he was no longer part of India's fertility problem. That incident was cheerfully elaborated upon by the mission raconteurs until it pictured McClure, at the end of a short day, instantly assaulting a handy male with all the fervour of a family planning zealot. It became another paragraph in McClure mythology.

The O.R. itself was a simple room, almost Spartan. The room had been built many years ago by Dr. Waters as a gift from the Maharajah but had not been well equipped. McClure was on a never-ending campaign to add better equipment to the O.R. without yielding to what he considered frills. During the McClure regime the O.R. never had a shadowless overhead light. For many years a 500 watt light bulb hung from a cord and was supplemented when necessary by one or two goose-neck desk lamps. The dangling bulb eventually gave way to a fluorescent strip and that was frill enough for McClure.

Each operation began with a prayer similar to the one McClure had become accustomed to use in Gaza. He never failed to personalize it with the patient's name. Some of the more devout missionary doctors did not care for McClure's O.R. prayer because frequently it was followed closely by a "damn", or "hell", or other expletive if the O.R. staff did not move with sufficient sprightliness onto the next phase. Dr. Naku claimed, jokingly, that the assistant who kept his eyes closed for an extra moment of meditation would open them to find the patient's abdomen already laid open.

During major operations the nurses and assisting doctors would find themselves peppered with a running barrage of questions from their Chief who was always teaching. He was also a stickler for detail. Every move had to be made strictly in accordance with *his* routine. A new staff doctor would be briefed by the theatre nurse on everything from how to hold forceps to how to tie a knot the McClure way before he or she would be permitted into the O.R. A doctor who held an instrument the wrong way would suddenly find it removed from his hand. When McClure requested an instrument the scrub nurse would repeat the order before handing the instrument. If she did not repeat the order the instrument would be refused. If it was the wrong instrument it would be thrown across the room. If an injection was ordered the person administering it not only had to repeat the name of the drug but had to show the ampoule to the surgeon. Instruments had to be slapped into the surgeon's hand with suitable force. A nurse who offered them gently would be told that such delicate courtesies were more suitable for a meeting in the park.

The surgeon was always under tension and the staff even more so. If anyone was not alert, or slipped up, there would be an eruption. They never knew when the eruption would come. From McClure's point of view he never knew what a green member of the team might do next. He stared in astonishment one day as a nervous and excited anaesthetist poured ether onto the patient's stomach. Once he stopped in the middle of an operation to stare balefully at a new assistant. "Who," he inquired, "is shaking? You, doctor, or the patient?"

"Both," came the agitated reply.

Flies were a curse in India. They penetrated into the O.R. forcing the circulating nurse to patrol the perimeter armed with a swatter. One day a fly got past the swatter while McClure was doing some bone "carpentry" using a chisel and a steel hammer. He used the hammer to make an impassioned pass at the fly and demolished the intruder, along with a glass-topped table.

McClure always worked as though driven by some inner demon but in the O.R. it was as though he was haunted by an image of all the ailing people of India lined up outside the door. As one patient was moved from the O.R. he wanted to see the next one already on the way in. He himself would break only long enough to look at the incoming patient's file and to re-scrub. He could work through without a break until one o'clock, go home for lunch all blood-spattered and dishevelled, and be back, refreshed, by two o'clock. Minor operations were usually kept for the afternoons and the normal routine was to complete O.R. by 4:00 o'clock. It was not unusual, however, to go until six and to have emergencies during the evening.

A legend grew in Ratlam, and it spread to Canada, concerning the enormous number of operations McClure performed "every day". It was *normal*, so ran the legend, for McClure to perform fourteen, eighteen, twenty *major* operations a day. Fortunately the O.R. log-book recorded the truth. Throughout the years at Ratlam McClure averaged 847 operations per year with an average of 312 being major. His peak year showed 1,084 operations of which 387 were major. On the basis of 3 O.R. days a week for 50 weeks one arrives at an average for that peak year of 7 operations a day. Even that figure reflects an enormous sustained effort not only by McClure but by his team. It reflects long weary days during some of which they did indeed perform fourteen, eighteen, twenty operations.

The Ratlam O.R. team developed a reputation for speed but simply because its Chief insisted upon frequent drills and rehearsals. He himself was gifted with great dexterity but nothing was ever left to chance. If a major operation was scheduled that had not been performed recently the team would be called into the O.R. the evening before and would go through a practice run. If McClure had learned a new technique or had obtained a new instrument the team members would rehearse until they were movement perfect. They rehearsed everything, from the precise spot the nurse should stand to receive the baby during a Caesarean to the way a sterilized bone saw should be unwrapped and handed to the surgeon.

McClure's team gradually realized that a strange thing was happening on O.R. days. Everyone knew that McClure was a dynamo but few members of the staff considered themselves to be unusually endowed with energy. And yet they invariably stood the strain of long hours. Some of them would go to bed as soon as O.R. was completed and not wake up until morning; none of them would go cycling or walking for recreation afterwards the way McClure would; but doctors and nurses looking back from the vantage point of later years say they never knew of a single instance of anyone breaking down from exhaustion while working with McClure in the O.R. On the contrary, it was as though McClure "gave energy". Certain words keep cropping up when Ratlam alumni describe the hours in O.R. with Bob McClure. Those words are craftsmanship, team-work, discipline and energy.

As time went by the doctors and the nurses of Ratlam Christian Hospital applied a name to their Chief. On formal occasions and in the O.R. they called him "Doctor", but elsewhere they called him *Dada*. It was a good name for McClure and it appealed to the subtle Indian mind. It was a word that was used in several of India's languages and had various shades of meaning. The gentler nurses said *Dada* meant "brother", or even "father". Others believed that *Dada* was more sentimental. It meant "grandfather". Some of the doctors maintained it meant all that but more. It meant "boss", "strong man", even "bully". It meant "godfather", as in Mafia. Alumni of Ratlam Christian Hospital could get into heated arguments over the meaning of *Dada* as applied to McClure but always the argument would be tempered with affectionate laughter.

With all meanings put together and mixed well, *Dada* meant "McClure".

22

The Bureaucrats

The Indian doctors and nurses of Ratlam Christian Hospital were coming to terms much more quickly with *Dada* McClure than were some of the Canadian members of the medical mission bureaucracy.

This was partly an accident of history.

Throughout the years it had been the custom for women workers to be sent from Canada under the auspices of the Woman's Missionary Society (W.M.S.) of The United Church of Canada. The W.M.S. recruited them, supervised, and paid them. The men had been sent by the Mission Board. The women missionaries were always fiercely loyal to the W.M.S. and considered it to be the ultimate arbiter of policy. It was equally as traditional, however, for doctors who were superintendents of hospitals to consider themselves the principal arbiters of hospital policy. In McClure's case that meant that when he had strong opinions concerning hospital policy he was dealing with other Canadian missionaries who did not necessarily recognize his authority.

McClure was an enthusiastic supporter of undergraduate nurses' training and was impressed by what had already been accomplished. He felt, however, that the training system was taking a dangerous turn. It was becoming too lecture-orientated without enough practical work. They were turning out administrators and bureaucrats rather than ward nurses. "We now have," he wrote, "six or seven of our senior nurses (Indian) on the field who could not possibly look after a sick person if they tried." He wanted a return to a greater emphasis on practical training and he wanted to launch a campaign at home to raise funds specifically to underwrite the costs of training nurses. It was at this point that he parted paths with some members of the Medical Commission.

An old dragon was raising its head—"special project funding".

The principle favoured at home was that people donated money to the Mission Board or to the W.M.S. and then the church administrators, responding to budgets drawn up on the fields, decided how the money should be allocated. But McClure wanted individuals at home to take on the financial sponsorship of *individual* girls training as nurses in India. The money would still be channelled through the W.M.S. but he wanted the girls and their sponsors to know each other's identity. He wanted them to write to each other. He wanted the missionaries to take pictures so the girls could send them to their Canadian sponsors. It was McClure's contention that mission should be personalized and he maintained that people who gave for special projects did not turn away from their general giving. On the contrary, McClure was convinced that people gave even more when sensitized by a special project. His opponents considered the system to be open to dangerous abuse, to be inefficient, to rely too heavily on personality, and to encourage glamorous projects to the possible handicap of more worthy ones. Personalized giving also smacked of charity, an activity that has been said to debase the giver and corrupt the receiver. It was a philosophical area in which McClure had a blind spot. When it was suggested that his approach was too sentimental he wrote: "They do not see that most of our work is all sentiment."

The Medical Commission hesitantly approved the personalized nursing project but some of its members resorted to Mahatma Ghandi's "non-co-operation" and for a long time no pictures of the girls or letters from them were forthcoming.

In Ratlam, Nurse Robson was the leader of the opposition until she was posted to another hospital. The posting was a wise move in which a little distance enabled her and McClure to become good colleagues. Nurse Robson was a gifted teacher and linguist and made a lasting contribution translating nursing text books into Hindi. She was one of a long line of Canadian nurses whose efforts made it possible for McClure to write: "Nurses' education . . . is the greatest single contribution made to Christian work in India by our mission."

Miss Robson's successor at Ratlam was another Canadian, Dorothy McIntyre. Nurse McIntyre won her way into the McClure heart one memorable day in the operating room when the Indian scrub nurse dropped an instrument. McClure exploded. He ordered the nurse to pick up the instrument and to leave the room and ordered another girl to scrub up. To his amazement Nurse McIntyre countermanded the order. Not only that, she placed her foot firmly on the instrument on the floor and informed the Chief Surgeon that none of them had to obey when spoken to in that manner. Her attack won McClure's instant respect.

McClure also ran into some of the realities of devolution.

It happened when the Medical Commission was restructured. The Canadian members were to act merely as advisors. At the first meeting of the reconstituted Commission the senior Indian members voted themselves a pay raise and then adjourned. The Canadian advisors, warm with the feeling of encouraging "self-expression" among their proteges, did not point out that this unseemly haste for a pay raise was undiplomatic, poor strategy and a financial error. In McClure's opinion it was one thing for the missionaries to relinquish control but it was quite another thing for them to abandon responsibility for ethics.

He was alarmed, too, because some of the Indians when given their head were going off with the bit in their teeth. One was Dr. Halla, a young male doctor at the mission station of Neemuch. Both he and Dr. Naku at Ratlam had been named, by the Commission, "deputy-superintendents . . . under the supervision of Dr. McClure". A year later McClure was complaining that he, as supervisor, was not being shown any financial statements of any kind, that the Neemuch Hospital was referring no cases to its better-equipped neighbour at Ratlam, that Halla was refusing to do public health work, would not co-operate with the system of TB treatment that McClure and Naku had set up and was not keeping adequate records of the TB patients he was treating. McClure admired Halla's personal drive but felt that his go-it-alone attitude was in direct contradiction to the idea of a system of mission hospitals that should become more and more integrated. He was also dismayed by the fact that young Dr. Halla was a member of a strong family that was showing an alarming tendency to take over political control not only of the Indian church's medical work but of the church itself.

To McClure it seemed that in India a thirst for power was a symptom of a peculiarly Christian ailment.

Every institution had its empire-builders but the Indian church appeared to be particularly vulnerable. Again, history was partly responsible. From the beginning the Canadian and other Christian missionaries had concentrated on the most disadvantaged members of society; on the outcastes and the tribal people. They had taught them to read and write. They had given them institutions in the form of good schools and decent hospitals. They had given them the major institution of the church itself. Within that institution the formerly disadvantaged people could now aspire to the coveted status symbols of college degrees, good salaries, and positions of authority. Within the new Christian "caste" the Bhil tribesman was as good as the Brahmin and keen to scramble for the top.

The focal point for McClure's ire was the automobile. By now every mission station had acquired at least one automobile. It seemed to McClure, however, that the ambition of every Indian who became a church official was to see that the job specifications included an automobile for his personal use. It was like the office carpet to a Canadian civil servant. McClure, who had had a life-long admiration for the bicycle, considered it a dangerous trend. To the Hindus, poverty was one of the earmarks of a truly holy man. The Hindu *sadu* arrived in a village walking on bare feet and leaning on a staff. In such a society, McClure felt, the Indian churchmen should ponder the effect of *their* arrival in the ultimate luxury, a car. In addition, as part of the status problem, there was the feeling that anyone who was in command of a car should not lower himself to the dirty job of servicing a car. The same went for equipment in general. McClure viewed the motor car on the Indian mission fields as having infinite possibilities for creating both spiritual and mechanical wreckage.

Some people claimed that McClure himself enjoyed status; enjoyed the heady feeling of being a well-known surgeon. But a Canadian clergyman put another slant to it when he said, "Of course Bob McClure thinks he's a bigshot. In his eyes *everybody's* a bigshot!"

Call it self-respect or a sense of individual worth, the fact was that Bob McClure had little time for bureaucrats in any institution, government or sectarian, who treated power and position as though they were a right rather than a privilege. Perhaps it was simply part of his Canadian psyche. Back home in Canada, in the spring of 1957, McClure's countrymen flocked to the polls to put the Progressive Conservative Party into power under John G. Diefenbaker who was almost paranoid in his mistrust of bureaucrats. Not long after that, McClure was in conflict with both Canadian and Indian bureaucrats and was becoming almost as paranoid as Diefenbaker.

It began with a polio outbreak in the summer of 1957.

The epidemic was very severe in Central India. Then, as now, the best cure was prevention and the best prevention was immunization by means of the recently discovered Salk vaccine. One of the principal manufacturers of Salk vaccine was Connaught Laboratories in Toronto. McClure placed orders for the vaccine knowing it would have to be shipped (under Church World Services auspices) from Canada to the United States to India and that the whole transaction could easily take a year. There were, however, many missionary children in danger and since they were Canadian nationals it seemed logical that the Canadian High Commissioner's office should be able to provide vaccine for them through more direct channels. He soon discovered that both the American and the British legations were obtaining vaccine for their people and doing it very promptly indeed. Nor were they intending to charge for the service. Full of optimism McClure visited the Canadian offices in New Delhi.

Canada's new High Commissioner to India was Chester Ronning. Like McClure he was a son of the China mission field and had been raised in China. McClure found Ronning to be an affable and charming man. They carried on most of their private conversations in Chinese, with a good deal of nostalgia on both sides. The High Commissioner, however, was not at all sure what could be done. It would all have to go through channels with due observance of protocol. McClure reluctantly came to the conclusion that the Canadian High Commissioner was, as far as his work went, a "completely stuffed shirt . . . in the hands of a 'protocol bound' staff that is quite un-Canadian and one would think one was dealing with something left over by the pre-World War II regime in the old government of India." McClure's written outburst would have made headlines at home if it had been mailed to anyone less discreet than the Board Secretary, but McClure was riled enough to suggest that the Secretary himself should not be *too* discreet. "Privately you can say that I am not proud at all of our Canadian High Commissioner's office in its work in Delhi. They do not visit Canadian institutions, they spend their time in the diplomatic social whirl of New Delhi polishing each other's brass."

What had really burned McClure's sense of national pride was that the British High Commissioner's office had already been quite obliging: "They have offered (Salk vaccine) to help us Canadians 'if necessary'. Imagine 'if necessary' when we are the ones who make the stuff! Really the folks in Ottawa ought to be wakened up in this line a little! I hate to have to think of Canada as one of the more backward countries."

That explosion came on a mid-September's day not long after the end of an unseasonably late and unusually heavy monsoon season. By the time one baked through May and June in temperatures that could soar into the Fahrenheit hundreds and then soaked through July and August in rains that could block vision across the compound one could easily become short-tempered.

The British were inoculating their people by November but the Canadian vaccine did not arrive in Delhi until the end of February, 1958. By then, McClure had simmered down enough to write a quite cordial letter saying how grateful they were to the Board, to the Canadian High Commissioner in Delhi and to the Department of External Affairs. He complimented everyone on the fact that the vaccine was well packed and in excellent condition and that it came in duty free. He would have trouble with polio and the bureaucrats later on but in the meantime his ire had switched to the government of India.

The mission medical college at Indore had been trying to get a "Cobalt-60 bomb", the latest and most impressive of the anti-cancer weapons in the medical arsenal and one that had been developed in Canada and was being produced there.* Two of the Cobalt units had recently come to India as gifts from the Canadian government. But no more were being permitted.

*The famous *Cobalt 60 Therapy Unit* was developed simultaneously by the team of Dr. H. E. Johns and Mr. John Mackay at the University of Saskatchewan and by Atomic Energy of Canada Limited.

And yet McClure's friend, Donald Fleming, who was now a cabinet minister in the Diefenbaker government and who should know, told him that the government had actually offered five of the therapy units to India but only two had been accepted. To McClure, who knew that India was "equipment starved", the Indian government's stand was irrational to the point of insanity.

It was fortunate for McClure's own sanity that he had the medical and surgical work as his major preoccupation. He was always delighted by the sight of student nurses diligently training in the wards at Ratlam. He rejoiced in every minute spent training village "compounders" as village laboratory technicians. It was even more pleasurable to see some of the compounders, who were little more than mediaeval herbalists, become so busy doing public health lab work that they abandoned their original activity. He rejoiced, too, when other missions sent young men to him for technical training from as far away as Assam on the borders of China. He pushed forward with mass TB screenings. He worked assiduously in the O.R. wielding his scalpel with speed and dexterity even through the months of high heat. He continued to cajole, harangue and berate.

To some extent the blur of action, the gruffness, the McClure noise and enthusiasm was an unintentional front masking the more compassionate man from public view. Over the years the staff and a myriad patients saw behind the front. It was not at all uncommon for McClure to return from a village trip bringing a crippled youngster with him whom he had simply met by the roadside. He would examine the youngster's deformity, discuss the possibility of correction and, if the child was willing, would then go to great lengths to contact the relatives for permission to perform the necessary surgery. There was seldom a question of payment. If necessary, McClure Fund money would be called into use thereby short-circuiting everybody's bureaucracy but his own.

And so operation followed operation. The monsoons followed the blistering heat. The greening, the flowering and the growing followed the monsoons. Mission Medical Commission meetings were endured, Rotary meetings were enjoyed and Bob McClure became a part of Ratlam without ever surrendering either to India or to the bureaucrats.

23

With Knife and Tampon

In December, 1958, the McClures enjoyed a brief holiday interlude and re-visited Taiwan and Hong Kong. By early January, 1959, they were "home" again in Ratlam.

McClure now found himself in a period during which most major obstacles seemed to have been overcome. He and his staff completed the Rotary-sponsored TB chest survey by X-raying almost 3,000 Bhil tribesmen. In addition to the portable X-ray the hospital now had a heavy duty machine. McClure had also been responsible for obtaining and supervising the installation of X-ray equipment in the other six mission hospitals. The Ratlam mission power plant was being equipped with new Diesels to guarantee reliable AC power. Similar plants were slated for the other missions and he was trying to obtain identical Diesel equipment so the parts would all be interchangeable and Ratlam-trained operators and mechanics could serve at any of the missions. In the meantime he was training lab technicians, X-ray technicians and pharmacists. The hospital had been granted a licence to manufacture certain drugs. A new building had been erected to house the out-patient department. It had a large hall upstairs for classroom use and social gatherings. McClure had also seen to it that the building had space for a dental clinic (in case he could ever find a dentist). By now he had managed to acquire a small supply of radium, some of it more or less smuggled in from Canada, and was treating accessible cancers.

Jovial Dr. Naku left to strengthen the staff at the sister hospital at Banswara but three other Indian doctors joined the

Ratlam staff. One of them, a recent graduate, female, with a name as attractive as herself, Dr. Charity Noah, soon turned out to have as much staying power as Naku. A fourth doctor, a young, keen chap, studying for his Master of Surgery, came to McClure for a nine month surgical internship. The hospital was full most of the time now, and there was a waiting list.

McClure was pleased with current relations between the mission hospital and the local provincial hospital. The medical chief there was most co-operative and both hospitals were referring patients to each other. In fracture work, however, the Ratlam Christian Hospital was building a monopoly. It was a monopoly based on a reputation for speed and efficiency. In the large, over-crowded government hospital the examination, X-raying and setting of a fracture could take as long as three days. The mission hospital, however, prided itself on swift reaction to such emergencies. As a rule, even in the middle of the night, a patient with a fractured femur would find himself X-rayed, given an anaesthetic, the bones pinned with traction wire and his leg up on a Balkan frame all within a period of thirty minutes from the time of admission. The staff had been known to handle a fracture involving both bones of the forearm in twenty minutes, including the time required for a general anaesthetic. The word got around that the Ratlam Christian Hospital was the place to go for swift emergency service even if it did charge a fee.

For McClure treatment of fractures was a specialty, but family planning was almost a calling. Every year it was becoming increasingly apparent that India was heading for more and more trouble because of multiplying population. In India as elsewhere modern medicine was making great advances against the killer diseases such as smallpox, TB, and cholera, thus extending life expectancy while at the other end of the spectrum the birth-rate continued to increase as well. Now, at the end of the sixth decade of the twentieth century, India's population was already 439,072,893* and was estimated to be increasing by six million a year. If unchecked, that rate of increase would accelerate in the years ahead.

Western economists liked to point out that a large population made for a large domestic market but their optimism was

---

* 1961 Census.

based on the Westerner's assumption that there would be employment and food for all. It was a shaky assumption. The Indian government was making great efforts to bring more and more fertilizer plants into production, to encourage the mechanization of any farms large enough to benefit from machinery and to extend and improve irrigation. Even so, food production was not keeping up with the increase in population. It was becoming apparent that the average Indian was consuming fewer and fewer calories. It was becoming equally apparent that there were only two possible solutions. Either India would have to rely on agricultural surpluses from abroad or India would have to limit its population.

Birth control had always created debate among missionaries. There had always been conservatives, even among the doctors, who claimed they had no right "to play God". It was an ongoing argument that cut across all denominations of the Christian church and one could find some Catholics more inclined to be lenient in their views than were some Protestants. The debate always left McClure feeling impatient. He had very little liking for abortions but he was downright enthusiastic for birth control.

One did not have to read long-term projections of population growth to appreciate the need for birth control. Every doctor saw cases where the personal need was obvious. If a woman was recuperating from TB, whether of the lungs, bones, glands or abdomen, and if she became pregnant before regaining full strength, it usually required an abortion to save her life. At that time in India abortions were illegal. Obviously even conservative doctors preferred such patients to take precautionary measures. The big problem was to find the birth control method that would meet all the requirements. It had to be culturally acceptable, technically efficient, readily available and economically feasible. It had to be something that an illiterate couple in a remote Indian village could use.

McClure's interest in family planning was shared by a doctor in Boston who had the appropriate name of Gamble. Dr. Gamble became a McClure sponsor, providing funds and supplies for family planning. It was an association that was to last for several years. One of the first contraceptive devices the "Gamble project" came up with was a foaming tablet. It seemed to suit all the requirements, being inexpensive, effective, and easy to use. All the woman had to do was to insert one small tablet a few minutes before intercourse. Body moisture dissolved the tablet and induced an abundant spermacidal foam. It was a patented formula.

A drug firm in Calcutta was commissioned to make a large trial order and McClure received half a freight car load for use at Ratlam and for distribution to the other hospitals of the field. The tablets, about the size of an aspirin tablet but coloured brown to avoid confusion, came packed ten to a vial and the vials were in large cardboard cartons. There was a two-year supply and after initial distribution to the other hospitals the remaining cartons filled a small storeroom at the Ratlam hospital.

Dozens of patients were introduced to the tablets during the remainder of the winter months and seemed to find them acceptable. McClure was highly pleased; until the monsoons came.

The monsoon rains managed to penetrate the tablet storeroom. The first indication that all was not well was the sight of brown foam oozing out around the wooden door. It was an alarming sight, particularly when everyone knew that during the monsoons all wooden doors swelled to a tight fit. McClure clothed himself in rubber boots and a raincoat and forced the door open. The room was truly impregnable. Wall-to-wall, ceiling-to-floor, it was a seething mass of brown contraceptive foam. Boston was informed that foaming tablets were not ideally suited to the Indian climate.

The sponsor was not daunted. He informed McClure that recent research had produced the perfect Third World contraceptive; one that simply required salt, water and a small sponge about half an inch thick by two inches square. Every bazaar sold salt. All a woman had to do was to put an ounce of salt into a ten ounce pop bottle and fill it with warm water to dissolve the salt. This bottle of 10 per cent saline solution could then be kept by her bed and before intercourse she could soak the small sponge with the saline solution and insert it into the vagina like a tampon. It was said to be 99 44/100 per cent effective.

The only real hitch with the tampon-saline method appeared to be the problem of acquiring the sponge. The answer was found in the bazaars of Bombay in the form of house-hold sponges made from synthetic rubber. Each sponge could be cut into eight tampons which put the price of the tampon at considerably less than 5 cents (Cdn). It was felt that each tampon should last anywhere from three to six months.

The programme was launched with considerable enthusiasm. The student nurses volunteered their spare time to slice sponges and an illustrated instruction sheet was printed so that even illiterate women could understand the method. The instructions and the tampons were distributed free of charge. Whole villages joined in the programme. Out in Bamnia, Dorothy Mackenzie's public health clinic could barely keep up with the demand.

Then the reports started coming in. Synthetic sponges seemed to have a great attraction for cockroaches. The folk around Bamnia claimed that cockroaches were migrating there from the neighbouring counties. At the end of two weeks sponges were being returned to the hospital no larger than a .25 cent piece.

McClure cabled the sad tidings to Boston.

Boston was equal to the challenge. By return airmail came rolls of 100 per cent latex sponge rubber sheeting that was unpalatable to cockroaches. The shipment was described as being "padding for orthopaedic appliances". (The sponsor had decided that a customs declaration claiming that great sheets of sponge rubber were for contraceptive purposes was going to create more bureaucratic problems that it would solve.) This new material was already in half-inch thickness and along with it came a "cookie-cutter" made of hardened steel with razor-sharp edges. The student nurses again fell to with a will and once again the tampons were distributed to the village women.

Dr. Gamble had access to a computer that ate statistics. He asked for detailed reports. Each patient who left hospital with a tampon was asked to return every few months for a free check-up and, ostensibly, for a new tampon. At the time of check-up a staff member would have the woman answer a Boston questionnaire: Is the method satisfactory? Is it suitable for use in a one-room home with older children sleeping in the same room? Is it uncomfortable for you? Does your husband object? Does it offend religious teachings? What is your religion? If Hindu, what caste? Does it cause any guilt feelings? Any other remarks?

It was two years before one of the original experimenters

finally volunteered "another remark" in the form of a minor complaint. The saline-tampon method, she said, was satisfactory in every way except that she found that holding the sponge in her mouth made her terribly thirsty!

Often, before a couple would use *any* birth control device, they had to be convinced that it would not cause imbecility, or impotency, or encourage infidelity. (McClure felt he could not give a written guaranty covering the latter possibility.) Sometimes a woman could be persuaded to have an intra-uterine device, the loop, installed. It was effective although exactly *how* it worked was still as much a mystery as it had been back in the Thirties when McClure had introduced the Graefenberg Ring into China. The loop was sometimes uncomfortable and occasionally it came out of place. An expelled loop could give rise to malicious rumours among village women to the effect that the doctors had installed a worm to eat up the babies. McClure, however, was no novice in the propaganda department. He sent a spokeswoman from village to village to tell the other women how pleased she was with her loop. With his usual directness McClure called her the "Happy Loop Lady".

Although couples would sometimes disagree over the spacing of children there was seldom any disagreement over the number of children they wanted. Once that number had been achieved then it was McClure's custom to advocate sterilization. He found it heart-breaking to know what some women had already been through; one patient had borne twelve children, only one of which had lived. If a woman was in hospital when she gave birth to what she hoped would be her last child McClure would recommend a bi-lateral tubal ligation, or "tying-off" of the Fallopian tubes. A BTL, as it was called, required an operation and several days in hospital.

The operation that McClure promoted just as much as tubal ligation for the woman was a vasectomy for the man. He could recommend it because he had had a vasectomy himself back in China. (A favourite picture among his old Ambulance Unit gang on the Burma Road had been a cartoon of McClure performing his own vasectomy; legend also had it that he had done his own appendectomy.)

Even though McClure was a long-time advocate, even a pioneer, in the sterilization field he moved cautiously in India. It was several years before he did a vasectomy but when he finally performed one he was guided by good fortune; his first candidate was a district court judge.

The judge came quietly one evening, ostensibly paying a visit. He asked that a vasectomy be done and that it be done secretly. He had no desire to have such a personal matter noised around the city.

McClure had his doubts about the secrecy. He suggested he simply schedule the operation for the end of an O.R. day and enter it as something innocuous on the O.R. booking. He assured the judge that by the end of a day the O.R. staff would be vastly uninterested in such a minor operation and that he would let most of them sign off early.

The judge was not to be persuaded. It had to be done secretly, when nothing else was going on, and there were to be no female nurses around staring at his genitalia. It was to be an all male operation. McClure agreed.

Late one evening the hospital staff saw the O.R. area ablaze with light as though an emergency had just come in and yet, strangely enough, not a female nurse was in sight; a most intriguing and unusual situation.

In the O.R., McClure made the two tiny incisions in the scrotum and cut and sealed the vas deferens, the tiny tubes that carry the sperm from the testes. A few minutes later the judge was able to climb off the table and walk out of the O.R. Before leaving he exacted a promise.

"Dr. McClure, assure me you will not tell anyone whomsoever about any of this whatsoever."

"Judge," said McClure, "I promise you I won't tell a soul."

McClure always had the impression that the judge must have gone straight from the hospital to the radio station and made a public announcement such was the speed and enthusiasm with which the word spread throughout the district concerning the "secret" operation. A few days later the grapevine also carried the information that the operation was not nearly so uncomfortable as the judge had feared and that he was well pleased. A few weeks later the word also spread that his wife was well pleased.

For McClure it was the first of many hundreds of vasectomies in the Ratlam area. In that district the judge had performed a psychological public service. "If it's all right for the judge," other men said to themselves, "then it's all right for me."

The Ratlam Rotary Club became enthusiastic and organized a vasectomy clinic.

Experience in other areas had shown that it was a good idea, when arranging a clinic, to have a big-name surgeon in to give a few preparatory lectures so that both husbands and wives knew what was going on. It was essential that they both be warned that the operation was irreversible and be assured that it did not lessen enjoyment of the sex act. The visiting surgeon would then return home while the local surgeon did the work. In this case an eminent Indian surgeon came up from Bombay, gave his pep talk and left. McClure was to do the actual surgery at the three-day clinic which was being held at a village about seven miles from Ratlam.

The night before the clinic was to begin some of the Rotary Club members suddenly thought of a complication. One of them 'phoned McClure.

"Bob, we are thinking you might have opposition. We are thinking you might even have a riot."

"It's just a vasectomy clinic!"

"But think of this, Bob. You, a white man, are going out to a village to sterilize brown men. How will that look?"

"You tell me."

"It will look like attempted genocide."

"The clinic starts in the morning!"

"We must have an Indian surgeon."

McClure hurriedly got on the 'phone to the Chief Surgeon of the provincial hospital and asked for his opinion.

"Goodness gracious, McClure, it could be very nasty. What some young radical will ask is, 'Have you sterilized any Canadians?'" There was a pause. "What will you answer?"

"In some things," said McClure, thoughtfully, "Canadians are a very backward people."

The two surgeons hurriedly came to an agreement. The Chief Surgeon of the provincial hospital would go out in the morning and take over the vasectomy clinic while McClure would take the routine clinics at the provincial hospital.

The next evening the Indian surgeon 'phoned McClure and reported that there had been no riots and that the first day of the clinic had been a success. By working a fourteen-hour day backed by a paramedical who closed the incisions he had performed 113 vasectomies.

The question about Canada gnawed at McClure. During any discussion of family planning he almost felt ashamed of being a Canadian. In Canada family planning was not a "nice" subject. It was illegal to sell contraceptives as such and sterilization was a taboo topic. A man wanting a vasectomy could not go to the nearest doctor or to a vasectomy "camp" as in India but would have to make discreet inquiries. He would probably have to write to A. R. Kaufman of Kitchener, Ontario, who was "the father of family planning in Canada" and who would brave the wrath of society and quietly name doctors who would deign to perform sterilization. One Canadian couple wrote to McClure, in India, for guidance. They received two pages of type-written detailed information which ended on a note of slight despondency: "Canada is very backward in these matters and among the more literate nations we are by far the most backward . . . Even a student nurse on our staff can talk to a man about vasectomy and a woman about tubal ligation with complete freedom and yet in Canada one has to look around to find someone to do this work almost like trying to find an abortionist."

McClure was a member of the Christian Medical Association of India. He eventually became its Vice President. He preached family planning to his colleagues of the C.M.A.I. and in particular he advocated vasectomy clinics. There were other like-minded doctors in the association, doctors who, like McClure, were capable of doing arithmetic and had the imagination to foresee what unchecked population growth would do to India and eventually to the world. Prodded by McClure and his supporters the C.M.A.I. began to encourage the establishment of family planning units in its member hospitals and began to find funds to subsidize sterilizations and loop installations.

McClure was also a member of the Provincial Medical Association and of the India Medical Association. These organizations had very few Western members but being a minority, sometimes of one, did not inhibit McClure. He lobbied, pressured and preached for family planning.

A family planning conference was held at New Delhi. McClure attended and came away greatly encouraged. The Indian government, he felt, and many of the missions, were beginning to take a very practical view of the whole problem of over-population.

Off in Singapore a Dr. Benjamin Sheares, an eminent Eurasian surgeon, was making a name for himself in the field of sterilization. McClure, following his ingrained habit of searching out the latest techniques, went to Singapore in July of '59 to work with Dr. Sheares. The Boston sponsor financed the trip.

Dr. Sheares had developed a sterilization method using an insulated electrode to cauterize the cornua of the uterus creating a small scar that sealed off the entry from the Fallopian tube. It was a way of performing an instant, knifeless, bloodless operation. In theory a woman could come in while shopping, climb on the table and be sterilized, get off the table and continue her shopping.

McClure returned to India with a set of diathermy electrodes for patterns and commissioned an Indian firm to make more. By mid-September he had a waiting list of fifty women and was envisaging Ratlam as a cornual cautery centre for India. Eventually, however, his enthusiasm for cornual cautery waned. It was, essentially, a "blind" technique which depended too much upon the doctor having an almost instinctive sense of anatomy. That was something he could not teach. McClure contented himself with encouraging the use of saline tampons and the loop for contraception and, when circumstances dictated, recommending vasectomies for men and tubal ligation for women, but he did not relax his efforts. It was as though the spectre of over-population haunted him; as though it had haunted him since his early days in China; as though he could always see, out of the corner of his eye, humanity multiplying itself like cells in a laboratory culture, at first almost unnoticeably and then more and more rapidly—spreading, swelling, seething, uncontrollable. Cells out of control. That was the basic definition of cancer. For McClure, who believed in a Supreme Intelligence and therefore in an orderly universe, cells out of control were an abomination. He saw, however, one strong glimmer of hope when he looked at the cancer of over-population. The cells themselves were *intelligent.*

24

The Witness

The rains came late that year of 1959 and once started showed no inclination to stop. Usually by mid-September everything around Ratlam was turning green. This year the waters were still coming in torrents. Even at the end of the third week of September the roads around Ratlam were impassable and the railroad to Bombay had been washed out. In other areas of the country floods were causing major dislocations and catastrophe. Bengal, a province that had suffered enormously from famine during the war years, now had floods and a refugee problem. McClure was temporarily seconded as an adviser to a Church World Service refugee committee in Calcutta.

He came away convinced that mission should do more in the way of providing trade schools for technicians and craftsmen of almost every kind. India seemed to have jobs for refugees if refugees could receive training. He had been amazed and delighted to discover that India, overpopulated though it was, still had large tracts of virgin territory heavy with forests, minerals, and even water. India had untapped water resources suitable for both irrigation and the development of hydro-electric power.

What India did not have was enough food rich in calcium. The only food that provided enough calcium was milk. Church World Service and other organizations had been in the habit of shipping great quantities of inexpensive surplus milk powder from North America to India. It had been a great boon but in the late Fall of '59, as though floods had not been enough, those surplus supplies of milk powder came to an end.

Governments rallied. In Ottawa, the Conservative government under John Diefenbaker was well-disposed toward India and donated nine million pounds of skim milk powder with more to follow. For the mission hospitals, however, who used milk as an important part of their supplemental diets, governmental gifts were of no assistance. Although most Canadians never stopped to think about it, official foreign aid *never* went through mission hands. It was a policy that McClure did not question. Aid too often had some kind of strings attached. Missions could not accept strings. He and Amy both began writing letters home pointing out to the Canadian church that while the government's gift of nine million pounds of powdered milk was generous it did not make up for the fact that in the eight months before supplies had ended Church World Service had sent ten million pounds of milk to India for use by church-related agencies.

There were other more routine but continuing frustrations.

McClure had forty village lab technicians now at various stages of their training but an order of Japanese microscopes, placed fourteen months ago, was delayed somewhere in a snarl of red tape. The lab course had lurched to a halt and McClure was becoming ever more paranoic about bureaucracies in general and that of India in particular.

An Indian professor of surgery from a large teaching hospital visited Ratlam and was surprised to see that McClure's cystoscopes for inspecting the inside of the bladder were not only in working order but were in use every day. "I have a cystoscope," said the visitor, then added, sadly, "it has been out of order for four years." The instrument needed a small, special lamp costing about $2.50 (Cdn) but the red tape to get that lamp was beyond belief and included the need for an import licence. The doctor had given up trying.

Even the provincial hospital in Ratlam had problems. It had a gas-and-oxygen anaesthetic machine that made McClure break the commandment about covetousness every time he saw it. The machine was worth about $1500 (Cdn) and had been in the hospital for three years without ever working. A bottle had been broken during shipment. McClure estimated the replacement bottle would cost about $1.00 (Cdn). Each year the government hospital had requisitioned a new bottle but it had not yet come through.

There was, however, another aspect to the problem. In McClure's opinion one should not always simply wait for government. There were some things that required personal initiative or, when you got right down to it, commitment. He spelled it out in a letter: "Not one of the well-paid doctors on the (provincial hospital) staff would dream of putting out five rupees from his own salary for the sake of getting things going. They are lacking in what their own statesmen refer to in every speech to medical conferences—'missionary zeal'. There is no reason for us to be stuck-up about it, yet it is the reputation that we are challenged to live up to. *If we were not different and if we do not stay different then there could be no call for our being here.*"*

Far from being stuck-up about the missions and their zeal McClure was inclined to be somewhat discouraged. He still felt that other doctors of his own mission were far too conservative and cautious and kept telling them so. He attended the all-India annual conference of the India Medical Association and discovered to his consternation that he was the only non-Indian doctor there and the only missionary doctor. Officials noticed the lack and one of them stated: "Missionaries are not much interested in medical progress in India." McClure was embarrassed for all missions, including his own.

More and more McClure was finding himself wondering whether the church was running out of steam, or whether missions were running out of a sense of purpose. There was a current debate raging over recent expansion of the flagship mission hospital at Vellore. "The institution is becoming larger and larger," McClure informed the Board Secretary, "and more impersonal in the process. The work, both in quality and quantity of its medical turn-out, is improving, there is no doubt about that. However, Vellore was originally founded to train Christian doctors, Christian nurses and to do Christian medical work of its own as its witness. Neither of these three functions has been improved in any recent expansion . . . Many mission representatives feel that growth is 'out of control'."

McClure was an interesting person to be questioning the validity of an institution that was, according to his own report, doing better and better medical work. He himself showed a great deal of interest in expanding and improving any hospital

*Author's italics.

with which he came in contact. McClure, however, had come a long way since he went to China as a twenty-two-year-old doctor "for the adventure". Now, at the age of fifty-nine, it was quite clear to him that he was not carrying on the work as a servant of medical science but as a servant of some higher authority. He felt the church's first responsibility to medical science was to instil *motivation*. The church would do well to get out of the big expensive institutions that could be run by government. Christian students, he suggested, should go to government schools but live in church-run hostels. After graduation these government-educated but Christian-motivated doctors and nurses would have maximum impact upon the quality of medical service.

It was difficult to describe the difference between the service in a Christian hospital and any other. McClure had already sensed in Canada that it was becoming a heresy among liberals to suggest that a Christian doctor or technician was any "better" than any other. In terms of technical know-how they were not. Sometimes, regrettably, they were worse. But McClure was certain there was a difference. He had seen it in China and he was seeing it here in India. It was a delicate subject about which to get specific. He did, partially, in a letter to a fellow doctor: "If a patient wants good nursing and good care they often, in the government hospitals, have to pay extra for it in the form of 'gratuities'. If a fracture wants prompt treatment there is a tip to the X-ray man, there is a 'fee' for a sedative injection, there is a tip here and tip there, all of which adds up in the long run that it is considerably cheaper for him to pay regular fees in a mission hospital and he knows he will get the best from the staff."

A Hindu doctor, an adviser to the federal government, told a visiting Canadian surgeon that the distinctive mark of a Christian hospital was "the compassion and sympathy expressed by the staff".

There were still mission doctors who thought of a hospital as a spring-board for evangelization. That was an outmoded concept which, in McClure's opinion, frightened good doctors away from the mission field. "They are scared off by questions on their theology," he wrote, speaking about potential recruits, " . . . I think there is still the feeling that as a medical missionary they are probably going to have to do a spot of preaching and evangelistic work as well . . . In this day and age a doctor's

'Witness' is in his work and in his life and the quiet guidance he can give to his students in the lab and the operating room."

McClure would have hesitated to attempt to detail what was meant by "witness" but an Indian woman articulated it. She did so by the simple expedient of writing a letter about Bob McClure. The letter was to the Board Secretary. It was written in English and was painstakingly typed. As any good business letter should do it carried a subject caption. The caption stated: "Dr. Maclure (sic), the great Surgeon."

The letter told how the writer's husband had been treated for several months by private practitioners and government doctors at considerable cost and with no results until he had travelled some distance to consult McClure. She said that McClure "did some minor operation and prescribed very 'cheap' medicines and lo! my husband began to improve . . . This way he miraculously saved the life of my dear husband and saved me and my eight children from starvation and poverty."

She elaborated concerning the "fine nursing" and then returned to her principal subject, McClure: "We also saw that even the lowest amongst human beings who came to this hospital was treated like his own kith and kin with great love and affection. We have seen some of the poorest being carried to wards by the DOCTOR himself in his own arms. His way of encouraging and treating the patients is really wonderful and amazing. This all through your spirit of serving humanity without distinction of caste, creed or COLOUR. We would always remember Dr. Maclure, as our great ANGEL and saviour, and hence your mission and the great work being done in this direction in this area."

25

Through Parsee Eyes

Other people judged Christianity by the Christians they met and McClure judged other religions by the people he met. Becoming aware of another religion by seeing its believers put their faith into action had been one of the continuing pleasures of his life. Through Manohar Nagpal he became aware of the Hindus' great capacity for tolerance. Through Parsee friends he became aware of the many virtues of the Zoroastrians.

Many centuries before the birth of Christ, in an almost mythical era, a very real person, Zoroaster, founded the Persian religion that was to bear his name. Zoroastrianism was a religion that conceived of the world as being ruled by two gods, the Lord of Good and the Lord of Evil, who were interlocked in a perpetual struggle for the soul of man. Man was free to opt for either good or evil but the gods kept strict accounts. After death the soul crossed the accountant's bridge and faced a reckoning of good and evil deeds. A balance of good passed the soul into heaven but a surfeit of evil opened the way to permanent torment. Some respected scholars maintain that the three wise men of the New Testament were Zoroastrians.

When Islam swept through Persia, Zoroastrianism fell into disfavour and many of its more dedicated followers migrated to other parts of the world. A number went to India. In India they became known as Parsees. They established themselves principally in Bombay and surrounding areas. Thanks to a sound business sense they became renowned as bankers, businessmen, and industrialists. The Parsee religion became monotheistic but remained ethically demanding. It put great emphasis on Truth and Law and considered Falsehood to be the essence of wickedness. Worship was conducted in temples known as "fire temples" because of an altar featuring a living flame.

At the risk of over-simplifying, one can say that the Parsees were *not* among the poor of India. They tended to be well-equipped with the good things of a materialistic world. McClure was not one to be overly impressed by wealth. He was, however, very impressed by generosity and in the Parsee community he found an open-handed generosity that amazed him. It was with two members of that same community, Mr. and Mrs. Gustad Anklesaria, that the McClures formed one of their closest Indian friendships.

Mr. Anklesaria gave generously to the Ratlam Christian Hospital and his wife could be found at random hours wandering the hospital wards and visiting with Hindu patients. The staff noticed that she invariably had more time for poorer patients than for the well-to-do. The hospital business manager became accustomed to Mrs. Anklesaria slipping into his office to request that a poor patient's bill be charged, anonymously, to her personal account. On such visits Mrs. Anklesaria would usually drop into the McClure bungalow for a cup of coffee and a chat with Amy.

Mr. Anklesaria ran an agricultural machinery store. In McClure's eyes Anklesaria and his fellow Parsees stood out as beacons of honesty in the merchandizing world. McClure never could come to any very clear understanding of the Hindu religion and tended to judge it by its practitioners. In matters of business he had little admiration for Hindu merchants. With them it was a case of "Buyer Beware". To them it was a novel idea that a merchant's responsibility for his produce should carry on after a cash sale had been completed. McClure showed an Eaton's catalogue to a Rotary Club group and the slogan "Satisfaction guaranteed or your money refunded" caused instant hilarity among the Hindu members. It caused respectful interest among the Parsees.

Culturally the Parsees were among the most Westernized minorities in India which made it easy for a Westerner to move among them. Even so Amy was on the receiving end of a Parsee lesson and it came from an Anklesaria bride-to-be. Amy knew, although the girl had had some say, that the match had really been arranged by the families. Amy, like most Western women, found it difficult to accept the idea of an arranged marriage. It seemed to be the ultimate violation of an individual's rights. She was not about to make any radical speeches to a member of another faith and another culture but she did permit herself to voice one quiet question.

"How do you know you will love him?"

The girl managed to smother a flash of anger but could not keep from sounding condescending as she replied. "You Western people think that love is something that comes down from a palm tree on a warm moonlight night beside a lagoon on a tropical island. That's not love. That's just chemistry." She launched into a short lecture. "Love, courage, faith, hope and trust are things that grow. My husband and I will cultivate our love and it will grow."

Amy reported the conversation to McClure who followed up with a look at some statistics. It was always difficult to know what lay behind statistics but the Parsees seemed to have about the highest marriage success rate in the world.

For one period of almost two years McClure had a medical associate on staff who was a Parsee. Her name was Manek Chenoy. She was a gynaecologist and an F.R.C.S. from Edinburgh. Chenoy gave up a lucrative private practice in Bombay in favour of being of more use to the poor in Ratlam. She felt that missionaries should not think that they were the only ones interested in service. In the O.R. McClure found her to be cool, skilful, decisive and blessed with excellent judgement. She gave lectures and demonstrations to the nurses and acted as sister confessor to junior doctors. (One greenhorn weathered McClure by taking a Chenoy-prescribed tranquilizer every morning he was scheduled to scrub for O.R.) In later years McClure would look back and assess the Parsee doctor as "the finest national colleague I've ever worked with".

The McClures went home on furlough in the late spring of 1960. They were followed by Mr. and Mrs. Anklesaria, themselves on holiday. The Anklesarias stayed with the McClures for a few weeks at 108 Strathallan. During the course of that visit McClure had an opportunity to look at Canada through Parsee eyes.

Mr. Anklesaria arrived already determined to check on Eaton's money-back guaranty. He made a bee-line for Eaton's, purchased a hundred dollars worth of costume jewellery and other trinkets and returned half of them the next day saying there was nothing wrong with the goods except that they were "unsatisfactory". He received his money. That evening at 108 Strathallan the chief topic of conversation had to do with the marvels of a society that was so ethical the major stores could stick to such an incredible guaranty.

The McClures and the Anklesarias went on a holiday motor trip through parts of Ontario and Quebec. It was July and the world was still green. The fresh, sweet scent of hay still wafted off the fields. Fat cattle grazed on rolling lands. Southern farmland was dotted with hardwood bush and up on the Canadian Shield evergreen forests stretched away beyond vision and almost beyond imagination. Lakes and rivers basked in the sunbathed Pre-Cambrian rock, not by ones or twos but by whole chains. The Parsee from India viewed the freshwater lakes of the Muskokas, the Kawarthas, the Rideaus; he watched the fresh waters slip down from the Ottawa River and merge with the great St. Lawrence; he stood beside Lake Ontario and saw to the east and the west and the south a horizon that was all water— *fresh water*—and his credulity failed him. He walked to the shore, knelt, and cupped the water in both hands. He stared at it a moment then looked at McClure, wonderingly. "God," he said, "has given to Canada with both hands."

McClure was spending a few voluntary hours a week at the cancer clinic at Toronto General Hospital and one evening at the supper table he described a case that had intrigued him. It had involved an elderly man who had been treated three years earlier for cancer of the lip. There was no evidence now of recurring cancer but the man had been referred to the cancer department because he was losing weight. McClure could find no medical cause for the weight loss so called in the Department Head. The Department Head, a rather brusque person, quizzed the old man and discovered that he was living in a one-room slum flat and was existing on poor grade canned meat and toast and tea. She referred him to the Social Service Department. McClure was intrigued by the way the case was so easily referred from department to department and he accompanied the old man to the Social Service Department to see what the outcome would be. The case worker in this department automatically went through an extensive questionnaire that re-established that the patient was living in poverty. It also established that he had half a dozen married children living in Toronto but that seemed to be an unimportant fact. The case worker said the department would try to get the man admitted to an institution where he would be properly cared for.

McClure was intrigued by the cool efficiency and the bureaucratic sterility of the system. It was humane in an inhuman kind of way. It was this he was commenting on at the dinner table. But Anklesaria hit on the existence of children who neither expected, nor were expected, to provide for their parent. While the story was being told the Indian had been changing colours. McClure finished the story and looked at his friend with some concern. A vein on Anklesaria's forehead was beginning to stand out.

The Parsee leaned across the table and pointed his finger at McClure's nose.

"Bob," he said, "raise your right hand."

McClure, puzzled, did as he was told.

"Now swear that you will never, *never* will you tell that story east of Suez. Children not looking after their parents is sub-human. No one east of Suez would understand that story."

26

Activities of a Soap Salesman

The Anklesarias left in July and McClure dove headlong into deputation work, that seemingly endless round of speaking engagements with which the church traditionally monopolized at least fifty per cent of a missionary's furlough. From the first of September to the fifth of December he spent only nine nights at home. "I have been travelling around Canada," he wrote to Anklesaria just before Christmas, "like a soap salesman." That was to be his last letter to his Parsee friend. Gustad Anklesaria died in January, 1961, leaving a void in McClure's India.

During the course of his soap salesman's travels McClure talked to many individuals and to many congregations who had helped support the work in India and who, after receiving a McClure pep talk, were determined to continue to support it. He also did some behind-the-scenes lobbying with government and industry. One result was that the Connaught Laboratories in Toronto agreed to donate enough Sabin oral anti-polio vaccine to protect ten thousand Indian children. Another result was that the Canadian government, through its Crown Assets Disposal Corporation, agreed to sell to the Mission Board some surplus army dental kits that came complete with chair and drill.

McClure was after those dental kits because he wanted to incorporate a modern dental clinic into the Ratlam hospital. He had already built the space for it. He had also found a qualified dentist ready to join him in India, a Dr. Morley Honey. McClure wrote to the church in India explaining, in decorous terms, the need for a dental clinic run by an experienced dentist who could teach as well as practise. He had already gone on record, less decorously, to the Board Secretary concerning that need: "Even in Indore there is no real dentist that I know of and much less in Ratlam. There is coming up a class of people now who are quite intelligent in these matters and they want something more than a dirty-handed half-trained dental quack—there are three in our city—to do their work for them. It would be quite a feather in our hat if we could be the ones to introduce modern dentistry into this part of the country."

It appeared that McClure's dental dream was about to come true.

The McClure enthusiasm was in such high gear these days that in a burst of enthusiasm (not untinged with nationalist pride) he decided to make a one-man assault on the problems of shipping directly from Canada to India.

In the past when hospital equipment or supplies were to be shipped there had been only two alternatives. The first alternative was quite unattractive. Equipment and supplies could be shipped directly from Canada to India but they would be treated like any commercial shipment. In India an import licence would be required as well as a Foreign Exchange Control Permit from the Reserve Bank of India. Duty would have to be paid of approximately 100 per cent. If licences and permits were not obtained (a long, tedious procedure) then the goods would be confiscated and a fine levied roughly equal to the value of the goods. "These little difficulties," McClure had once explained, "I should like to avoid."

Using the second alternative an officially registered charitable organization, such as The United Church of Canada, could send its goods via Church World Service in New York. Under the terms of a U.S.-India agreement the goods would then be shipped to India with the U.S. paying the ocean shipping and with India paying the overland charge. There would be no duty. There were two problems with this. One problem was that it put an entire intermediate trans-shipping stage in the middle at New York which caused interminable delay. The other catch was that regardless of place of origin everything arrived on the Bombay quayside clearly marked, "Gift of the American people to India". That label on the crates had galled McClure from the very outset. "I am sufficient of a nationalist," he had complained, "that I don't like to bring out Canadian donations to a Commonwealth country through American channels." But he also understood his fellow Canadians well enough to know they would balk at having to pay duty to India on relief goods donated to India. "Rather than pay duty (a Canadian) will direct his gift to some other country," he had warned.

From the time the Diefenbaker government had first come to power in 1957, and made it clear they wanted to untie Canada from American apron-strings, McClure had been badgering the Canadian High Commissioner to instigate action to get a Canada-India shipping agreement. The High Commissioner had seen the logic of it and Canada had tried. But finally, not long before McClure had left India on furlough, the answer had come. No such treaty was possible.

But now, suddenly, while McClure was home on furlough, a notice came through to the effect that the Government of India had liberalized the customs terms for relief supplies from *all* sources. It was great news. McClure and the Board Secretary made a frontal attack on the major shipping lines sailing between Canada and Bombay and received generous concessions for the shipment of donated equipment and supplies. Within a few weeks McClure was able to dispatch five tons of donations, including most of the equipment required to establish Dr. Honey's dental clinic. It was a marvellous, fruitful furlough. It seemed as though the world at large was becoming most generous.

After a good furlough McClure was always itching to hightail it back to work. This time, with direct shipment now possible and with a dental clinic to be established and with 10,000 doses of polio vaccine to be used he was even more impatient than usual. His restlessness was not helped by a cheerful letter from Dr. Anderson. Anderson was holding the fort at Ratlam and was living in the McClure bungalow. The bungalow was beginning to disintegrate around his ears: "The cracks in the dining room and pantry end of the house are increasing so much that next week ... they are to start tearing that whole section down, dining room, pantry and store-room, your bedroom, dressing and back room and the side verandahs up and down—that whole quarter of the building. . . . What dirt and havoc there will be during the tearing down, and the kitchen right there—plaster soup and brick sauce!"

Anderson was not worried about the thought of the soup and the sauce. "What worries me," he wrote, "is that at the present nothing will be replaced!" Apparently the residence committee, following the new wave of missionary thinking that came along with each new group of younger missionaries, had decided that the old bungalows had too much space. In Anderson's opinion the committee was ignoring the fact that in a community like Ratlam where there was a great deal of church-related traffic and no hotels those old bungalows did yeoman service as guest houses. He now urgently recommended that the McClures move quickly to catch the ear of the Board Secretary if they wanted the bungalow to be rehabilitated, not just amputated.

The McClures were having housing problems on two continents. This time when they returned to India they would be leaving 108 Strathallan standing empty; or they would have to rent it and be absentee landlords. They decided they should sell. But Bob did not want Amy to go back to eat "plaster soup and brick sauce" in a bungalow that might or might not be standing. In addition two family weddings were coming up in the summer. Patricia was marrying Jack Ebbs, a chartered accountant, and Doug was marrying Margaret Jackson, a fellow teacher. It was decided that McClure would return to India in April but that Amy would remain in Canada for both weddings and would sell 108 Strathallan before leaving. It was an old familiar pattern that seemed to be unbreakable. Once again McClure was missing family weddings and once again Amy was in charge of major family business.

Walter Anderson had included some other information in his letter, writing in a chatty, newsy way and without any intention of alarming McClure. He had listed the names of a few of McClure's ex-patients who had died and he had commented on the fact that the out-patient department was going until 7:00 p.m. every day and he had casually mentioned that the hospital beds were almost empty. The news of an empty hospital might well have put McClure into shock. He had turned that hospital around, changing it from not much more than an out-patient clinic to a surgical hospital with an O.R. supported by good lab and X-ray departments. It was also a teaching hospital for nurses, technicians, and interning surgeons. The Ratlam hospital could no longer tolerate too many empty beds. Not only would it not fulfil its teaching functions, it would go bankrupt. To McClure's mind the only justification for empty beds would be the discovery that all the physical ills of the people of Ratlam district had been healed. That was about as likely as a monsoon in January.

McClure was back in Ratlam a day before his furlough expired and a day before anyone expected him. He came in on the early morning *Frontier Mail*, ate breakfast at the railway station and took a *tonga* to the hospital. He baled out of the *tonga* just inside the compound gate and asked the *tongawalla* to take his bags to the bungalow and to deposit them on the verandah, if there was one. He went directly to the hospital.

The staff went into turmoil, not because they were caught slacking, they were not, but because they had planned to greet their Chief the next morning at the station with all the customary garlands and greetings of Indian courtesy. "I had your welcome when I first came to Ratlam," said McClure, checking the O.R. schedule. "Welcomes are no longer necessary."

There was such a spate of activity that morning around Ratlam Christian Hospital that Rotarian Sapat strolled across the street to see what was afoot. He, too, was astonished to see McClure. He pointed out that the Rotarians had been planning a railway station reception for the next morning and were going to be mightily disappointed to miss the pleasure of giving a red-carpet welcome.

McClure was unimpressed.

"I am not," he said, "the President of the United States."

The flurry attending that arrival in the spring of 1961 was misleading. The Indian members of the hospital staff soon sensed that in some mysterious way a watershed had been crossed. Although *Dada* McClure had returned as full of drive, enthusiasm and energy as ever before there had been a subtle change in the McClure character. He was less abrasive and more patient. It was one of those metamorphoses that used to be referred to as a "sea change" and that was impossible to explain. Had he been more than usually touched by the generous co-operation he had received at home not only from churches and individuals but from the Canadian government? Was it that he had passed his sixtieth birthday while on furlough and that fact, combined with the marriages of two more children, had given him pause for thought? Or was it the loss of his good friend Gustad Anklesaria that had tempered him? Had McClure finally felt the tremors of mortality? No one knew the reason but his associates knew that *Dada* had mellowed.

27

Surgeon in Governmentland

McClure's alarm over the possibility of finding an empty hospital was unfounded. The emptiness had been a temporary phenomenon brought about by a burst of cold weather inducing prospective patients to stay at home. Before long McClure was able to report: "For the last few months we have been running at nearly full occupancy. By accident or design of Walter Anderson, the proportion of 1st-class paying patients to 3rd-class poor and subsidized patients is exactly right. Thus when our hospital is full there is enough money made on first-class patients to pay the necessary subsidy to cover losses on third-class patients (who) fill the wards . . . We do not get, nor can mission hospitals ever expect to get, any assistance from government."

Walter Anderson not only had the balance correct, he had been pushing the TB work among non-Christians. McClure found himself scurrying to follow up Anderson's added impetus. The TB work was proving most rewarding. Almost every week he was able to list two or three TB patients as "cured".

The big bungalow was rescued without too much friction. A compromise was reached on size and McClure had the happy idea of putting a picture window in the dining room, which faced west. He agreed to pay for it himself. The Indian contractor was puzzled by the idea of such a big window. A house was supposed to enwrap you and exclude the outside world. He could see more sense in McClure's request for a special window in the bedroom. The bedroom window was to be paned with frosted glass.

The contractor worried about the picture window and finally came to the conclusion that the Canadian doctor was obviously mad. He solved the problem with a neat bit of personal initiative. McClure returned home one afternoon to find that the large dining room window had also been installed in frosted glass. McClure dug a little deeper into the family pocket and paid for a replacement. By the time Amy arrived in Ratlam the bungalow was looking rejuvenated.

Amy rejoined her mercurial husband to find that he had been involved in complications far more monumental than a mere window. The complications were international in scope and even McClure knew that the bureaucrats finally had him on a limb. At the beginning of September he sat down with a heavy heart and wrote a letter to the Board Secretary. He typed in a heading: "Direct shipment from Canada to India" and then underlined it. He sat for a moment staring darkly at the paper in his typewriter and then plunged ahead: "This will always be remembered as my greatest blunder in my missionary career."

The five-ton shipment of equipment and supplies that McClure had so proudly dispatched from Canada during the late winter of his furlough had made record time from Montreal to Bombay but was now sitting in a Bombay warehouse. It had been sitting there for three months. "We have been officially refused an import license ... The outlook is grim. There is a good chance that in sticking to red tape they may confiscate the whole shipment." It was even more aggravating since the dentist, Dr. Morley Honey, was now on hand and doing what he could without most of his equipment. An Indian Christian dentist had come up from South India to join the staff and Honey was already training an oral hygienist. As far as McClure knew there were only two other graduate dentists in an area inhabited by 24 million people. It was a poor time to be into a shipping snarl. McClure, as yet, had not quite figured out what the error had been but he had come to a very clear understanding of the lesson: "The lesson for us is that there is one channel and one only by which any goods for the hospitals can be admitted duty-free and that is Church World Service." The lesson had a moral to it: "Whatever our Canadian nationalism may make us feel about it we must eat humble pie and send all our stuff through New York."

By mid-September he reported that customs had made

their decision and that duty would have to be paid. "The advice of the Indian High Commissioner's office in Canada has been entirely wrong," McClure wrote. "There has been no 'liberalization' of regulations at all. In fact one would think, without being paranoid about it, that instructions have been given to clamp down on mission hospitals and missionaries."

He admitted that there had been a complication over and above the problem of lack of "liberalization". Someone in a department store in Toronto where some mechanic's tools had been purchased had made a slight error. They had accidentally included 500 cartridges of .22 calibre ammunition! If the customs officials suffered from a little paranoia themselves it was no wonder they were taking a long hard look at what, to them, was an "unauthorized" shipment.

McClure thought the whole shipment might have to be returned via New York where Church World Service could process it and ship it back again. Before taking this backward step he wrote a humble letter to the Central Board of Revenue in New Delhi. He pointed out that the government's press notice earlier in the year had given the impression, by omission, that certificates and licences were not needed but he admitted that he (and several church executives) had overlooked the word "consumable" referring to the kinds of goods governed by the supposedly liberalized regulations. "I must confess," he wrote, "that all this difficulty is due to my enthusiasm on one hand and my ignorance of customs regulations on the other combined with lack of intelligence and interpretation of the word 'consumable' in the press notice." He asked them, please, to confiscate the cartridges and to permit the rest of the shipment to come in duty-free.

In retrospect one can hardly believe that men as intelligent as McClure and the Board Secretary had not seen and understood the word "consumable". One is sorely tempted to suspect that they had hoped to bluff their way around it. Canadians afflicted by nationalism could embark upon strange ventures. At any rate, McClure was suitably contrite. "Being merely a surgeon . . ." he explained to the Indian government, "I find that I have broken all the laws except the universal laws of goodwill and brotherly love."

Finally, early in December, the shipment arrived in Ratlam. It included the Army Dental Corp kits for Dr. Honey as well as a steam sterilizer and many other items for the hospital. Storage and duty came to about $1,000.00 (Cdn). McClure sent an unnecessary warning home: "No more experimenting, please. That was the big 'goof' of my missionary career."

It tells much about the McClure character, however, that while he had been in the midst of the "goof" he was not averse to joining battle over the duty-free admission of polio vaccine. The gift of Sabin oral vaccine from the Connaught Laboratories had sparked a large scale polio project. Before McClure had completed his furlough he had convinced Canadian Rotary and Kiwanis Clubs to join forces to take care of shipping costs and all other overheads connected with an ambitious immunization project. Liaison was established with the Rotary Clubs of Ratlam and Indore and the Indian end of the project was organized as a co-operative effort between The United Church of Canada mission hospitals, the Rotary Clubs, the government medical college in Indore, and the communities. The amount of donated vaccine had been increased by Canadian Kiwanians from the dosage for 10,000 children to enough for 20,000 children.

Early in September, McClure reported to the Board Secretary that everything was ready. Connaught Laboratories were holding the shipment in readiness for cabled instructions. Now, with the advent of jet aircraft on the world's air routes, it would take a mere twenty-four hours for the cargo to come from Canada. It would be shipped refrigerated. Facilities were ready in India to put it immediately into refrigerated storage. All that was required was the import licence to allow duty-free entry but even this was being applied for by the Provincial Deputy Director of Health Services. Government laboratories were standing by to take delivery. McClure could not contain his enthusiasm. "It is the biggest public health thing that has ever been done by missions in these parts," he crowed.

A few weeks later not only had the necessary import certificates not been issued but McClure was being asked to guarantee the payment of duty. He avoided a head-on confrontation and asked the Canadian High Commissioner's office to intervene. He suggested that their diplomatic talents should be directed toward the education of the Indian government. "India should realize that it is highly repugnant to Canadians to think that a gift to India for the children of India, with all overhead covered by service clubs in Canada, should pay a customs duty levy to the Indian Government." He went on to say that he recognized that he himself might be a little paranoidal on the subject of such duty but that his feelings had been reinforced by a Canadian Kiwanis spokesman who stated: "If the Indian Government feels no more grateful for a donation of this type than to charge customs duty on the gift then do not bring the vaccine to India but instead call off the campaign and notify us in Canada and we shall give the polio vaccine instead to Malaya, Korea or Angola where we know it will be appreciated."

"Tax, tax, tax," wrote McClure, "is the routine of life in India. That their toleration for this kind of thing is not shared by their Canadian fellow members of the Commonwealth will probably have to be told to them in words of one syllable." He was angry but he gave the High Commissioner's office the challenge of turning his anger into productive channels. It was a challenge that required "that diplomacy for which you gentlemen are famous," he told them.

A few weeks later there was still no sign of a customs clearance. Instead there was a directive from the Central Board of Revenue to apply to the provincial Joint Director of Industries. Then the Canadian High Commissioner's office wrote to say they had found McClure would have to get a "No Objection" permit from the Reserve Bank of India.

McClure exploded.

"None of my Indian government friends," he wrote to the High Commissioner's people, "have as yet thought up this one." He referred to the "writing marathon sometimes referred to as a Polio Project," and he made an announcement: "I find myself near the end of my tether. I am about ready to quit . . . If India wants this stuff from Canada, and every doctor in India feels that India does want it, then she can receive it or turn it down. It is a relatively simple thing. The time element has completely gone out of our project."

The project had been scheduled for mid-September, 1961. Eventually diplomacy prevailed. The Indian government managed to overcome its own inertia and in the Ratlam area 5,000 children received their first anti-polio dosage just before Christmas. McClure, as usual, forgot the administrative frustrations in the light of the human achievement. Not only were thousands of children protected but in his area he had seen a Christian mission hospital, an "ecumenical" Rotary Club and a predominantly Hindu community all co-operating in a spirit of service.

"We shall take on more in this line soon," McClure promised the home team.

The members of Ratlam Rotary had been blissfully unaware that brother McClure had been fighting in the bureaucratic jungles. Being unscarred they took great, and justifiable, pleasure in a project well done. They told each other that McClure was teaching them the meaning of service.

McClure liked "projects". To him projects were the thing that created human interrelationships. When a group of Canadian children wrote asking for a project he told them about a Hindu school-teacher who needed an artificial arm. The children raised enough money for the arm and McClure then challenged the local Hindu community to finance the man's travel to a distant rehabilitation centre. The challenge was met.

In his own mind McClure classified money gifts into two categories, the "hot" and the "cold". The cold gift was preceded by a letter from the potential donor asking if there was a particular project for which money could be sent. The hot gift came along in the form of hard cash that could be used immediately for the need of the moment. In the interests of efficiency McClure preferred a hot gift but always tried to let the donor know how it had been used. The size of a gift was unimportant. The McClures would write voluminous letters explaining what had happened to the money; a patient's hospital fee had been paid; an instrument had been purchased for O.R; a second-hand microscope had been given to a village lab technician; a TB out-patient had been given enough protein supplement to last six months; a polio victim had received leg braces; a little Hindu boy had had his TB spine straightened; a young woman had had her nose remodelled.

To a donor in Canada cosmetic surgery on a nose might not have appeared to be among the charitable concerns of a Christian hospital. The need arose, occasionally, because of a custom that was tolerated in the Hindu culture. It was a custom that permitted a husband, when he felt he had been cuckolded, to cut off his wife's nose. It was a rural habit and usually involved the use of a handy sickle. The custom was looked upon with some leniency by the courts; it was obviously a crime of passion and passion was an ephemeral thing.

McClure had been doing about two "nose jobs" a year. He always found it an intriguing challenge. So did the surgeon at the provincial hospital. They competed to see who could rebuild the best nose. While McClure was involved with the Direct Shipment Project, the Polio Project and the Dental Project he performed a nose operation the memory of which remained with him because the result offended his sense of aesthetics.

The victim came from a village fifty miles from Ratlam. She was about sixteen years old, as was her husband. Even with her nose missing the little woman was brazen. McClure explained that the operation was both difficult and time-consuming but was told that he was supposed to be a real doctor and, in essence, to get cracking. McClure plodded patiently on with his explanation of the operation and particularly of the fact that it had to be done in three stages, the first two fairly close together and the third about three months later. He was told in no uncertain terms that a real doctor could do it in two stages and how about getting on with it!

The technique used was one that had been developed half a century earlier by a British doctor in the Indian Medical Service. It was called, appropriately enough, "The Indian operation". Stage one involved a preliminary build-up of the nose done by folding in skin from both cheeks and by turning down a flap of skin from the forehead. McClure called it the "Ganesh stage" after the name given an elephant-headed Hindu god. The patient always remained in hospital until the Ganesh look could be removed during stage two, at which time the elephant trunk was removed and skin was grafted from the thigh onto the forehead. Stage two ended with the creation of a bulbous nose that might or might not shrink somewhat in the next few months. The bulbous appendage would then be tailored to size during stage three and a hockey-stick-shaped piece of cartilage, taken from a rib, would be inserted into the nose as a bridge.

Much to McClure's astonishment and professional chagrin his strong-willed patient left the hospital as soon as the bandages and stitches were removed after stage two. She announced that she would not be back for stage three. McClure argued with her, but to no avail. He was appalled at the thought that his handiwork should go unfinished.

The patient made matters worse. She took that potato of a nose directly out into public view and attended court where her husband was receiving a hearing. McClure was pleased to hear from an enthusiastic messenger that she had gone to her husband, had thrown her arms around him, and had achieved a reconciliation in spite of her proboscis, but he was mortified to learn that the judge had discussed the surgeon's handiwork in open court.

The judge had asked an unnecessarily pointed and totally irrelevant question: "Is that a McClure nose or a government nose?"

The girl had announced, for all to hear, that it was a McClure nose.

The judge had thought about it a moment and then had contented himself with one mild comment. "McClure," he said, "is very generous."

McClure was still squirming from the messenger's report when the girl and her family returned from court to pick up her few belongings. This time her mother was with her. McClure could hardly believe his eyes. The mother, too, had a large bulbous nose. Unwittingly, he had recreated a perfect family protuberance. He was one up on the government surgeon.

28

Period of Paradox

The twentieth century moved on into the turbulent Sixties and India's problems did not seem to be going away. The biggest problem of all, excessive population growth, was getting worse. Prime Minister Nehru and his government had launched into family planning with high hopes. The government had promoted sterilization with more candour and forthrightness than had any other government in the world only to be undermined by conservative politicians representing large segments of society. The programmes had been toned down and cut back and the population statistics were still zooming. Even Ratlam would soon have doubled its population from the forty-five thousand of McClure's arrival to eighty thousand. The great optimism of the Fifties was gradually giving way to the doubts and concerns of the Sixties. Even the optimists were beginning to concede that there appeared to be no way India could feed itself if population went unchecked.

It was an enormous task that Prime Minister Nehru had set for himself; to lead the huge sub-continent of India, which was striated by the caste system, compartmentalized into religious factions and beset by drought and flood, into a reasonably self-sufficient and truly secular state. He had also set out to lead the country to a position of eminence among the nations. In this he had been amazingly successful.

Nehru had inherited Gandhi's platform of non-violence. He added his own international platform of non-alignment. He was anti-colonial and believed in the principle of self-determination. Nehru's powerful personal presence on the international stage, preaching co-operation and conciliation, helped the Dutch and the French move out of Asia without too much loss of face. India took an active role as a conciliator during the Korean War. India recognized Communist China from the very beginning and, as soon as Stalin was dead, Nehru visited Russia. He also visited China. And he invited the Queen to India. Nehru could not conceive of the world as being composed of two sides, the East and the West, with Russia face to face with America. For him each country was a link with another. Russia, China, India, Britain and the United States were links in a chain and each link was an intermediary between its neighbours on either side.

Nehru had no military might behind him, but he had personality and a striking command of the English language. He was a rational man in a world that seemed inclined toward madness. He was, in the words of John Kenneth Galbraith, "luminous and lonesome". For awhile, through sheer moral strength, Nehru gave India international stature and a sense of purpose.

The world was surprised in 1961 when "non-violent" India violated international law and occupied Portuguese Goa. But the world was inclined to suspect that the little enclave of Goa, a cyst on the side of India, was an anachronism from another era and that the Portuguese were a thick-headed folk insensitive to the trends of history.

Then, in 1962, pushed on by the nationalism of his self-conscious new nation, Nehru indulged in a military adventure against the Chinese on a remote portion of disputed border. He was also pushed on by his Defence Minister, Krishna Menon, a man later described by Canada's John Diefenbaker as having "all the attributes of Mephistopheles". It was said in India, and echoed by the West, that the Chinese were the aggressors. If so, seldom in history had an aggressor been so docile. With embarrassingly little effort the Chinese army broke through the Indian lines and found before them the plains of India and an almost unimpeded route to Calcutta. But, in a move that received very little play from the Western press, the Chinese declared a unilateral cease-fire and withdrew from the area. With a fine sense of brotherly condescension the Chinese released their Indian prisoners and returned their arms.

Throughout India the border war created a surge in national

sentiment. In the beginning citizens responded with considerable enthusiasm to the government's request for support, even going to the point of contributing personal jewellery to the national effort. One saw groups of young men learning military drills with make-shift weapons. But the war enthusiasm soon subsided; a psychological downer.

At the height of the frenzy a call had gone out across the nation for blood for the troops and this call had some impact on McClure's work. All hospitals found themselves functioning as blood donor clinics and the crisis did something to popularize the idea of giving blood. Medically the war made a positive contribution.

In 1964 Prime Minister Nehru died and the world wondered whether his passing was the death of a giant or the final disintegration of an already fallen idol. (An historian has since written that Nehru's contribution to India was that "he gave her a sense of purpose for the future as well as pride in her past",* surely an enormous legacy to be left by one man.)

Nehru was followed by Shastri, a gentle man wearing the spiritual mantle of Mahatma Gandhi. He died before two years was out and was followed as Prime Minister by Mrs. Indira Gandhi. The tides of history were ebbing and flowing across the sub-continent but McClure was in a backwater where national politics made no radical impressions. The China years, when his whole medical career had had to respond to the vagaries of politics and revolution, now seemed so very very far away. Those distant years had been so violent, so tumultuous, that the memory of their drama tended to obscure the hard human realities that underlay the theatrical action. Here, in Ratlam, it was all different. There were wars and skirmishes on the frontiers which radically affected some missionaries. In other regions there were language riots, racial riots and killings. But Providence decreed that McClure, having served an early apprenticeship in violence, should now be tried in the less spectacular trials of a slowly worsening economy, increasing poverty and drought, famine and disease. It was (and is) fashionable in some missionary circles to dismiss McClure as being too restless, too prone to pyrotechnics and to action and not capable

*Percival Spear, *India*

of the long, patient, hard grind required of the "true" missionary. His entire career in India was contradicting that smug
assertion and the years of the mid 1960s leading up to his
retirement called for more stamina and more patience than ever
before.

When McClure had arrived in India the statisticians were
anticipating a population of 408 million by 1961, but the census
of 1961 showed a population of 439 million. The growth rate
was 12 million a year and increasing. Statisticians were project-
ing a population of 500 million by 1970.* During the Fifties the
national income had increased but now, in the Sixties, it was
declining. Industrial production was beginning to stagger. Food
production was not only falling short of increased targets it was
dropping behind the accomplishments of previous years. A
great weight, invisible but all-pervasive, was bearing slowly
down upon India. That weight was also bearing down upon The
United Church of Canada's missions and, in particular, upon its
hospitals.

The Canadian hospitals had managed for years to be largely
self-supporting, relying on the Canadian church for staff
salaries and capital for equipment while drawing daily operating
expenses from patients' fees. But all that was changing. Patients
who might once have demanded a private room were now
settling for a public ward with lower fees. Medical services had
improved but costs had risen. The United Church of Canada had
been increasing its grants a little each year but there was pressure from within the church in Canada to decrease grants in the
interests of weaning the Indian church into a state of self-
sufficiency. But the Indian economy had worsened and there
was less chance than ever of Christian hospitals receiving much
financial support from Indian Christians.

McClure recognized all the inherent paradoxes. In the face
of rising costs the only way for the Board to decrease grants and
for standards to be maintained would be to close down some
hospitals. If a hospital closed down it was required by law to pay
separation allowance to all employees. The sums involved were
staggering to a mission budget, sometimes working out at more
than double the capital cost of the entire hospital, both plant and

*The 1971 census reported 547,949,809

equipment. It was difficult to imagine a campaign at home to raise money to close down hospitals.

It was obvious to any thoughtful observer that India would be much the poorer without the Christian hospitals. Their contribution in the field of nursing alone was staggering. Now, in the mid-Sixties, only 2.3 per cent of the population of India was Christian but 85 per cent of all nurses in India were Christian. (Hindu girls were only beginning to think of nursing as other than low menial work.) In 1946 there had been one trained nurse in India for every 45,000 of population. Now the figure was approaching one trained nurse for every 11,000 of population. It was one of the few statistics that was showing a positive and steady improvement and most of the effort that made it possible had been mission effort, with more than a little of it being Canadian.

Throughout the years, as though to compound all paradoxes, the Indian government had been exerting pressure, both subtle and overt, to get missions and missionaries out of India. Irrationally, those pressures now increased as conditions worsened. McClure responded with a dictum that was both pragmatic and prophetic. "No missionaries," he said, "no money."

Medical policy was a matter to be decided by the Indian church, not by the missions. The United Church of Canada did, however, send a doctor to the field to conduct a survey and to give a personal report. He was Dr. C. W. M. (Bill) Service, a surgeon from Lindsay, Ontario, who had been born on the West China mission field and who had served in China during the Forties, overlapping with McClure in the Chungking area. Service presented a thoughtful, well-considered report in which he suggested that some hospitals could indeed be closed and that others should make an even greater effort to complement the government institutions. He also suggested that the mission hospitals could do more to relate to the non-Christian community and that their Boards might well contain some public-spirited non-Christian members of the communities in which they were located. It was advice that seemed sound and rational to McClure but which was debated endlessly throughout the councils of the Indian church.

So non-productive were the debates that six months after

Service's visit McClure wrote a letter to the Board Secretary and labelled it "Confidential". It reeked of disillusionment: "There is no thought about 'What is best for the Christian Church in Malwa?'* That has never crossed people's minds. The whole attitude is 'What will this do to me and my family?' 'How am I faring compared to others?' 'What more could I get out of it by some other arrangement?' This is the attitude of the doctors involved. There will be no progress, I feel, by having the matter brought to Mandal or Church Council for within these bodies each person is related in one way or another to one of the doctors or to some group of interests and will merely ask the same questions. Sides will immediately be taken. Who will take what side could be predicted with 99 per cent accuracy... In neither medicine nor in nursing do we have a single Christian in Malwa who can think in non-personal terms about the medical work except some of those who come from Canada and many of them have been here so long that they too tend to react in an Indian way.

"Without wishing to feel like a pessimist one must say what is my advice then? My reply would be that since no satisfactory solution can be found within the medical fraternity on the field it should be necessary to draft certain terms for the future by those in Canada and hand these to the Church of India. This sounds like a backward step but it is a step."

McClure showed this verbal blast to Walter Anderson who also wrote a letter to the Board Secretary. In it he gave support to McClure's contention that a dead end had been reached in discussions, but he thought it possible that everyone was not as self-seeking as McClure said and suggested that nothing be done in haste and that discussions be resumed after the hot season had been passed. In his gentle fashion he described a few more paradoxes that had been overlooked and implied that what looked like a time of pending drought and famine was not perhaps the best time for the church to be thinking of getting out of the hospital business. Irascible McClure and quiet Anderson were perfect counterweights for each other.

Dada McClure may have mellowed but he had developed no inclination to use velvet gloves. He was still incredibly blunt

*The Presbytery.

with his staff. "Indians profit," he told a visiting Canadian journalist, "by having their eardrums tickled by a bit of reproof now and then." He also explained that he had not come to India carrying a message that said, "God loves you, so sit on your butt". It was precisely because McClure did not sit on his butt that his staff and the people of Ratlam had learned to adore him.

Now, as he was moving well on into his sixties, he was not slowing down. Late one October evening he was on his way by train to the mission station at Rasalpura to attend a meeting of the Medical Commission. The train did not stop at Rasalpura but it slackened speed as it passed through. McClure, wishing to save himself time and expense, leaped from the moving train. The next morning he led opening devotions in the Rasalpura chapel and spoke on the need for adaptability. Miss Sonu Canara, the Indian Nursing Superintendent from Ratlam hospital, listened with amazement. At that moment she was the only one present who knew the speaker was trying to adapt to a broken leg. When the service finished she blew the whistle on her Chief and rounded up Dr. Anderson, Stephen Haider Ali and other commissioners who carted McClure off to the nearest railway station and forced him into a first class compartment. The men turned their backs for a few moments and McClure disappeared. They found him in a third class compartment. He said his leg was too painful for him to move again and that he had already sent a runner off to claim a refund on the first class ticket. A few hours later, in Ratlam, Dr. Charity Noah and two junior associates had the nerve-wracking job of putting McClure into plaster. They were so nervous they completed the job but forgot to install the iron peg for walking. Not daunted they added the peg along with more plaster. They were certain that at last *Dada*, with a broken leg and wearing a monumental cast, would be out of action for a few days. Dr. Noah wrote on the cast with a firm hand stating the date for removal. It was six weeks away.

That same evening patients watched McClure practise walking with crutches along the hospital paths. The next morning he made the rounds as usual. A few days later he told Sonu Canara that a new book had come out in which it said that for certain breaks three weeks in a cast was quite sufficient. The Nursing Superintendent was having none of it. She tapped the

had been sitting cross-legged on her cow dung floor grinding meal with a little mill when she had been seized by a terrible stomach pain and had collapsed. Her husband had taken her to the provincial hospital, which was free. She had been given an injection and sent home. McClure assumed the injection had been morphine because the pain had eased for a few hours. Then it returned. The woman and her husband wanted to come to the mission hospital but had heard that it was not free. They spent the next two weeks weaving as many baskets as possible and finally took them to market, the woman still wracked with pain. Now she offered the doctor their total savings; ten rupees or about $2.50 (Cdn).

McClure comforted her as best he could and assured her that in spite of what she had heard the money was not important. When he operated, McClure found an ovarian cyst the size of a large grapefruit. It had twisted upon itself and had cut off its own blood supply so that the growth itself was rotting inside her. The surgeon estimated that if it had gone another two days she would have died, and in agony. As it was she responded excellently to post-operative supportive treatment.

By the time the patient was ready for discharge her hospital bill (actual costs) was about $20.00 (Cdn), or almost eight times her life's savings. McClure dipped into his "special project" funds for the $20.00 and Haider Ali explained to the patient that the bill was being paid by a Canadian lady in a city called Regina.

One of the major foes that frequently made it to a show-down battle in O.R. was TB. Tuberculosis was not confined to the lungs. It frequently attacked the lower intestine. A patient would come in complaining of loss of weight, afternoon fevers, vague pains in the midline lower abdomen or, sometimes, more specific tenderness in the region of the appendix. They were symptoms that in the Western world would make a doctor suspect appendicitis but in India appendicitis was very rare. If the case was well advanced the doctor could feel the growing mass with his fingers. As the patient grew thinner the TB mass grew larger. Without surgery the patient would die.

The success of the surgery depended not only upon the skill of the doctor but upon the facilities of the hospital. The advice given by many Western teachers, and repeated in many Western textbooks, was to remove the entire section of diseased intestine and then rejoin the healthy sections. This advice ignored the fact that an equipment-starved hospital (like most in India) would have inadequate blood bank facilities and poor anaesthetic equipment and consequently the textbook operation would inevitably kill the patient. It was quite possible, however, to use another TB technique, that of simply putting the diseased part to rest, as one did with lungs. This could be accomplished by making a bypass from the healthy part of the small intestine down to the healthy part of the large intestine. There was very little operative shock and not much risk of post-operative complications. In addition, the operation could be done under a spinal anaesthetic which had little after-effect. The Ratlam team could do it in thirty minutes. They always sent a portion of the neighbouring lymph gland off to the lab for a biopsy to confirm that the lesion was TB and not cancer.

Whenever possible the hospital kept track of its patients during the following years. Occasionally some who had had the bypass operation were opened later for other reasons. In every case it was found that the disease had been completely cured and the normal channels had been re-established by nature.

TB also attacked bones. TB of the spine, if left unchecked, always crippled and often killed. Complete paralysis of the legs would usually precede death. TB crippled by curving the spine, forming the "hunchback" that was once familiar in all parts of the world. The modern drugs and vaccines were of small consolation to those already afflicted with gross deformation.

McClure had pioneered with spine straightening operations in North China and while in Cairo had learned what was called the "Albee technique". It centred around the use of a double-bladed sterile circular saw. He had ordered one of those saws shortly after arriving in Ratlam but by the time the order had been approved, had gone through the Board at home, then to the Church World Service organization in New York, then to the suppliers, then to the shippers, then through Indian customs and internal shipping, it was several years before he had the instrument in hand. Then came the training period. Sometimes it seemed to both McClure and his staff that while they were working full time they were also at school full time with the Chief Surgeon acting as Head Teacher.

To straighten a TB spine they began on the lower leg. A long incision was made and, using the double-bladed saw, a piece of bone about eight inches long by a half-inch wide and a half-inch deep was removed from the shin-bone. This strip of bone was then immersed in a dish of warm saline solution while an assistant closed the leg wound and the surgeon prepared the spine. There was some elaborate spinal carpentry using hammer and chisel and then another groove was sawn to receive the eight-inch splint of bone. When dropped into place the graft was firmly bedded in several vertebrae above and below the rotting TB bones. Eventually all three areas would weld themselves into one solid whole. The spine would not be flexible in that area but it would be straight. As a deforming hump it had not been flexible either.

McClure was always elated by the successful completion of corrective surgery. The psychological effect upon a patient when freed from physical deformity could be exhilarating for all persons concerned. Nowhere was this more evident than in the treatment of leprosy, and in no other field was the struggle more difficult or drawn out.

McClure's first confrontation with leprosy in India had come shortly after he had first arrived in Ratlam. He had received a message, channelled through one of his own nurses, from a nurse who worked for the late Maharajah's family. The message had asked Dr. McClure if he would make a private, unobtrusive house-call at the nurse's apartment, inside the palace grounds. (The old Maharajah had died just before Independence but his son still lived with some semblance of pomp in the local palace in line with Nehru's treaty with the princely states.)

McClure had gone along on a hot afternoon about two o'clock when most people were having siesta. It was a time of day when the streets of Ratlam were as deserted as though the city had been abandoned. He had pedalled his bicycle to the palace, an imposing structure that was now beginning to decay. The high-arched elephant gate was guarded by a sleepy detachment of the Ratlam constabulary armed with Lee-Enfield rifles. They had passed him through without showing any signs of curiosity.

The palace was a multi-storey structure housing some two hundred bedrooms and suites. It still housed the big Durbar Hall used in the grand days of princely gatherings. Now the portraits of former Maharajahs were draped with cloth and elegant furniture was sheeted in plastic to fend off the ravages of both time and democracy.* McClure's destination, however, had been what used to be a guest house on the palace grounds. Here he had met the nurse and had followed her to an apartment on the third floor. She had opened the door to a small room and had asked him to enter.

The room was dark and airless. The shutters were closed and the curtains were drawn. There was a reek in the air that had jolted McClure's memory back to a small dark shack on the coast of Taiwan where he had once found two Japanese youths locked away in shame and misery to die of leprosy. And indeed, the situation here was not much different. On a bed, in the dark, lay a boy about fifteen years old. He was in the last stages of leprosy and TB. The nurse was his mother but all she could do for her son was to take him out every night around midnight for a short walk in a secluded part of the palace grounds. Other than that she could only watch him slowly die, outcast, a victim of what Indians called *Mahag Rog*—"the greatest of diseases".

McClure had done the best he could for the lad but by then it was not much. Before long the boy had died. His case remained in McClure's mind, not because it was typical, but because it marked the end of an era. Radical changes were underway.

The big break-through in leprosy treatment had come in 1948 with the development of the Sulphone drugs. These drugs were capable of arresting the spread of leprosy through the body. They could not rehabilitate the damage already done but invariably they would prevent further progression. They were truly "miracle" drugs. The miracle they could not achieve was to cause an overnight change in society's attitude to the "leper". The name itself continued to be a curse. The disease was actually less contagious than TB and no more deadly but so visible and grotesque were its ravages that the leper continued to be driven from the hearthside while the undetected tuberculosis victim stayed on to spread contagion.

The traditional way to handle victims of advanced leprosy had been to gather them together into "colonies". Missions had been active in this work for years in many parts of the world. The

---

*In 1978 the Durbar Hall housed the main Ratlam postal depot. The author bought stamps where the Maharajah had held assemblies of state.

Sulphone drugs were changing all that. The challenge now was one of re-education. Doctors and missionaries had to be re-educated along with everyone else.

McClure made a point of meeting the leprosy specialists at the two Christian medical colleges of Ludhiana and Vellore.* At Vellore, Dr. Paul Brand was becoming recognized as the father of modern leprosy work. By means of reconstructive surgery Brand was demonstrating that even the crippling aspects of leprosy were highly curable.

The school of thought led by Dr. Brand was one that appealed to McClure. It was direct, practical and aggressive. Do not send patients to colonies, McClure was told. Do educate the patient and his family. With proper treatment and instruction all the deformities associated with leprosy could be avoided. What was needed was a vigorous programme.

McClure began to re-educate his own hospital staff.

"Every patient," he said, "is a potential leprosy patient. We will not hold leprosy clinics. Every day is leprosy day. Every patient will be given leprosy tests as a matter of routine. Any patient even suspected of having leprosy will be referred directly to me."

They set aside a four-bed ward that bore no identification. Each new leprosy patient underwent hospitalization for a preliminary ten-day period of treatment and observation during which time X-rays, blood, and other tests established whether there were any complicating factors present such as syphilis, TB, intestinal parasites, chronic malaria, chronic dysentery, anaemia, diabetes or dental caries. All such ailments had to receive attention before leprosy treatment could be effective. The leprosy medical treatment was simple. The Sulphone drug (usually one called DDS) was administered orally. Gone completely were the old days of painful oil injections.

What was not so simple was educating the patient as to the nature of his or her disease. Leprosy in India was usually of the anaesthetic variety. There was usually a loss of sensation in the hands and feet. The victim would burn his hands or cut his feet without knowing he had caused any damage. Through constant, unattended injury the hands and feet would ulcerate.

*Both were union colleges and hospitals in which The United Church of Canada participated with other missions.

Subjected to frequent injury and deep infection the bones of the fingers and toes became thin and tended to shrink in size, creating the impression of "rotting away". Hands and feet became grotesquely mis-shapen. The main thrust of the Ratlam programme was to catch the disease early, before such obvious destruction had begun.

It was one thing to arrest the disease. It was quite another thing to restore the use of hands and feet that had already been crippled or to re-create a face that had lost the elasticity of the skin so that eyelids and earlobes sagged; a face that was heavily wrinkled and that had lost its eyebrows; a face that appeared to have no nose. Rebuilding from such ruin was a major surgical challenge.

McClure was fortunate. A young Canadian surgeon from British Columbia joined the mission in the mid-Sixties and spent some time at Ratlam. His name was Dr. David Kennedy. McClure sent Kennedy post-haste to Vellore, to Dr. Paul Brand and to Brand's associate Dr. Mary Vergheese, a surgeon who in spite of being a paraplegic had become, in Brand's own words, "an absolute master of her craft".

Kennedy returned from Vellore and set to work. To begin with, McClure, in his customary brusque way, was inclined to be impatient of the tedious time-consuming techniques brought back by Kennedy; until he saw the results. McClure then set to work to learn from Kennedy. It was an example of something McClure had stated many years before when he had explained that what a mission doctor leaves behind is not grateful patients but "a trail of men who have worked with him, who have got something that took time to give them".* The process applied to so many doctors and was still continuing; from Brand, to Vergheese, to Kennedy, to McClure.

McClure was also learning about the psychology of the disease and its social consequences. A woman arrived one day with feet, hands and face all showing the effects of advanced leprosy. She had hobbled thirty miles on foot, managing about ten miles a day. McClure asked her to choose what should be corrected first; hands, feet, or face. He thought she would probably elect to have the right hand rehabilitated but she said, "No".

*Vol. 1, page 406.

"When I get on a bus," she said, "they see my nose. Every-body cries out, 'She's a leper! She's a leper! Throw her off!' The driver puts me off. I can hide my hands and even my feet. There are other people who limp. I can't hide my nose. Fix my nose first and then I can come by bus for treatment."

Leprosy caused the ridge-bone of the nose to disintegrate. The skin remained intact but collapsed, like a tent that had lost its ridge-pole, giving the illusion of a cavity in the centre of the face. External skin grafts did not work on a leper so the surgeon worked from within, moving up from inside the upper lip, and gradually molded a new ridge in whatever fashion the patient wanted—Greek, Roman, Chinese—any style was possible. The result was a miracle of facial and psychological rehabilitation. In comparison, reconstruction to take the sag out of eyelids and to remove wrinkles was relatively minor cosmetic surgery, but reactivating an eyelid that had ceased to blink was a major challenge. In advanced cases the diseased eyelid muscles would cease to function. The eye, remaining constantly open, became dry and scarred. The inevitable result was blindness. There is, however, a muscle running upward from the jaw just forward of the ear. By means of delicate surgery a piece of this muscle could be led to the corner of the eye. There it would be split and led around the eye, above and below, and be reunited and anchored at the inside corner of the eye. When the jaw moved, the eye would close. Even restless jaw movements during sleep would keep the eye blinking and moist. It was a delicate piece of surgery but McClure, now rapidly approaching retirement age, learned to execute it with precision. He then set about learning the tricky tendon problems involved in reactivating leprosy hands.

For McClure there was something symbolical about lep-rosy. The disease destroyed the person physically, socially, and then spiritually. But it could be stopped and the body could actually be remade. The physical results were often somewhat mis-shapen and scarred but the mental results were amazing. Thanks to medicine and surgery the leprosy patients were in-deed "reborn". Moreover, during the years McClure had been in India even the society had been changing. Gradually the rehabilitated leper was finding it possible to be accepted.

A young married man, a farmer, came to the hospital with one foot "dropped", its muscles no longer able to lift it. His feet were ulcerated. His body was blotched with the all-too-familiar anaesthetic patches. Both hands were frozen into claw-like positions so that he could not grasp tools or even cup his hands to drink water in the traditional Indian fashion. His face was normal but he had a desperate, pinched look and his eyelids were beginning to sag. A year and a half later the disease had been arrested, he was lifting his foot by means of a "new" muscle, the tendons in his hands had been re-routed and he could cup his hands. The day finally came when he gained the courage to offer water to his relatives (a deeply symbolic act) *and they accepted it.* In his case, *Mahag Rog,* "the greatest disease", had been defeated in more ways than one.

30

The Homestretch

The McClures were home in Canada for a fleeting mid-term break during the summer of 1965. They now had nine grandchildren and were missing the privilege of watching the little ones grow. Amy was feeling particularly frustrated by not being close enough to babysit or bake cookies or perform any of the other grandmotherly rites. They were "Grandpa" and "Grandma" to the children of the hospital staff in Ratlam and McClure fixed tricycles and made tiny furniture and led wanderers home by the hand but it was not the same thing as being near one's own grandchildren.

Quite apart from the joys of family reunion, 1965 was an interesting year during which to sally forth into the outer world. It seemed as though the pace had changed; accelerated. The world was spinning faster. In Canada the edges between national and international events were becoming more and more blurred. Perhaps electronic communications were indeed creating McLuhan's "global village". In England Sir Winston Churchill died and most of North America watched the funeral "live" via satellite TV relay. An era had ended but a new one had already begun. Canada hoisted a new flag. There were Liberal scandals, avalanche disasters, airplane crashes and a postal strike. Canadian Roman Catholics began to hear mass in English, a committee of Anglican and United Church clergymen agreed on the guiding principles for a prospective church union and Prime Minister "Mike" Pearson outlined a startling proposal for universal medical care. A Soviet astronaut became the first man to "walk" in space and the slow starting Americans followed five days later with their first two-man space flight. Soon the launching pads at Cape Kennedy looked like the Fourth of July as American two-man rockets went off to space for "walks", orbiting records and practice dockings. China exploded her second atomic bomb, the Vatican denied that Jews held a collective guilt for the crucifixion of Christ, United States Marines intruded into a Dominican Republic revolt under the guise of heading off communism and "Mike" Pearson called, unsuccessfully, for a United Nations Peace Force to avert a major war in Vietnam. The Province of Quebec was well into its "quiet revolution" under Jean Lesage and was probing to see how far it could go in making its own international agreements. Quebec Separatists were probing further with demonstrations. A Dominican bomb damaged the American Embassy in Montreal and a Separatist bomb exploded on Dorchester Boulevard in the same city. Although the Montreal Canadiens won the Stanley Cup it was gradually dawning upon Canadians that their world was no longer stable.

McClure found that in spite of what appeared to be escalating chaos the members of the United Church were still interested in helping less fortunate peoples. He also found that service clubs were still interested in service. He returned to Ratlam knowing that Canadians still drew upon an apparently bottomless reservoir of goodwill for others and as yet had not put padlocks on their pocketbooks.

McClure had been so eloquent on at least one platform in Canada that a young Canadian doctor and his wife, Jerry and Sandra Shime, journeyed to India and joined the Ratlam staff for a year. Dr. Shime was young, keen, observant and blessed with a social conscience. He was also a Jew. One of the Canadian missionaries objected to the idea of the church hiring a Jewish doctor. She went so far as to put her concerns into a letter. Dr. Shime was temporarily and understandably depressed but McClure was enraged. He let it be known that any Canadian who objected to a Jewish doctor on a Christian mission field could henceforth refrain from appearing inside the Ratlam compound. Fortunately the furore subsided.

McClure was often criticized as being naive and unaware of the true facts of life. It would be closer to the truth to say that he often over-simplified a situation or described things with such energy as to create an impression of over-simplification. He was not naive. He saw the world and his associates with great clarity and commented accordingly. His comments were seldom meant as judgements. There was a young Indian doctor whose career McClure had followed with interest. The doctor went, on church scholarship, to study in England and eventually headed for further studies in Canada. He made the mistake when he left for England of booking an expensive passage. That burst of self-indulgence brought him under the McClure scrutiny and a laconic letter went off to the Board Secretary simply suggesting "strict budget control" for the mission's protege.

By the time the doctor was ready to head for Canada McClure had come to a slow simmer and there was nothing laconic about his next warning to the Board Secretary: "Before leaving and now in letters he has told his friends that he is 'going to get out of the church every cent that he can'. He has told folks here that he has found out that there is lots of money in the United Church and that if you address meetings and then speak in the right way to the influential people afterwards that you can get lots of money. Other Indian delegates have done it and he has more of the gift of the gab than any of them. He has too. His plan then is not to cramp his style by limiting himself to the Canadian $4,000 of scholarship and the full salary with all benefits that is being paid for out here while he is away but he hopes to milk the United Church cow and he has his pail and suction all ready . . . Take him behind the barn and tell him the facts of life at a rather early date after his arrival. You will have to be very plain and explicit with him and speak in words of one syllable. You will not be able to get any help in this matter from missionaries on furlough for none of them want to get in wrong . . ."

The hopeful young cow-hand may have been off with his toy bucket to do a little illicit milking but if so he was being headed off at the pass by a dusty, crusty, hard-riding old timer. Presumably the talk "behind the barn" took place because the doctor completed his studies. The following year found him back in India and in charge of one of the mission hospitals. It was an achievement for all concerned because not every doctor who went abroad on post-graduate scholarships returned to India. Of those who did, too many often chose more lucrative private or government practice.

During the mid-1960s the pressures seemed to increase and

to come from all directions. The Canadian Broadcasting Corporation sent a film crew to Ratlam to film McClure in action. They arrived at the height of the hot season when everyone's nerves were drawn thin. The crew members were appalled by the poverty of India and by what struck them to be a ramshackle hospital. Some of them had expected to find a gentle stereotype missionary and were shaken to find a muscular man with an abrasive tongue and the bearing of an R.C.M.P. officer. He found them too demanding of his time in the midst of the heavy dry season schedule. Behind the scenes Nurse Canara and Stephen Haider Ali had to convince McClure that the crew members were there to help and were suffering physically to do so. The final film product was well-balanced and reflected none of the personality clash. The director allowed himself the pleasure of including only one shot of real vintage McClure. This gem captured the Chief making ward rounds and looking at a baby's chart. There was a sudden on-camera flare-up. "Where's the lab sheet!" the doctor roared, "Come on, come on. One baby, one lab sheet!" An arm nervously extended into frame with the missing lab report. "That's better," growled the doctor.

At home in Canada on Thursday, September 1, 1966 at 9:30 p.m. (E.D.T) the CBC television network burst into colour for the first time. At 10:00 p.m. Canadians from coast to coast were watching *McClure in India*. By September 3rd they were reading an illustrated article in the *Star Weekly* by the film's producer, Dale Barnes, and by mid-September a lengthy article in *Maclean's* by the film's writer, Kenneth Bagnell. McClure and the Ratlam Christian Hospital were getting a good press.

All publications were not so favourable. Dr. John McIntyre, a Canadian surgeon, and his wife, Shirley, a nurse, joined McClure for a month of voluntary service. The couple wrote lively and informative letters to *The Uxbridge Times-Journal* in Ontario which printed them in full. The letters did not mask the cultural shock felt by the McIntyres upon encountering conditions in a mission hospital. They were not accustomed to a society that did not seek medical help until an ailment had reached almost terminal proportions. They were not accustomed to patients who turned up with mutilations received as a result of treatment by local medicine men. They were not used to a "poor" hospital where the surgeon had to save his scalpel

blades and re-sharpen them for re-use and where tongue depres-
sors were boiled and re-used instead of being thrown into the
waste basket. They were not used to making emergency burr
holes in a skull with an instrument that came apart unless one
had a free hand with which to hold it together. They were not
used to the spectacle of a missionary who began breakfast every
morning by putting the toast in the toaster and then reading a
passage from *The Upper Room* and saying grace in precisely the
time it took the toast to cook. (McClure would permit no one else
to ask the blessing because an Anglican prelate had once prayed
so long the toast had burned.) They were not used to having flies
in the O.R., goats in the courtyard and visitors sleeping under
the ward beds. The McIntyres' reports did not ruffle McClure
but they caused heartburn among some of the Indian staff. An
Indian nurse sat down and shot an irate letter off to the Board
Secretary describing how much assistance the McClures and the
entire staff had given to the visitors. "They were treated like our
honoured guests," she explained, "and as far as possible were
included in our working programme to make them feel very
much at home and useful . . . I am surprised that educated and
cultured people should be so unappreciative of all that was done
for them."

It was too bad. The visitors had merely been following the
McClure principle of telling it the way they saw it. The main
drawback of the McIntyre letters was that they were not published widely enough. It was almost impossible to convey to
Canadians a real appreciation of the work being done by medical
missionaries in India. McIntyre wrote a voluminous letter describing the work of a typical mission doctor: "The pile of letters,
orders, import forms, licenses, government forms, priority
slips, requisitions, and other paper work is quite unbelievable to
our minds . . . It would be difficult enough if a missionary doctor
had only to attend to the medical needs of the hospital. But it
seems almost invariable that he must also assume all the administrative and financing work as well . . . Then there is the task
of organizing and attending mission meetings, religious meetings, Indian medical meetings, family planning meetings, and
inevitable meetings required to satisfy the Indian government.
Then in his spare time there is his public health work—
organizing and carrying out immunization projects, education
in public hygiene, sanitary sewage disposal, clean water supply,

prevention against parasitic diseases . . . To add to their miseries doctors must work within a strict and always inadequate budget. To supplement monies coming from home he must raise what he can from the patients . . . All things considered, it takes quite a man to be a mission doctor. In fact the present generation isn't producing enough of them, and mission hospital after mission hospital finds its doctors retiring or going home, and no replacement taking his place . . . It is no wonder that many churches, including The United Church of Canada . . . are considering closing their mission hospitals."

If McClure had seen that letter he would have been saying "amen" to everything written. There was only one paragraph where he and McIntyre would have parted company and that was in a summation: "Having seen a fair bit of India I cannot but agree that there . . . is much to suggest that all foreign interests withdraw all aid of every sort, and leave India to sink or swim, rather than bungle along."

McClure had no intention of abandoning India until retirement forced him out. Many of the missionaries who had been afraid that the foot-loose surgeon would come to India only for a year or two had long since gone home. Indian doctors had come and gone, visitors had arrived and departed but Bob and Amy McClure were still there. One of the most promising of the Indian doctors, who was being groomed to take over Ratlam, went to study in Canada on a privately donated scholarship and chose not to return, but McClure remained in Ratlam. The medical councils within the Indian church continued to debate endlessly and vested interests continued to oppose change so that even Indians were getting fed up and were resigning, but McClure hung on.

Why?

A father brought his little son to the hospital. The lad had fallen down a dry well and his leg was broken with a compound fracture. The bone ends were showing through and the dangling limb was a bleeding, torn mess. McClure made his preliminary examination, ordered sedatives, and had the boy taken to the O.R. Before following, he turned to the father who was distraught and weeping. McClure took the man's hands in his and said, "I'm going to fix your son's leg. He's going to be okay." The father did not comprehend and was even more distraught. McClure threw his arms around him and told a nurse to translate. "Tell him I have children of my own," he cried. "I won't let anything happen to his boy!"

McClure was compassionate and that was why he was in India.

That same day, inside the O.R., a staff member who was monitoring a new anaesthetic machine let his eyes and his mind wander. He was thrown out. McClure was ruthless. In the O.R. a person's life depended upon efficiency. Split-second timing could make the difference between long life or a swift death. One had to learn that in the operating room there was no place for either cultural sloth or sentiment. That, too, was why McClure was in India.

The Bougainvillaea beside the study door struggled for moisture. Amy's zinnias and nasturtiums died in their pots before transplanting time. Out in the villages the earth hardened and cracks opened wide and deep enough to break a man's leg. Wells dried up and refugees fled to the cities. Water buffalo died in the river beds and people died in rural streets. The vultures moved closer to town. Temperatures soared to 113°F. The monsoons failed and famine came to the Malwa plateau but the McClures stayed on.

The rain began, a few hesitant drops at a time. No one dared notice. No one dared look or rejoice. The rain might not last. But it did. Floods came, and instant greening, and the McClures remained in Ratlam.

Bob and Amy McClure's 40th wedding anniversary came and went. Amy was counting the months to retirement. McClure's 66th birthday arrived and the hospital staff, headed by theatre nurse Dorothy McIntyre and Nursing Superinten- dent Sonu Canara, gathered together in the ward courtyard to pay birthday compliments to *Dada* McClure. There were nurses there like Maya Ishwardan who once, many years before, had burst into tears and said she would never again go into the O.R. with McClure. To Maya, an orphan, *Dada* now meant "father", with no shadings, and to her children it meant "grand- father", with no reservations. Sonu Canara, who had been an auxiliary nurse in the British Army and whose Colonel had once had to disarm her, had entered McClure's employ with ap- prehension and trembling. Her fierce loyalty now typified that of many others. When a visiting Canadian surgeon chided her for being too particular and said, "I'm not McClure," she snapped back with, "You are so right. God only made one McClure." Another doctor once dourly referred to "your McClure" and Sister Canara flared again. "Don't you dare call him my McClure," she protested. "He is my doctor and my boss and my friend but not *my* McClure."

Again she was right. He was *their* McClure. By now a roll call of McClure supporters would have included a large cross-section of Indian society on the Malwa plateau and a majority of the Canadian missionaries in Malwa Presbytery.

Now, on this 66th birthday, the Indian nurses and trainees of Ratlam Christian Hospital performed an unprecedented and, for Indians, an almost immoral action. One by one they came forward and kissed the Chief Surgeon. Amy was even more moved than was McClure.

In the spring of 1967, a young woman came to McClure, quite openly, accompanied by her husband. She was worried by a touch of eczema on her face, and no wonder; she was one of the most beautiful women McClure had ever seen. He found slightly discoloured patches on her face and on her back. They were anaesthetic. She could not tell the point of a pin from the head of a swab. McClure diagnosed early leprosy and told her so. He expected a flood of tears but she took it quite calmly. They conferred with her husband and it was apparent that this couple were going to be able to face the disease without any personal trauma or social ostracism. Then McClure discovered the identity of the beautiful young lady. She was a sister of the boy he had visited on first coming to Ratlam; the boy who was dying of leprosy and TB; the boy who had to be kept locked away in the dark, hidden with his disease and disgrace. Mankind was learning. The human condition was improving.

Or was it?

In the Middle East open warfare broke out once again between the Arabs and the Israelis. After the Suez War of eleven years earlier the Israelis had occupied the Gaza Strip and the whole of the Sinai but had later withdrawn. In violation of the withdrawal agreement the Egyptian army had immediately moved back into the Strip. During the following years McClure's beloved Gaza Strip had become one of several germination centres for Arab terrorist activity. Now, in the spring of

1967, Arab armies were massing on Israel's borders as they had done in 1948.

"The existence of Israel is an error which must be rectified," announced President Aref of Iraq.

"Our basic objective will be the destruction of Israel," declared President Nasser of Egypt.

"The Arab people are firmly resolved to wipe Israel off the map," reported Cairo radio.

The Israelis were alarmed by such pronouncements as well as by the arrival of 100,000 Egyptian troops in the Sinai armed with 1,000 tanks and 500 heavy guns. Other Arab armies massed on other borders. Israel launched a pre-emptive strike and six days later had occupied the West Bank, the Golan Heights and, once again, all of the Sinai and the Gaza Strip.

McClure was heartsick. He thought of Mustapha and wondered if the colossal international vendetta in the Middle East would ever end.

It seemed ironic that at that same time Canada was enjoying its most euphoric moment since Confederation. It was Centennial Year in Canada. There were celebrations coast to coast and, in Montreal, Expo '67 was proving to be the exhibition triumph of the century. Canadians of a myriad racial backgrounds were walking around in a happy daze, amazed that they had been able to bring such a wonder to pass.

Up in the Lachute area of the Province of Quebec members of the Rodgers clan, descended from Dr. William McClure's maternal grandfather, bestirred themselves in search of a Centennial project. They raised $2,800 and sent it to India via The United Church of Canada. In India the money was used to establish a "Rodgers-McClure" scholarship fund to pay for the entire medical education of an Indian student. It gave Bob McClure a psychological boost as his own retirement descended upon him. His father had contributed half a century of his life to China and had been dead more than a decade but in memory of the old doctor relatives and friends in far-off Quebec were educating a medical person in India. It was proof that the vibrations from a good life rippled out in all directions with an energy that was never spent. McClure knew that he could go into retirement with a light heart. There were no endings, only beginnings. Life not only had continuity but a definite forward progression. Even now, in McClure's final months, a junior doctor joined the Ratlam staff. There was nothing unusual about that except that this bright, keen-eyed young medic with the brilliant smile was the son of the lame sweeper woman with whom McClure had locked wills thirteen years ago.

On November 19th, 1967, a dinner party was held in the hall above the O.P.D. building. The room was packed with hospital staff along with friends from the community and missionaries from other stations. After the dinner Bob and Amy McClure were escorted to the railway station. Hundreds of people surged onto the platform to say farewells. The guards at the gates gave up asking for platform tickets. Small girls and old men came bearing garlands. There were Hindus, Sikhs, Moslems, Christians and Parsees. The Ratlam Rotary Club was there en masse to say good-bye to the foreigner they had twice honoured with the office of president. There were *pranams* and handshakes and little speeches and the McClures were weighed down with garlands. The train pulled in and the big station rocked to the sound of hundreds of Indian voices singing "For he's a jolly good fellow", in English, while more garlands were hung upon the outside of the McClures' coach. By the time Bob and Amy broke away and entered the coach they found that their compartment, too, was lined with sweet-smelling, vibrantly beautiful flowers.

As the train pulled out of Ratlam station the sound of the engine and the clatter of wheels was penetrated by a voice calling, "Three cheers for Dr. McClure," and the noise of the accelerating train was swamped by a triple hurrah of human affection.

Three days later, in Bombay, the McClures celebrated Bob's 67th birthday. They were joined for the celebration by Walter Anderson, four members of the Ratlam hospital staff and three members of the Ratlam community, all of whom had followed them to Bombay to usher them through the Gateway of India and to see them safely aboard ship, bound for Hong Kong, Vancouver, and home.

In Ratlam Christian Hospital a new, younger, Canadian doctor was in charge.* In the big bungalow, surrounded by the gulmohar trees, the Bougainvillaea and the roses, his wife was beginning to make a home for himself and their three small children. In the O.R. the team was beginning to adapt to the

*Dr. Douglas Marriott.

demands of the new surgeon. In one corner of the O.R. there was a series of shelves carrying gowns, masks and gloves. At one end of one shelf was a neat pile of large gowns bearing the simple monogram "MC". A label on the shelf proclaimed, "Dr. McClure's gowns". In the years ahead many doctors would come and go and Canadians would give way to Indians but, as though by instinctive agreement, no one would remove from the shelf either the proprietary label or the gowns with the "MC". Ratlam was McClure territory.

31

We Are Not Alone

In the autumn of 1967, while the McClures were packing to leave India, Canadians were enjoying, via TV, a pastime that was rapidly becoming a national sport; a political convention. After an orgy of metaphorical blood-letting the Progressive Conservative Party deposed the fiery, flint-edged, visionary leader John George Diefenbaker and replaced him with soft-spoken, gentlemanly Robert Stanfield. The following spring of 1968, after the McClures were home and able to join the TV audience themselves, the Liberal Party staged a convention to find a replacement for fatherly "Mike" Pearson who was going into voluntary retirement. The Liberals chose a charismatic playboy, Pierre Elliot Trudeau, who was soon installed as Canada's fifteenth Prime Minister.

That same spring of 1968 Bob McClure was asked if he would consider entering the ecclesiastical political arena by running for leadership of The United Church of Canada. It was an astounding proposal and one which, in the words of a member of the family, left McClure "a shaken man". He was being asked to consider trying for a job that had nothing to do with medicine; a job that, if he won it, would make him top man in the church bureaucracy; a job that had *never* been held by a layman! McClure knew, however, that winning would offer both a challenge and an opportunity for service. There may also have been a leadership virus loose in the Canadian air because John Diefenbaker had recently noted that the craving for high office was an "affliction" that came to many. Afflicted or not, McClure agreed to contest the election for his church's highest office.

The governing body of The United Church of Canada, the General Council, met every two years. Its first order of business was always the election of a new moderator. In August, 1968, some four hundred General Council delegates (called commissioners), representing all regions of Canada as well as the United Church "fields" in Brazil, the Caribbean, Africa, East Asia and India, converged upon the old "limestone city" of Kingston, Ontario, and crowded into Sydenham Street United Church. In line with the United Church constitution the delegates were supposed to be evenly divided between clergymen and laymen, an almost impossible achievement. That year the laymen were four short.

The assembled commissioners presented an interesting spectacle. Here were no black gowns and purple cassocks; no trappings of ecclesiastical pomp or hierarchy. A few of the older clergy wore the traditional dark suit and clerical collar while others wore the collar with ordinary business suits, even sport jackets. The majority of the clergy shunned the collar. Some of the clergy were women. It was impossible to tell the shepherds from the flock. Members of that august assembly were adorned in everything from brightly coloured sport shirts to turtle neck sweaters and mini-skirts. Most observers chose not to speculate on the way such an assortment of delegates might vote.

After McClure had decided to let his name stand he had tried to put the pending contest out of his head. He arrived in Kingston supremely indifferent to the outcome. There was a certain air of competition to the whole election event that bothered him and he was made uncomfortable by the fact that there were indeed factions supporting various candidates.

There were five candidates. Votes were cast by secret ballot and, as in a political convention, after each ballot the low man on the totem pole dropped off. Unlike a political convention there were no announcements of the numbers of votes being accumulated by individual candidates. No one knew who was front runner and consequently delegates were relieved of the temptation to switch votes en bloc to favour or to oppose an apparent winner.

When the results of the third ballot were announced McClure was astonished to find himself one of the two survivors heading into the final and fourth ballot. He was in the contest along with a Rev. Bruce McLeod. McClure had no way of knowing whether he was neck and neck or merely still on the track.

During the preceding months and throughout the church there had been a "youth" ground swell of considerable proportions. Bruce McLeod, at forty, was the youngest of the candidates. He was also personable, bright and articulate, in many ways a perfect spokesman for a liberal church soon to move into the decade of the Seventies. There had been, however, another ground swell and it was in favour of electing a moderator who was a layman.

As the fourth ballot was cast one thing was obvious—the winning candidate could not be both young *and* a layman but, whichever man won, the United Church would certainly have a moderator who was articulate. He would also be a "Mac".

The commissioners voted for Bob McClure and made him the first lay moderator of The United Church of Canada.

"Moderator" was a term inherited from the Presbyterian Church at the time of Union. The job, however, not only included the original Presbyterian function of presiding over the church parliament, General Council, but also the Methodist function of being a general superintendent. McClure was not to be merely chairman for the next eight days of deliberations but was to be the principal spokesman for the United Church during the next two years. Any public statement he chose to make as moderator would be considered to be a statement by the United Church unless repudiated by his executive or the next General Council.

As moderator, McClure was the elected representative of the whole church. Any congregation or individual member of the church could go directly to the top because the top man was "their" man, democratically chosen. As moderator, McClure had influence if he chose to use it, and he had prestige, if he wanted it. He also had a unique opportunity to take the church to the people. That opportunity was one McClure was intending to seize with both hands. But first he had to pilot the ship of ecclesiastical state through eight days of policy debate.

McClure knew that he could have little influence on this 23rd Council. Its agenda had already been prepared and its committees had already been making their deliberations. He was merely a chairman. The General Secretary was in the wings and *he* knew what the business was all about and could be relied upon to give swift advice concerning procedure. McClure felt it was a silly business this, electing the moderator at the beginning of General Council and immediately making him preside as chairman. He felt it would make much more sense to elect a moderator at the end of the session so he could have two years in office before presiding.

McClure managed to survive the next eight days. Some of the commissioners thought he was a little rusty on his parliamentary rules. Others thought he was not rusty but merely lax. The majority thought he did extremely well and a few confessed to being amazed. He was, for McClure, the epitomy of patience. Only once did he really lose his temper and that was after a session had bogged down for an hour-and-a-half while delegates debated the spelling of names. He should not have worried. The weary reporter for the the United Church *Observer* would have told him that the length of any General Council debate was always in inverse proportion to its importance.

McClure had little to do with the formation of policy statements made by the 23rd Council but there were a number of resolutions passed that dealt with the international scene. These resolutions could not have been more in keeping with the spirit of the new moderator had he drafted them with his own hand. There was a resolution calling upon the Canadian government to increase aid to developing countries and one calling for the United Church to continue to support the World Council of Churches in giving assistance to "refugees and migrants, especially in the Middle East, Africa and in Vietnam". There was a resolution asking the United Nations "to urge that high priority be given in developing countries to programs of health, education and family planning" and urging the Government of Canada "to offer assistance for population control programs where these were requested by other nations".

Every General Council since 1952 had called upon the Canadian government to recognize the People's Republic of China. This one repeated the cry, not only calling for such recognition to be made "without delay" but making a further request that the government then support admission of Red China to the United Nations. Another section of the same resolution called for "recognition of the right of self-determination by the people of Taiwan".

A strongly worded declaration was made concerning the volatile situation in the Middle East. It called upon the Arabs to recognize the State of Israel and to permit that State "to live in peace, secure from threats or acts of force". It also called upon

Israel to "withdraw from territories she has occupied by force since June, 1967, with minor boundary changes" and either to permit displaced persons to return to their homes or to provide compensation. The lengthy resolution went on to affirm the right of the public freely to express its view concerning the Mid-east conflict: "We deplore suggestions that those who criticize Israeli policies are necessarily anti-Semitic and that critics of Arab policies must be unsympathetic to the plight of the Arab people. The policies of Arab and Israeli governments are always open to the judgment of public opinion."

The commissioners were not content with mere resolutions. Under the enthusiastic chairmanship of McClure they called upon every member of the United Church to donate "one day's pay" toward a special fund of $1,750,000 for world relief and overseas development. To McClure that was almost the ultimate "special project".

The 23rd General Council did not content itself with the heady world of international affairs. It delved vigorously into theology. During the previous few years a committee had been assiduously studying the various creeds of Christendom. In its constitution the United Church had acknowledged "the teaching of the great creeds of the ancient church" but had avoided locking itself off to any specific creed. The Apostle's Creed was the one most likely to be heard recited by a United Church congregation but even it, with direct references to the virginity of Mary, to heaven, hell, and the resurrection of the body, could cause literal-minded Christian liberals to think twice before parroting it. Many United Church members, including ministers, had found themselves justifying the words to themselves with interpretations that would make even a Hindu's brain bubble. And yet a creed, by definition, was supposed to be a concise, formal, and *authorized* statement of belief. It was quite possible that the United Church, being a very Canadian organization, would never be able to agree on an official creed but the courageous committee presented one to the Council for its consideration. After vigorous debate the commissioners, under the chairmanship of Moderator McClure, won their parliamentary epaulettes; they sent the proposed creed back to committee for further study and approved its publication for experimental liturgical use.

Barring the legal nicety that the statement was not "authorized", and probably never would be, The United Church of Canada had a new Creed:

Man is not alone; he lives in God's world.*
We believe in God:
  who has created and is creating,
  who has come in the true Man, Jesus,
    to reconcile and renew,
  who works in us and among us by his
    spirit.
We trust him.
He calls us to be his church:
  to celebrate his presence,
  to love and serve others,
  to seek justice and resist evil.
We proclaim his Kingdom.
In life, in death, in life beyond.death,
  he is with us.
We are not alone; we believe in God.

It was reported that a principal of one of the United Church's own theological colleges called the Creed "poetic but un-Christian". In the United States a conservative theological journal announced that the new Creed should automatically disqualify The United Church of Canada from membership in the World Council of Churches. It was fortunate for the editor's blood pressure that he did not realize that in addition to tolerating the allegedly heretical Creed the commissioners of Canada's largest Protestant communion had elected a *Karma Yogi* as moderator.

---

*The Creed, with some later amendments, is widely used today and many congregations, more concerned with diplomacy than with etymology, find it fashionable to begin: "We are not alone; we live in God's world."

32

Don't Blame God

McCLURE IN FAVOR OF 'MERCY KILLING', screamed the headline in the *Kitchener-Waterloo Record*. McCLURE SAYS 'SLUG THE PUSHER', said the headline in the *Times-Globe* of Saint John, New Brunswick. McCLURE SAYS SEX EDUCATION NOT DANGEROUS, announced the Edmonton *Journal*. McCLURE SUPPORTS YOUNG MARRIAGES, said the Niagara Falls *Review*. UNITED CHURCH 'THE CHEAPEST', chortled the Toronto *Globe and Mail*. For two and a half years Canadian newspapers from Newfoundland to British Columbia had a field-day quoting Bob McClure. From the small-town weeklies to the big-city dailies the newspapers found that McClure made good copy. Radio hot-line hosts loved him as a guest. TV talkshow producers vied to have him appear on their screens. Magazine writers interviewed him extensively and quoted him at length. The United Church had had moderators before who made good copy but they had always been theologians and had somehow maintained a slight air of diplomatic distance. The idea of maintaining distance never occurred to McClure. Whether he spoke to a men's club or to a church congregation he never worried whether the press was present and whether he was being diplomatic. He spoke about subjects and about the world from *his* viewpoint, that of a missionary-surgeon who had spent forty-five years of his professional life actively and aggressively engaged in fighting human suffering. He had been a "foxhole Christian" for so long it never occurred to him now that as a commander he might function from headquarters.

All moderators travelled but no moderator before or since travelled as much as did McClure. *Time* magazine referred to him as a "Mandarin in motion". A previous moderator had been billed by the General Secretary for half the cost of a hotel room because he had taken his wife along on a ceremonial occasion but the General Council that elected McClure recognized there were many occasions when the moderator's wife should accompany him. Amy accompanied McClure to British Columbia and to the Maritimes. She toured Federal penal institutions with him. They were both guests of the Presbyterian Church of Scotland for the 200th anniversary of its General Assembly and together they met not only the Queen but the Queen Mother. Amy accompanied her husband to Africa—to Zambia, Kenya, South Africa and Angola. She did not go with him on a three-week trip to the Middle East nor did she try to keep up with him on his myriad speaking engagements and appearances in Canada. That schedule set a pace only McClure could stand. He spoke to students, health leagues, service clubs, Bible societies, family planning groups, presbyteries, medical conventions, Anglicans, Catholics, Zionists, relief organizations, cancer symposiums and (via the media) the general public.

McClure suggested it would be a good idea to do away with most sermons and that there was no reason church services had to be confined to Sunday. He wondered aloud whether the United Church had too many pipe organs and buildings. He told Canadians that they were too affluent and that affluence did not make for happiness. He told Canadian doctors that they were overpaid and not sufficiently dedicated to serving others. He gave the back of his hand to his large, smug, middle-class, affluent United Church following by telling them that their average member gave 25 cents a week to the church making the United Church "the cheapest church in the world". When attacked on that one he cheerfully admitted that members actually averaged $1.25 a week but that only the 25 cents was for use outside the congregation. He also said he did not really care for the "collection plate" method of raising funds and saw no reason a church should not accept credit cards. He himself refused his moderator's salary of $16,000, accepting only some cost-of-living assistance and the amount he would have received from his pension had he in fact retired. That act moved one ecclesiastical mandarin to announce that the church may have had better moderators but it had never had a cheaper one. He may have been correct. Moderator McClure and wife were invited to Ottawa to participate as platform dignitaries at July 1st celebrations on Parliament Hill. Even the most modest of previous moderators would have booked an Ottawa hotel room for overnight but the McClures went to Toronto airport early in the morning of July 1st and waited around for low-fare standby seats. In Ottawa, McClure changed into his moderatorial regalia in a public washroom.

McClure could savage his people at one moment by quoting their weekly giving statistics to them and encourage them the next by enthusiastically supporting the "One Day's Pay" special project for overseas relief, a project that had $1,750,000 as its target and cleared more than $2,000,000.

McClure enjoyed a good relationship with the press. He had a high profile with most Canadian newspapers, although almost a year after he had been knocking around as moderator the Vancouver *Province* managed to refer to him as "United Church Moderator Donald McLure". He once had occasion to thank media representatives for their warmth and courtesy and he did so with enthusiasm, then put his tongue in cheek and quoted the New Testament: "I was a stranger and you took me in." The moderator recognized that there could be pitfalls built into journalistic accounts. "Please do not judge me entirely from newspaper reports," he wrote to a parishioner. On the other hand the succinct newspaper reports sometimes reflected inconsistencies that could creep into the McClure position. A young and very irate United Church minister mailed two clippings to his moderator. One quoted McClure as saying that religious missionaries were outdated in this age of technology. The other quoted McClure as implying that young ministers today were more interested in the pension plan than in evangelism. "Dammit all man!" said the accompanying letter, "You can't have it both ways. Keep 'em above the belt, Bob."

As a rule, the headlines were wrong and the accompanying articles were correct. McCLURE IN FAVOR OF 'MERCY KILLING', was followed by an article that pointed out he was not in favour of mercy *killing* but that he was in favour of not prolonging life support in cases of irreparable damage and of agonizing terminal illness, a delicate but important difference.

McClure felt quite strongly that there were times when deformed babies should be permitted to die but it was a point that
was almost impossible to debate in Canada. Everything had a
tendency to be turned into absolutes. He knew that a deformed
baby that might be rescued and even live a useful life in Canada
would be doomed from birth (if it lived) to a beggar's life in India
and be used by a manipulating master as little better than a
performing animal. Where was the kindness in performing a
"miracle of science" at the time of that infant's birth? Questions
such as those were not, for McClure, matters for philosophical
debate. He had run into them all as matters requiring the application of swift, practical, personal decisions. And yet it was
precisely because he had seen so much and done so much that
he had little tendency to pussyfoot around Canadian sen-
sibilities. McClure suggested that a good case could be made to
justify the state sterilizing unfit parents, either because they
were child beaters or were mentally retarded. He made the
statement to the Family Planning Federation and said he was
speaking as a doctor and not as a moderator but almost everyone
(outside the Federation) jumped on him. He staunchly upheld
the right to abortions, even though he had always hated performing them, and was unswerving in answering the "right to
life" cry with the bald statement that the greatest crime is to give
life to a child who is unwanted. His supporters always pointed
to the broad scope of McClure's experience and his critics always
did the same, claiming that he based all his opinions on India or
China and that it was a fallacy to transplant his conclusions to
Canada.

McClure was not perturbed by such accusations. He felt
Canadians had a lot to learn from Confucian courtesy, from
Japanese self-discipline, from Arab generosity, from Chinese
resiliency, from Hindu forgiveness, from Moslem devotion,
from Parsee honesty. He advocated early and arranged marriages not because he did not understand Canada but because he
had seen early arranged marriages work very successfully in
several other cultures. He always hastened to add that a necessary corollary was that both families should play an active and
supportive part in the marriage. Marriage was between families
not just between individuals. To the question, "What about
love?" he would cheerfully say, "Just a matter of concentration
of hormones. You can test for it in the blood and urine. It shows
up in the frog." He could get away with such replies. Journalists

were so well disposed toward McClure and he himself was outspoken in such a friendly fashion that interviewers seldom pressed him. They would accept a statement that love was merely hormones without pointing out that perhaps while they were asking about love he was talking about the sex drive and was it not possible there was a difference? Seldom was he challenged; he made such good copy.

The Toronto *Star Weekly* wanted to know what the moderator thought of Prime Minister Trudeau. McClure obliged: "He played a little trick on the public with all this 'swing, swing, swing'. I don't see anything dramatic in Canadian political life done by a man of 49 that couldn't have been done by a man of 99."

The *Star Weekly* reporter also was interested in the moderator's views about sex. He gave her a stunner: "We're not getting enough natural sex in North America. Sexual activity here is very low by Asian standards; they'd consider the average Canadian almost a paraplegic."

Some people might have expected a man who was both a surgeon *and* a moderator to waffle on any statement concerning the physical resurrection of Christ. Not McClure. The Church wanted a statement for the Easter Sunday *Bulletin*. It got it, and printed it: "The bodily resurrection means much to many people. I respect their belief. It is something that, personally, I can't understand. To me the important thing is that the Spirit of Jesus was resurrected on Easter morning."

On Christmas Eve of 1968 American astronauts circled the moon. A goodly portion of their fellow earthlings followed the voyage on TV and the explorers returned with astounding colour photographs. To McClure, the breath-taking vision of earth-rise over the mountains of the moon, the view of the world hanging suspended in space like a milkshot sapphire on a velvet cloth, confirmed what he had known all his life. All humankind was but one family in one house, and only a loving God would provide a mansion of such beauty.

Russian astronauts, after their first ventures into space, had come back and reported that they had not seen any God. The Americans, catching their first moonview of Earth, saw God's handiwork and read the opening words of the Book of Genesis into the Apollo 8 records: *"In the beginning God created . . ."*

The astronauts in Apollo 8 were reacting with the same burst of faith that McClure had felt for years every time he peered into a microscope. The United Church *Observer* challenged the moderator with the suggestion that a doctor who had worked amidst great suffering for many years must find it difficult to believe in God. "The God I recognize," said McClure, "is the God I came to know down a microscope; the God I came to know in a laboratory. He's big, a tremendous power, and so big I believe he can take a personal interest in everybody ... When I look down the microscope I feel, 'here I'm seeing examples of God's handiwork'. To me what Jesus came to tell me is that God is a God of love, and he's the father of all men. And this is what I believe."

It was inevitable that McClure should be asked to voice an opinion concerning radio journalist Gordon Sinclair's views of God. Sinclair, a professional iconoclast with a devoted following equally divided between those who loved him and those who longed to see him deflated was reported to have referred to the suffering and poverty in India as evidence that God was "a tyrant and a bully". A reporter for the *Hamilton Spectator* caught Moderator McClure coming out of church and asked him what he thought of Sinclair's evaluation of God. The moderator was equal to the challenge. "Speaking with great charity and a smile," reported the journalist, "he said this was a very primitive stage we usually go through when we are three to five years of age, and the mind is far from developed. It is the five-year Sunday School stage, he added. We need to grow up, and learn to meet the crises of Life without blaming God in this way."

McClure's own experience in India had not made him cynical as it had some. It had not made him pessimistic, fatalistic, or inactive. If anything, it had clarified his ideas about God and about the role of the modern missionary. When a writer for *Maclean's* challenged him about a missionary's function McClure referred to Mahatma Gandhi, the man who, in McClure's opinion, was one of the greatest men in history to follow in the footsteps of Jesus. "We follow Gandhi's ideas," he said, "that to a hungry man God will appear in the form of a loaf of bread, to a drought-stricken farmer in the form of a tube well, to the mother and father of a little boy who is crippled, God will appear in the form of an orthopedic department with a rehabilitation centre." In the same interview he said, disarmingly, "My theology is positively childish and I'm very proud of it."

McClure's unadorned theology, his frankness, his humour and his friendliness endeared him to Canadians. He took the church to the people the way no other moderator before him had ever been able to do. Those who listened to him, who read him, who agreed with him or argued with him were not necessarily United Church folk or even Protestants. Many Canadians were willing to forgive him for being either of those things because he was always himself—McClure.

33

We deplore...

Moderator McClure may have thought his theology was simple but there were those who thought his view of certain aspects of international affairs was simple-minded.

The Vietnam war was at its peak. Many American youths, unwilling to fight in what appeared to be an unjust war, sought refuge in Canada. Most made it past Canadian immigration officials but some did not. McClure and the General Council executive ran headlong into an argument with Canada's Minister of Immigration over alleged discrimination by border officials against the American deserters and draft dodgers. McClure felt the church had a special responsibility towards genuine pacifists who were such because they had been indoctrinated by the Christian church. In a telegram to the Minister of Immigration, Allan MacEachen, McClure accused the department's officials of "bending the law" by applying "secret guidelines". It was, he said, "an immoral and intolerable evasion of public responsibility." The Minister countered by saying that the moderator's charges were "ill-founded and erroneous to the point of irresponsibility". He maintained that guidelines to immigration officers were not secret, but he refused to release a copy of them or even to table them in Parliament. McClure refused to back down.

As moderator, McClure also ran headlong into Zionism. It was a confrontation not of his own making and one that he found highly distasteful. A more subtle moderator might have circumvented it. For McClure it was unavoidable.

The confrontation had been in the making for some time

and was a result of numerous articles that had been written over a span of several years by Rev. A. C. Forrest, the editor of the *Observer*, the journalistic voice of the United Church. Forrest, a seasoned reporter, had made several trips to the Middle East, visiting both Israeli and Arab-occupied territories. He had been struck by several things, not the least of which was the indisputable fact that the Israeli government showed a remarkable tendency to flout both the Geneva conventions and the United Nations and to cling to most land gained during the spasmodic Israeli-Arab wars since 1948. The Israeli government also flouted the United Nation's instructions by building settlements in occupied territories and was less than enthusiastic in complying with its own agreements to let displaced Arabs return to their own soil. (Forrest also recognized that the various Arab countries were not above flouting international law and playing politics with refugees.) He was intrigued by the fact that although he heard criticism of the Israeli government while in Israel he seldom heard any such criticism in Canada. He was also impressed by the fact that the real victims in the whole Mid-east mess were the displaced Palestinians. He felt that somehow, somewhere, in the name of humanity and common sense, a journalist should attempt to put some balance into the flow of information coming to the Canadian public. In the *Observer's* October issue of 1967, just a few short months after the famous "six-day war" in which Israel had launched her incredibly successful pre-emptive strike against the five Arab armies massing on her flanks, Forrest came out with a full-page editorial with a banner headline proclaiming, INJUSTICE, and a sub-heading stating, IN HER PRESENT POLICIES ISRAEL STANDS CONDEMNED BEFORE THE WORLD. In the body of that editorial he said: "Our criticism is not of the way Israel fought the war last June . . . What we condemn is the treatment of the Arab people in occupied territory in the weeks that followed the war and the harsh, inhumane treatment of the refugees now, and the 19-year-old record of inhumanity to Palestian refugees."

Forrest was immediately deluged with accusations from Jews (both Zionist and non-Zionist) of being anti-Semitic and of hating Israel. The *Globe Magazine* quoted an official of the Jewish congress as saying Forrest was "a dupe of Communist and Arab propaganda". (The official 'phoned Forrest and apologized, saying he had been misquoted, that he never accused him of being a

Communist dupe.) Accusations were also being hurled at the United Church in general claiming that it, too, was anti-Zionist (which was probably true) and that it was anti-Semitic (which was nonsense).

The dust continued to fly for many months and Forrest, unrevised and unrepentant, ran an article headlined, HARSH LIFE UNDER THE ISRAELI BOOT. It appeared in the same issue that reported on the doings of the 23rd General Council and the election of Bob McClure as moderator. McClure inherited A. C. Forrest.

There was a clandestine, underground movement in some corners of the United Church head office to get rid of Forrest, to depose the *Observer's* Editor and Publisher from his journalistic pulpit. The people favouring that action did not reckon with the fact that the new moderator was not just a cheerful, humorous, tolerant figure-head. McClure was incredibly tough and had knocked around a little himself. Although he had had no experience with the Israelis he had met more than his fair share of Palestinian refugees and he knew with absolute conviction that human suffering was impartial to race, creed or political affiliations. He also knew that he either had to support Forrest or support the pressure for his resignation. The idea of a liberal, democratic church asking its leading journalist, a man of great integrity, to resign for calling it the way he saw it was, to McClure, patently absurd. Besides, one of the resolutions passed under McClure's gavel at the 23rd General Council had been one which began: "We deplore suggestions that those who criticize Israeli policies are necessarily anti-Semitic . . ."

McClure dug in his heels. Forrest not only remained at the *Observer* helm but headed back to the Middle East to do more extensive research.* While Forrest was away McClure received an invitation to appear before the Jewish community in Toronto at a public meeting and to explain the United Church's alleged anti-Semitic stand. McClure accepted.

The invitation had been extended by the president of the Toronto Zionist Council. He and his wife invited the moderator and his wife to a pre-meeting dinner at the Primrose Club. Their other guests included a former moderator, E. M. Howse (the minister of Bloor Street United Church), and Rabbi Gunther

---

*His studies eventually culminated in a searing book, *The Unholy Land*.

Plaut. It was a congenial group of intelligent, compatible people. McClure sensed that his hosts were worried but there was no indication of the storm that was to come.

After dinner the McClures were driven to a Zionist hall in the Bathurst-Dufferin area. Here they moved from the atmosphere of social affabilities into that of political realities. There was a large crowd gathering and it was obvious that the organizers of the meeting were concerned for the safety of the moderator and his wife. A six-man bodyguard escorted the McClures into the building, by-passed the one flight of stairs and isolated them in the elevator. There was no sign anywhere of city police but there were considerable signs of vigorous self-policing. McClure was intrigued by the fact that the organizers had been able to round up so many big men. It was not reassuring to see all the doors to the meeting hall being locked just before the meeting commenced and it dawned upon McClure that his hosts did not relish the thought of the moderator of the United Church being assassinated in a Jewish hall. He smiled to himself, conjuring up some possible headlines, then decided it was no smiling matter.

The meeting was chaired by Rabbi Plaut who disliked confrontations and was uncomfortably aware that the moderator was being embroiled in a debate that had its focus on politics, theology and history whereas McClure's focus was strictly humanitarian. The agenda called for McClure to make a short speech explaining the position of the United Church in relation to the *Observer* and to Israel and the Jews. After that there was to be a question period. McClure had prepared this speech in detail. A copy had been prepared for release to the press. He had no intention of wandering off in his anecdotal way or of making facetious remarks. Nor did he. He stuck to his text.

McClure began by recognizing the difficulty inherent in any one person attempting to speak for a large, diffused, nationally sprawling church like his own. He stated that mail coming across his desk demonstrated that the United Church membership represented "every shade of the spectrum of opinion from extremely anti-Semitic on the one hand to the ardent Zionists on the other". He stated that he felt that he himself was about "as free from racial prejudice as any WASP can be" and pointed out that his father was from Quebec, his mother from Pennsylvania and that he had been raised in China speaking Chinese; he had worked in Taiwan under Japanese occupation and in Gaza under Egyptian occupation; he had worked in India where he had been elected vice-president of the Provincial Medical Association of 4,000 Indian doctors. "I, personally," he said, "hold very positive views on racial interrelations. I am a great admirer of the other cultures that I have come to know. I believe that each nation can enrich its own life by borrowing liberally from the surrounding cultures."

He went on to point out that to the Canadian Gentile the Canadian Jew wore "three different hats"; that of a neighbour, that of a member of a sister religion, and that of "one involved politically and emotionally in the State of Israel". He assessed the first two aspects in a very warm, positive fashion and then he bore down on the third:

"Even the most 'venomous' anti-Israel people in Canada do not share the Arab nationalist idea that the abolition, liquidation or 'choking' off of Israel is to be considered as a solution . . . As the victors in 'the six-day war' I think there is no doubt that Israel had Canada's sympathies and admiration . . . In the long run the Canadian Gentile, I think, is more concerned to see peace in the Middle East than he is to see Israel expand her territorial boundaries. On the other hand the nationalistic enthusiasms of the Canadian Jew seems excessive to the Canadian Gentile . . . We think that we detect a slight 'guilt complex' in the Canadian Jew caused by his living a rather comfortable and affluent existence in relative peace in Canada.

"In seeking for peace in the Middle East the Canadian Gentile realizes the plight of the Palestinian refugee. He would like to see this refugee have some minimal human rights guaranteed to him. He would like to see him resettled somehow. He wants to see a just solution to the Arab refugee problem. Naturally he wants to see such a solution done with a minimum of fuss and bother to the Canadian Gentile . . .

"I submit that because of the excessive interest of the Canadian Jew in Israel a certain element of paranoia exists. The rest of us in Canada are interested in the Middle East generally and not exclusively in the welfare of the State of Israel."

McClure recapitulated some of the many official statements that had been made by various General Councils since 1948, ending with a lengthy quote from the resolution passed by the General Council that had elected him as moderator: "We also express our deep fear that if Arabs continue to refuse to recognize Israel, and if Israel continues to occupy the lands she took, to obstruct the return of the homeless, to insist on meeting directly with Arabs without UN assistance, and to declare that Jerusalem is not negotiable, there will be war again in the Middle East, and a million and half displaced persons will be condemned indefinitely to exist on the meagre subsistence of the world's charity, without homes and without hope."

McClure was given a hearing. His speech was interrupted by some heckling and groans but it was during the question period that things turned sour. There were calls for the replacement of A. C. Forrest and McClure was asked if the *Observer* reflected United Church opinion. He said that by and large it did and reiterated what he had already made clear to his own executive—it would be unconscionable for the United Church to fire Forrest. (It was impossible in the course of a platform confrontation to explain to non-Protestants the paradox in which the editor of an "official" church magazine must have journalistic freedom.)

Some observers say that even at this stage there were only groans and polite cries of disbelief while others say there were many boos and loud cries of anger. For Bob and Amy McClure the memory of the evening was to linger more as one of an atmosphere than of precise events. There was noise and a seething of angry people; the ever-present body-guards; a path cleared to an adjoining room where an attempt was made to have coffee; angry faces in close-up and jabbing fingers and emotional voices reminding them of Auschwitz and Belsen; a cigar burn through the back of McClure's suit; a protective escort out a side entrance to waiting cars; a swift drive home with the escort going all the way to the apartment door and the 'phone ringing a half hour later as their worried hosts called to make certain all was well and another 'phone call the next morning from the same concerned source.

The McClures never liked to talk about the incident and denied that there was much to it but members of their family who saw them the next day said their parents were in absolute shock. They had never seen them so low, so depressed, so traumatized. It was no wonder. McClure had outfaced General Li, the Warlord of Hwaiking; he had been bombed and strafed by the Japanese; he had disarmed a Burma Road bandit; he had wandered plague-ridden jungles and had once braced himself for a Chinese firing squad. But that night of January 15th, 1969, in Toronto, had been the first time he had ever been the personalized focal point for political hatred. And Amy had been with him.

In retrospect and in perspective one knows that the scene in the Zionist hall was not nearly as violent or aggressive as many a political meeting that had taken place on Canadian soil. A few years earlier both Lester Pearson and John Diefenbaker had been subjected to far more vigorous treatment. In the annals of Canadian political meetings McClure's experience would hardly merit a reference. It only merits reference in the annals of McClure. The most tolerant man in Canada had run up against intolerance and had been accused of prejudice. That, too, was no new phenomenon for the politician, but it was a new experience for McClure.

He was not helped by a headline in the *Toronto Telegram*, JEWS PARANOIC OVER ISRAEL: McCLURE. *The Toronto Daily Star* also bannered the word "paranoia". McClure decided that as far as bridging any gap between the United Church and the Canadian Jewish community the whole evening had been a futile exercise.

A year and a half later he paid an extensive visit to the Middle East accompanied by a couple of young, light-hearted United Church clergymen. McClure was greeted with great courtesy by the Israeli authorities (who knew all about him) and he was given every assistance. He talked with Jews and Arabs, with politicians and prelates. He visited his old haunts on the Gaza Strip which was now under Israeli occupation. McClure and his companions also visited Jordan and were guests at an advanced political training camp for crack guerrilla fighters. While there McClure became involved in a lengthy argument about the use of violence. The guerrillas listened to him with the respect due a man who had seen violence in the past. He told them that once on a trip to Chinese Communist headquarters in Yenan he had seen Chairman Mao order the execution of a guerrilla fighter for lack of discipline and McClure questioned whether the Palestinians, having seized the world's attention with violence, would have the necessary self-discipline to put their guns down and speak with the voice of reason. Two years later, at a meeting in Beirut, McClure's name was mentioned and Palestinian guerrillas still wrestled with his arguments.

During McClure's regime as moderator the tragic Biafran war was underway in Nigeria. It was a civil war in which Biafrans were attempting to secede from the Nigerian federation. Federal forces were able to use blockade tactics and there was very real danger that the Biafrans and principally the Ibo tribesmen would be wiped out by starvation. To many informed observers it appeared to be a war with genocide as an objective. It was a war that was said to be an "internal" affair but which saw Britain and Russia providing arms to the federalists and saw France backing the secessionists. The casualties escalated to a point that far exceeded the most inflated statistics from Vietnam. (A Dutch relief expert estimated that in September, 1968, 12,000 Biafrans were dying every day from starvation.)

International non-governmental agencies and church groups responded by airlifting supplies to Biafra. Canadians (Christians and Jews) formed a relief agency called Canairelief and bought a Super-Constellation aircraft to fly supplies to starving Biafrans. Moderator McClure and the United Church were whole-heartedly behind Canairelief and quickly pumped money from the "One Day's Pay" fund into keeping the Super-Constellation airborne. McClure was quoted as saying that Canairelief was "one of the promptest ways I have ever seen of meeting an urgent need".

Moderator McClure and the other religious leaders soon realized that their churches were running counter to the unofficial policy of the Canadian government. McClure sat in horror one day as, along with other churchmen, he heard Canada's Minister of External Affairs, Mitchell Sharp, subscribe to the popular theory that a "quick kill" by the Nigerian federalist forces would soon put an end to the problem.

While the Canadian government dragged its feet the churches persevered with relief and on the larger scene the world was treated to the spectacle of a war in Africa to which major powers sent arms while common people, through Joint Church Aid,* sent relief. To McClure it was a prime example of religion at work as a positive force. The fact that religion happened to run counter to government was no surprise to him.

McClure's own position in favour of Biafran relief caused

---

*Joint Church Aid: 27 organizations from 17 countries, cutting completely across denominational and inter-faith boundaries.

him to lose several friendships and he was surprised that the United Church membership in general did not become particularly incensed over the Biafran horrors. His church gave generously as an institution but it was the Presbyterians who burned with the flames of outrage and compassion.

The Biafran War ended with the collapse of the secessionists in January 1970. Before the end of 1970 Canada was into a minor secessionist crisis of its own as separatist F.L.Q.* "cells" in Quebec kidnapped James Cross, the British High Commissioner, and Pierre Laporte, a minister of the Quebec Government, events that eventually led to the murder of Laporte. The response of the Quebec and federal governments to the threat of political blackmail by the use of violence was to call in the army to aid the civil authority, followed almost immediately by the federal imposition of the War Measures Act.

The War Measures Act, a sledge-hammer of an act that gave the government the power to suspend practically every freedom fought for since the days of Magna Carta, had never before been invoked in peace time. It was invoked now to prevent "apprehended insurrection".

Once again the Canadian churches were faced with taking a position with or against the federal government. This time they had no concrete information other than that issued by the authorities. The Canadian Council of Churches issued a statement that was concurred in by the Executive of the General Council of the United Church under Moderator McClure. The statement recognized the need for swift and decisive action but also issued a warning: "It is our hope that, in our pre-occupation with the immediate crisis, none of us will lose our perspective. Much as we deplore and must resist violence, we must also recognize the urgent need for positive action in response to the discontent which is born of economic and cultural deprivation."

Strangely enough the membership of the United Church, which had always been more inclined toward civil liberty than toward "law and order", seemed in general to be undisturbed by the War Measures Act. There was at least one notable exception. When the government asked Parliament to replace the War Measures Act with an almost equally severe Public Order Act and still refused to document proof of the apprehended insur-

*F.L.Q.: le Front de Libération du Québec.

rection it was a United Church minister, Rev. David Mac-Donald, the Member for Egmont, Prince Edward Island, who stood alone in the House of Commons to vote "Nay" and, in the words of Prof. James Eayrs, "saved Parliament from shame". But the spirit of MacDonald did not ignite the United Church membership at large. In the halls and mail baskets of head office there was not enough agitation to make any impression upon McClure's memory. Eight years later he could recall no flurry of 'phone calls or letters of protest coming to his office and the moderator's correspondence files bear that out. He himself was not surprised or emotionally upset by either the kidnappings, the subsequent murder, or the suspension of civil liberties. He had seen too much violence in the world to be amazed by any of it, physical or legislative.

As the "October Crisis" of 1970 was unwinding, a CBC reporter for the radio network news programme *The World at Eight* asked McClure what he thought of the F.L.Q. and their demands. McClure automatically reached for a global perspective: "Some people ask me, they say, 'Bob, be more specific, what is it the black man in the southern States wants? What is it that the North American Indian wants? What is it that the F.L.Q wants? What is it the Vietcong wants? What is it that El Fatah wants? All around the world these groups, what is it that they want?'

"How simple. What you've got. They'd like a little chunk of that, that's all. It's very simple. And they don't want the whole thing. They just want a little chunk. And they won't take your rationalization, 'Oh, but what I've got, they might not be able to use it properly, it might do them harm and damage.' Oh, you can't get away with that now. They don't believe that, that waffle."

34

Dear Moderator

When Moderator McClure was not travelling, or speaking, or attending committee meetings, he could be found in Toronto in his ninth floor office at 85 St. Clair Ave., East, in the building cheerfully referred to by United Church clergy as "the Vatican" and, more accurately, by United Church lay people as "Cloud 85". He drove a four-cylinder car but preferred his old friend the two-cylinder bicycle and so pedalled to work whenever Toronto's capricious weather would permit. He wore a batterd peaked cap which seemed to complement the bicycle and he carried a battered leather briefcase held together by two frayed straps. Sometimes he carried his own portable typewriter with him, a sure sign to his secretary that he intended to write a few personal letters if time permitted. (It did not occur to executive McClure that the boss might impose on a secretary to type a personal letter.) In the course of a normal day, however, there was always ample moderatorial correspondence to keep him busy. Some of that correspondence was with senior clergy and church officers across Canada but a surprising proportion of it was with ordinary lay people who wrote to their moderator for help, or to congratulate him, or to get his opinion, or to chastise him. Those who needed the help or advice received it if it lay within the moderator's grasp. Those who administered the lash reaped as they sowed.

McClure appeared on CBC-TV's *Front Page Challenge* and made an offhand remark concerning the irrelevance of clergymen's pulpit gowns. An irate lady from Saskatchewan ticked him off and he replied: "I do not know why you think that because I said I thought a sixteenth-century clergyman's gown was not necessary to clothe one when thinking of the problems of the twentieth century, that I was denying my belief in Jesus Christ or His teachings. I think this is a ridiculous assumption... I admire the way you are trying to turn the clock back and hold the old line. I wish you all success, but I don't think you have a ghost of a chance... Sorry to disagree with you in your reactionary thoughts."

A lady from the patriotic heartland of Ontario soundly berated the moderator for saying that Canada's new maple leaf flag "looked like a beer sign" and received a little advice for her pains: "The fact that I can still crack a joke about our national flag and our national emblem does not impair my patriotism... I did not intend any insult in my remarks, and I do hope and recommend that you try to develop a sense of humour... and enjoy life much more."

A doctor from the University of Alberta raked McClure over the coals for being flippant and glib on TV, for questioning the motivation of interns, and for suggesting that doctors made too much money. The moderator apologized for allowing himself to be misunderstood concerning interns but the apology stopped right there: "In my T.V. methods I shall accept advice from experts just as I should in the matter of anaesthetics. Therefore I do not accept your criticism nor your advice on this point. I have suffered watching the T.V. image of several medical men. I should reply to your criticism that there are some few subjects left on which medical men are not masters... When you talk about doctors not having 'the big house on the hill', I suggest you travel around Canada a bit with your eyes open... I am fairly well aware of medical incomes in Canada. As we say in India, 'My heart bleeds for them, but it is a well-controlled hemorrhage'."

On the other hand, to a Manitoba doctor who wrote a thought-filled letter voicing concern over the encroachments of state medicine the moderator wrote a concerned reply: "I think we might as well realize that inevitably we will find ourselves deeper and deeper into the welfare state... if we see the inevitable coming, we may be able to shape it more by going along with it than by trying to oppose it head on."

When an almost illiterate letter came in, addressed simply to "Dr. Rober" (sic) and asking personal questions concerning his views on psychiatrists and vegetarians, McClure answered with great care. It had been his observation, he said, that many vegetarian diets ran to too much use of deep-fried cooking. On the other hand: "In Madras and Bengal there are vegetarians who eat fish and eggs. I think if I had to be a religious vegetarian I should prefer the Madras and Bengal type of theory. Ordinarily though I eat meat I find that I eat only about half or a quarter of the meat that the average Canadian uses. I am not against heavy meat eating on religious grounds but I do think that most Canadians eat far too much meat for their own health. I have spent some time in the post-mortem room and there we think we see the results of this heavy meat diet." As for psychiatrists: "We have benefitted greatly in our family when one of our children became ill mentally in university. The psychiatrists took her in charge and even though she had a relapse, that too was dealt with satisfactorily. After all if I broke my leg I should go to an orthopaedic doctor and if I have trouble with my mind I should go to a psychiatrist. To me it is just as simple as that. I am sure that sometime before I die I shall probably have to go to a psychiatrist also but just now I feel fine."

A personal question concerning income received a forthright answer: "My present salary is equal to what my pension would be as I retired from the Board of World Mission in November, 1968. My present remuneration is $2,600 per year, plus $196 per month rent on my apartment, as I have to live in Toronto. Over and above this I get help for my car at the rate of $500 per year. If you think this is too exorbitant, I would be glad to cut down further."

The moderator's views on sex, appearing as they did in headlines and brief journalistic quotes, caused some of the flock to think their shepherd was a lunatic libertine rushing around breaking down the walls of the fold. In letters McClure conducted careful fence mending: "I am as strict in my views about sex outside of marriage as anybody can be. I base this strictness, not only on the fact that it is a breach of Christian discipline, but also on the fact that it is a thing that destroys happiness and can very often destroy the personality. At the very least, it destroys the dignity of two people."

He was called to task for his comment about "not enough natural sex" and for calling Canadians sexual "paraplegics". He replied in detail: "young people reach their zenith of hormone activity at 17 to 19 years of age. From sexual maturity until normal married sexual life is a period of ten years during which young people, consciously or not, have sexual tensions and frustrations. During this ten-year period they are over-stimulated sexually by all possible means, drama, the press, radio, television, and even by dress. Some take to drugs and hippie life, some to homosexual activity, some to unusual sexual practices. These not only bring injury to themselves, but nearly always detract from normal marital life after marriage. I believe that early marriage with parental help in both choosing the partner and financing the living after marriage is more healthy than our present system.

"Thus I believe natural sex life in many other cultures is better than it is in Canada, and that with family planning and affluence combined Canadians should be able to design a better pattern of family life.

"This is what I am trying to say to Canadians. You have to say it in extremes in order to get Canadians to listen and pay attention."

Many of the more conservative members of the moderator's flock were concerned that the United Church was going soft on communism. It was holding a China "study year" and persisted in calling upon the Canadian government to recognize the People's Republic of China. McClure wrote in detail to a worried inquirer in Nova Scotia: "The reason why the Church has China for its study this year is presumably because one-quarter of the world's population live there. If a country is good enough to trade with, she should be good enough to recognize dip-lomatically ... Let me assure you that I have little love for the Chinese Communist leaders, for most of my friends were tor-tured to death by them. My former home and my hospital were wrecked and carted away by them. My wife and I lost all our personal possessions commandeered by them ... believe me that I am not an ardent supporter of Chairman Mao." And again, in answer to an inquiry from a lady in Saskatchewan: " 'Pure Communism' is a theoretical thing that is actually not practised in any country or by any party. Political Communism is practised in many Eastern European countries, Soviet Russia and China. I have seen the practice of political Communism and I have lived under it briefly. I do not like it as well as democracy. I think it is a much more harsh way of doing things, though perhaps in times of crisis it is more efficient. I sincerely do not believe that Communism gives a more rapid development of the human spirit, either individually or collectively, than does democracy. I quite agree with you that the more we apply our Christian principles the better democracy we will have."

To an accusation that the United Church's world outlook was being shaped by a group of ivory tower intellectuals, he replied: "Having just returned from forty-five years of service on the overseas field, and being of a very low order of mentality myself, I am living proof that neither intelligence nor detachment from everyday affairs is characteristic of The United Church of Canada today."

Letters came to "Mr. McClure", to "Moderator McClure", to "Bob McClure", to "Dr. McClure", to "Reverend McClure" and to "Rev. Dr. McClure". To the ones who gave him the accolade of "Reverend" he always pointed out in reply that he was not entitled to it and that he was "just a layman" or "a mere medical man with surgical training." But he never ducked inquiries concerning his theology. And he resented suggestions that he should keep his theological mouth shut: "You are quite wrong when you think one can keep his theological views to himself when he is in public... When I am asked a simple question, do I believe this or do I believe that, I have to give a simple answer, yes or no... I believe that there should be as many theological views in the United Church as there are church members. I think a person's theological views should be based on his education and experience. Since our education and experience is different in every person, so I think the views will be different...

"I do not regard the Bible as a text book in physics, chemistry and geology. I do think it is a marvellous revelation of how men have learned to know God. I believe I have come to know God through my study and my work and the God I worship is perhaps a slightly different God from the God you worship. I still think He is the same God to all of us, and we can trust Him."

McClure refused, absolutely, to engage in any special pleading that might suggest that the United Church had any monopoly on enlightenment: "I think you are legally quite entitled to resign from the United Church and join the Presbyterian Church, and I see no reason you should not do so... Each Christian, I feel, should attend and give his support to that church in which he finds his spiritual home most naturally . . . Somebody else's choice might be the Anglican, the Baptist, or the Pentecostal Church. I think everyone should try to find the right church to meet his spiritual needs."

And, a continuing plea: "We must remember that we are widely divergent people and the rights of each one must be remembered if the church is to succeed."

For two and half years Moderator McClure served his unusual pastorate in his own unusual way. The 24th General Council assembled in January of 1971 and McClure was succeeded by the Rev. A. B. B. Moore. In the interests of an ecumenical effort to synchronize with the meeting of the Anglican Synod the United Church had extended McClure's tenure of office by six months. A former moderator, when asked by the *Observer* for his opinion concerning the length of time any one person should hold the office, replied: "It depends on the man, and if it's Bob McClure you're talking about, I'd say life is none too long."

35

McClure's Law $\left(S = \dfrac{s}{i}\right)$

Bob McClure was seventy years old when he completed his term as moderator of The United Church of Canada. It occurred to himself and to Amy that their needs now, in that period of life referred to by some as the sunset years, were modest. They had their savings, partly based on life insurance they had stringently budgeted from the day of their marriage, and they had the Canadian old age pension plus a modest pension from the church. In their opinion they had all of this world's goods that any reasonable couple could want. It seemed to both of them to be the time to put *McClure's Law* to the acid test.

For several years McClure had been verbalizing a philosophy he delighted in calling *McClure's Law*. References to it had cropped up at various times during his term as moderator. It was a companion to the *Risk* formula developed during his China years which declared that *Adventure=Risk with a Purpose* (a=r+p). The new *Law* was more cumbersome to state: *Satisfaction gained from a job is in inverse proportion to the money earned.* As with many McClure statements it was one that had to be taken in context and that suffered from too close scrutiny. It cheerfully ignored the fact that many people derived a great deal of satisfaction from being able to feed, clothe, house and educate their families in a relatively prosperous way. It blithely ignored the fact that to a large percentage of humankind the "job" was the equivalent of the cave man's "hunt" and, no matter how great the sport, a hunt that was all sport and no kill made for a depressing day in the jungle. *McClure's Law* also seemed to be

tinged with a suggestion that money itself was not quite wholesome. Somewhere behind *McClure's Law* there lurked dour Presbyterian ancestors who knew in their bones that it was man's
destiny to labour but not to prosper. On the other hand, when
one considered the *Law* in terms of there already being a basic
income sufficient for one's needs then it began to make sense.
And when one considered the nature of McClure's own "job" it
made even more sense. As a doctor McClure was not only in a
service industry he was in a humanitarian industry. There were
only two things a doctor could do. He could *a)* serve humanity
and *b)* make money. It was obvious that if service dwindled and
money increased there was something askew in the balance. It
was McClure's contention that, for true satisfaction, service
should increase and income should dwindle. The *Law* could be
stated as "*S*atisfaction equals *s*ervice over *i*ncome $(S = \frac{s}{i})$" in
which equation it is obvious that the value of *S* will flourish only
if *i* is kept properly subservient to *s*.

McClure had been studying the phenomenon inherent in
this equation ever since he returned to Canada from China in
1948. He had watched his fellow physicians and surgeons with a
keen interest and had come to the conclusion that the equation
was valid. He had been applying it as moderator and now, in his
allegedly declining years, he decided to continue doing so. He
and Amy reasoned that if their savings and pensions could
support them in Canada they could support them abroad. The
McClures resolved to look for work in the Third World as volun-
teers. They would not ask for salary but would hope for some
assistance with travel costs. The only question to be answered
was, "Where?".

There was Africa, of course, and there was South America.
The logical place for McClure, however, was South-East Asia.
He ruled out mission work connected with the United Church
on the basis that it would not be sporting to inflict an ex-
moderator on people employed by the institution he had
headed. He had no more than cast his eyes toward Asia than he
was there, once again thanks, in part, to those remarkable
people, the Quakers.

For some years the directors of Oxfam* of the United Kingdom had been studying the world population statistics with

*An international aid agency strongly influenced by Quakers.

increasing apprehension and had begun to funnel money into agencies that were encouraging family planning. McClure had been observing the world's population explosion at first hand and had been preaching and practising family planning since 1932. Now, in 1971, Oxfam wanted to survey family planning in South-East Asia and in McClure they found the volunteer surveyor *par excellence.*

During the months of April, May, June and July, McClure visited Hong Kong, Korea, South Vietnam, Pakistan, India, Thailand, Indonesia, Taiwan and the Philippines. He completed the survey with a personal visit to England that coincided with the Oxfam annual meeting where he was billed as the star speaker. The salty, unorthodox, platform style that had endeared McClure to Canadians was not appreciated by the erudite audience at that meeting in Oxford but his written reports, full of stimulating insight, helped shape much of Oxfam's family planning efforts in South-East Asia throughout the 1970s.

During the course of his Oxfam survey trip McClure had been the happy recipient of two interesting items of information. The first, and most personal, had reached him in Pakistan and was conveyed in a telegram from the Oxfam representative in New Delhi. It relayed a message from the Canadian government to the effect that the Governor-General had named McClure as a Companion of the Order of Canada. McClure was touched by the fact that his own government and Oxfam had seen to it that the news should reach him in Asia. He was also quietly pleased to be a recipient of Canada's highest honour but managed to react, like a true Canadian, with outward indifference. "After all," he wrote to a friend, "you can't eat it."

The other item of information was that there was great need for a surgeon at a jungle mission hospital in Sarawak, Malaysia. The hospital was run by American Methodists and McClure promptly applied as a volunteer for a two-year stint of service. The Methodists, who were eagerly looking for someone to fill the breach while their resident surgeon took a brief furlough, were quick to accept.

December, 1971, found Amy and Bob McClure en route to Sarawak. Amy, suburban to the core and longing for a quiet retirement with her husband, was once again accompanying McClure to an area that most North Americans thought of as exotic, remote and primitive. Sarawak, a province of Malaysia, was on the northern coast of the island of Borneo. The hospital they were headed for was ninety miles upriver in a jungle area populated by tribal people who were members of a larger group known as Sea Dayaks. The Sea Dayaks of Borneo had once been head hunters. The last trophy had been collected as recently as 1946. But Amy McClure endorsed *McClure's Law* and had been heartily supporting all McClure endeavours since their marriage in 1926. She could see no reason to change now.

They flew, via the Pacific, to Singapore and then boarded a Malaysian Air Service 'plane for the flight to Kuching, the capital of Sarawak. It had been difficult to suppress all the preconceived notions that Westerners had about Sarawak. Exotic and fearsome words ran through one's head; "the wild men of Borneo", "head-hunters", "cobras", "jungles". But the aircraft was immaculate. The stewardesses were tiny, immaculate and pretty. The officers were immaculate and handsome. The crew members spoke numerous languages. They graciously served free champagne without reference to race, colour, creed or airline classes. Before the 'plane touched down at Kuching most of the passengers were convinced that Sarawak was incredibly civilized.

The city of Kuching was also small, immaculate and pretty, an unusual capital of a most unusual state. In the early 1800s the north coast of Borneo had been ruled by a Malayan Sultan who was an absolute ruler. Kuching, and the area around it, Sarawak, had been merely a small western corner of the larger "Sultanate of Brunei". The Sultanate had been plagued by rebels and pirates, most of the latter being Sea Dayaks from the rivers. During the 1840s an English adventurer, James Brooke, who owned and captained his own ship, assisted the Sultan in defeating rebels and suppressing pirates with such success that the happy Sultan of Brunei ceded Sarawak to Brooke, making him Rajah and absolute ruler of Sarawak in return for an annual tribute of $2,500 and on condition he would not change the Malays' Moslem religion.* Rajah Brooke ruled what was recognized internationally as an independent state. He was dedicated to even-handed justice and gained the respect not only of the

---

*Even today the foreigner who attempts to convert a Moslem is deported within 24 hours.

Malays but of the Chinese traders and the proud Dayak tribesmen. His rule was so non-exploitive that when he eventually
retired his friends in England felt compelled to raise funds so
that he could live out his life in some semblance of comfort.
Under the next Rajah Brooke, Sarawak signed a treaty with
Britain that brought it under the empire's wing for international
purposes but left all internal affairs in the hands of the Brooke
family. Sarawak was an astounding anomaly; a privately owned
country within the British Empire. It did not become a British
Crown Colony until after the Second World War.

In 1963, with considerable reluctance on the part of its
Dayak and Chinese peoples, Sarawak joined the Federation of
Malaysia. The following years were turbulent. Singapore, with
its large Chinese population, dropped out of the Federation
leaving the Moslem Malays of peninsular Malaysia dominant. In
Sarawak the Dayaks were in the majority with Chinese and
Malays almost equally balanced. There was unrest within
Sarawak, some of it attributable to Chinese and tribal discontent
with the federation and some of it attributable to Communist
organizers. There were spasmodic flare-ups from pockets of
guerrillas. The Federation of Malaysia was walking a typical
modern tight-rope, trying to maintain balance between three
major, and very different, ethnic groups while functioning in
several languages.

The McClures flew from Kuching to the city of Sibu, at the
mouth of the Rajang River, where they boarded the *Express*, a
boat headed for their destination, the community of Kapit,
ninety miles upriver. The *Express* was a long, steel-hulled boat
with a cabin and inside accommodation for ninety passengers
on hard, straight-backed wooden benches. There were Chinese
businessmen, Malay officials, Dayak farmers, grandmothers,
school children, young mothers with babies, pedlars, rubber
merchants and plantation owners. Other boats along the Sibu
waterfront ranged from deep-sea freighters to forty-foot native
longboats and one-man dugouts. In its long rakish lines the *Express* appeared to have ancient longboat ancestry but as it read-
ied for departure twin Diesels roared to life in an engine room aft.
The boat backed out into the great river, swung its bow up-
stream and shuddered forward for a few moments, breasting the
heavy current. The pilot, fully exposed to passenger view in his

wheelhouse at the front of the cabin, thrust the twin throttle levers full forward. The Diesels bellowed in their pits and the boat lifted forward and upward, surging onto the surface. One hundred feet of heavy steel hull carrying ninety passengers, baggage, and crew was on its way into the heart of Borneo, *planing*. McClure, who had had a lifetime love affair with engines, ambled aft on a tour of inspection. A narrow door opened directly into the engine room and there, nestled on either side of a narrow walkway, squatted two gleaming, green, GM Detroit Diesels. He stood for a few moments admiring them, bathing his senses in the roar and the heat and the smell, an engineer paying homage at the shrine of Power. He then rejoined Amy to watch the river unwind before them.

From the air between Kuching and Sibu they had seen several large rivers, all of them twisting and looping like convoluted intestines. The Rajang was different. It seemed wider, bigger, more regal. Its bends were majestic curves, never turning back on themselves but always thrusting forward, southeastward, toward the equator, ever farther into the jungle. And jungle it was. The heavy dark green foliage of the tropical forest flowed to the very edge of the river. This was a land of perpetual summer. There were two seasons, wet and dry, but the "dry" was always green, always warm. They were only three degrees from the equator.

The *Express* had not penetrated far upriver before native longhouses began to appear in clearings on the river banks. The McClures had heard of these and were watching for them. One of the major tribes among the Dayak peoples was the Iban tribe which inhabited much of the Rajang basin area. Although jungle dwellers the Iban were a water-orientated people and built their homes beside the rivers that were their highways. Those homes were the famous longhouses of Sarawak. They were multiple dwellings built under one long roof and behind a long communal verandah. Each house was in fact a village. To count the families one merely counted the doors opening off the verandah. A longhouse could have anywhere from a dozen to a hundred doors. Regardless of length every longhouse soared high above the ground, built on stilts. There, rising above the river bank on their airy perches, the homes were clear of snakes, rodents, garbage, excrement, and flood waters. It was a system that had worked for hundreds of years and was still working. Some of the longhouses were ancient and precarious and decrepit. Others were as proud as the latest surburban bungalows of Kuching, with clapboard siding and painted doors. In the head-hunting days the Iban along the Rajang had been among the last Dayaks to be convinced of the error of their ways and the proximity of their dwellings to the river had been their downfall. When they sallied downriver and took heads, Rajah Brooke made punitive expeditions upriver with a gunboat full of marines and simply burned the longhouses. The Iban were a very intelligent people who connected cause with effect (take a head, lose your village) and so adapted to more peaceful ways. One could still enter longhouses that contained baskets of old human skulls and one could still find longhouses where those skulls would be taken down periodically to be smoked over a fire to keep them contented, but Iban men had adopted other ways of proving their prowess. One favoured method was to take a very long journey. A man who had journeyed up other rivers or into other countries would have that message tatooed in exotic symbols on his throat. Although Amy and Bob McClure did not as yet understand the signs there were men on the boat now whose necks were totally wreathed with intricate designs. The Iban were a proud, adventurous, and independent people. It was the Iban McClure had come to serve.

In the course of the next two years McClure would become enamoured of the Iban and particularly of their longhouse way of life. He would extol the longhouse abroad as being the example of true communal living and would thereby give a slightly incorrect impression. Although the longhouse folk lived under one roof they lived in separate quarters and had a highly developed sense of *private* property. It was not unknown for a family to move and take their own planks with them, thereby leaving a ragged gap in the "communal" walls and roof. There was also a distinct pecking order in a longhouse, ranging outward from the headman and the wealthier citizens. A family could build onto a longhouse only with the assent of all the others. A family that was black-balled would still be accepted as a member of the community but could always be spotted because its house was the lonely one on its own stilts on the edge of the jungle several yards away from the end of the communal verandah. What the Ibans had developed was perhaps not so much communal homes in the small "c" communist sense as prototype horizontal condominiums in the small "c" capitalist sense.

The Ibans were fishermen, hunters, and farmers. They grew rice and cash crops of pepper and rubber. As the boat neared Kapit the jungle-covered terrain became hillier and pepper plantations stood out in stark relief, their clearings etched onto the hillsides, their crops marching in dark green regular rows supported on six-foot stakes.

Only four hours out of Sibu but ninety miles upriver the *Express* thundered into view of Kapit town. The craft decelerated, wallowed a few moments in its own wake and then rumbled gently alongside a modern cement pier. Nearby two signs proclaimed "Esso" and "Shell". The McClures did not know it but they were fortunate it was the wet season and a time of high water. That same cement pier sent its steps searching downward some thirty feet or more and in the dry season even that was often not far enough to reach the water. During those times the *Express* would pull in alongside a derelict freight boat across which the passengers would disembark. They would then walk the plank to a large log leading across the muddy shore and from there would climb a narrow path to the town on the riverbank above. But today the McClures walked easily ashore.

The two Canadians were welcomed by Sister Lydia, a German nurse driving an English Landrover, and were whisked off through what was essentially a Chinese town to an American hospital that was built to serve a clientele that was mostly Iban. To McClure, there was something vaguely familiar about the small town as he passed through it. It had the open store fronts of an oriental bazaar. It was spread out and rambling. Much of it seemed new. Its architecture was uninspired but functional. Its streets were unpaved. It looked like no other place McClure had ever seen but its atmosphere was familiar; it was that of a bustling, booming, Canadian northern frontier town.

36

Up the Creek with Ah Tong

McClure soon realized that this medical mission was like no other in which he had ever served. That knowledge first dawned upon himself and Amy as they were shown into their apartment. It was neater, brighter, better laid out and better equipped than any other mission quarters they had inhabited. Then they met Dr. Loreto Crisologo, the Chief Medical Officer of the hospital, and McClure was taken on a tour. The hospital, he discovered, was also better equipped than any other mission hospital in which he had served.

The equipment was better because the mission philosophy was different. The Canadian and English hospitals in which McClure had practised were *adaptive* hospitals. They were not financed by wealthy missions and the intent had been to create hospitals that were in keeping with the resources of the country in which they were established. One used Western technology and know-how but tried to adapt it to China, or the Mid-east, or India, always with the long term hope that the indigenous people would one day take complete charge. Christ Church Hospital in Kapit was not *adaptive*. It was a *transplant* hospital. The United Methodist Church, U.S.A., had followed the philosophy that facilities provided for patients in the States should be provided for patients in the Third World. The American church had the funds to back its philosophy and had transplanted to this jungle community in Sawawak the facilities that one would expect to find in any small community hospital in up-state U.S.A. It was a philosophy that ran counter to McClure's instincts but he was here in Sarawak to assist for a two-year term, not to alter mission philosophy or policy.

The staff of Christ Church Hospital was composed of that global mixture that by now had come to typify modern mission hospitals. There were Malaysians, Americans, Filipinos, English, Chinese, one German, and now one Canadian. Dr. Crisologo was Filipino. He had been the Chief here since early 1961.* The matron was Miss Soeng Hai King, a Chinese lady of indefinite age, infinite resource and unbounded enthusiasm. She spoke Mandarin and several other tongues, all of which she blended into English to create a unique "Soengalese", a remarkable language that moved one visitor to remark, "You always know what Miss Soeng is saying but never what language she is saying it in!" In addition to running a tight ship, Matron Soeng raised pigs and chickens, baked delicious cakes, and worked with enormous energy. She and her girls "cared". They were the epitomy of everything McClure considered good about a mission hospital.

Like Miss Soeng, the O.R. nurses were also of Chinese origin and all spoke Mandarin. To their great surprise they discovered that the doctor who had now joined them was also fluent in Mandarin. With that innate courtesy orientals show toward senior citizens the nurses called seventy-one year old McClure, *Ah tong,* "grandfather".

It was four years since McClure had handled a scalpel, a fact that worried him. His eyesight was still good, his hands were still firm, but how much had he forgotten? It was a question that the staff, too, were asking among themselves. McClure did not know it, but his first few hours in O.R. were watched with keen interest. The word then circulated throughout the hospital. "*Ah tong,*" went the message, "has not forgotten *anything!*" The O.R. staff also noticed something else. As a surgeon *Ah tong* was very gentle with the living tissue. His fingers treated the open flesh with delicate consideration, never bruising unnecessarily, never bunching layers into one single hurried closing. That word, too, went out from the O.R.

There was no "compound" at this Methodist outpost. There were no gates, no fences. The hospital and its residences, the boarding school, the playing field, the student hostels, were

---

*There had been only two superintendents before him; the American founder, Dr. Harold Brewster, who established the hospital in 1957, and Dr. Ding Lik Kiu, born in Sarawak of Chinese parentage and a graduate of Johns Hopkins in Baltimore.

all part of Kapit's miniature "suburban sprawl". The schools dated from an earlier era but Christ Hospital itself still looked new. It sat on a little plateau that had been bulldozed onto a hillside to accommodate the hospital's three low parallel wings which were joined by a central breezeway. Cream-coloured walls and red roof made a pleasant contrast to the rich green of the tropical foliage that swept down the hillside, circling the hospital's tailored lawns like green waves folding around a mossy rock. Farther up the hillside and a good stiff walk from the hospital were the apartments housing the nursing staff and the McClures. On a level lower than the hospital, and across a shallow ravine, were three houses occupied by Dr. Crisologo and his wife and children, and by the families of two American missionaries, Richard Schwenk, an agriculturalist, and Rev. Andrew Fowler. Both American men were married to energetic and vivacious Filipino ladies. (Over the years McClure had gradually come to the conclusion that Filipinos were among the world's most perfectly adapted people. In his opinion they moved with the greatest of ease between Western and Asian cultures, at home in both worlds and yet uniquely themselves. He saw nothing in Kapit to change his opinion.) An American, Miss Lorraine Gribbens, was the pharmacist and the business administrator. She, like Miss Soeng, had been with Christ Hospital from the day it was built.

McClure assisted Crisologo in O.R. and alternated with him between O.R. and ward duties. It was the first time McClure had been number two on the surgical totem pole for many years but now, whether assisting or alone, he followed established routine to the letter. The staff did not realize what a miracle was taking place before their eyes. In comparison with the pre-retirement McClure he was equanimity personified.

The hospital served an enormous area, some of its patients taking as long as seven days by outboard-powered longboat to reach Kapit. In the late Fifties the hospital had launched a mobile medical team that had travelled the rivers five days a week and did so until 1967. It had been strenuous work, difficult to fund, and difficult to staff. The clinic members also had found that they were doing more and more curative work and less and less preventative work. The mobile clinic had been abandoned. Now, however, McClure had not been around more than a few weeks before he was dreaming about reaching into the *ulu*, the remote jungle, with preventative medicine and family planning.

The Iban men were not inclined to line up for vasectomies the way Indian men had done because there was a popular myth that a vasectomy rendered a man physically weak and incapable of strenuous work, but Iban women had little fear of having their own tubes tied. The first solo operation McClure performed in Kapit was a bi-lateral tubal ligation for an Iban woman. The number of BTLs increased and by the end of May he had done 45 of them in contrast to 6 vasectomies.

A small Canadian film crew tracked McClure to Kapit and had enjoyable sessions "shooting" him on location in and around the Kapit hospital. Their film, optimistically entitled *They'll Tell Me When The Tread Is Gone,* correctly showed McClure full of enthusiasm about the work ahead. Early in May, Amy wrote home and referred to the "three awfully nice Canadian men" from Berkeley Studio.* Everyone was relaxed, little knowing there was trouble in the offing.

Dr. Crisologo left on furlough early in June, 1972, and McClure laid plans for a public health onslaught to be launched as soon as Crisologo returned. McClure pictured longboat teams each with a nurse and a midwife going into the *ulu* every three months to administer shots of a contraceptive called Depro-provera.† The renewal of the Depro-provera shots at three month intervals would give them contact with many Iban homes and they could teach public health at the same time. In August, McClure invited a family planning expert, Dr. E. B. MacDaniel from Thailand, to address the staff. MacDaniel was doing a great deal of work with Depro-provera. MacDaniel had hardly gone, leaving McClure feeling enthusiastically gung-ho, when news arrived from New York and McClure's dreams collapsed. Dr. Crisologo would not be returning as planned. He had an opportunity to further his studies and the Board in New York had approved an extended furlough. Crisologo might not be back for another year and a half. The Board would try to find a replacement.

Berkeley Studio: the audio-visual unit of The United Church of Canada. It has won numerous national and international awards in the audio-visual field.

†Depro-provera is still used as an estrogen but in North America it is not in favour as a contraceptive because of some side-effects and physician resistance. In Thailand some 7,000 women are on semi-annual injections and it is said that China has over 1,000,000 women on annual injections.

Christ Church Hospital was again a one-doctor hospital, but this doctor was a volunteer, retired, and in his seventies. There could be no question now of vigorous public health work until a replacement arrived. McClure would do well simply to hold the surgical fort.

On top of the news about Crisologo came a letter from Toronto. It was cheerful and encouraging and innocently prophetic. McClure's former classmates from the University of Toronto had held the 50th reunion of the Class of '22, or, as they liked to write it, the Class of "2T2". Each of the twenty-six had donated ten dollars to the McClure Fund which was still being faithfully handled by the United Church treasurer. Along with news of the donation they sent a "citation" to their absent classmate:

CITATION
Robert B. McClure, M.D.
Versatile Physician and Surgeon,
International Tube Hunter, (Fallopian, that is)
Expert in Population Control,
Healer of the Sick in Many Lands,
Benefactor of Mankind,
Awarded the "Paddle" Appropriate to the Creek
up which he has gone in Sarawak, Malaysia,
by friends and classmates of 2T2.

In the weeks ahead it became apparent that the McClures were indeed "up the creek". Another doctor was recruited. He was Dr. Rajaratnam Meganathon, a Malaysian Methodist of Indian parentage who had recently completed his studies in India and married an Indian girl, the daughter of a Methodist pastor. He was no sooner accepted by the Kapit hospital than he ran into Malaysian regulations that required him to intern in peninsular Malaysia. He was also eligible for Malaysian national service. It was obvious that Meganathon could provide no immediate relief. The McClures dug in.

They moved down the hill and into the house vacated by the Crisologos. From there McClure could walk across the front lawn, down a steep driveway skirting the edge of a banana-treed ravine, across a roadway, up a flight of cement steps, and into the hospital. Amy could walk to town in about fifteen minutes. Their house was two-storeys, with the lower floor set apart for guest accommodation. There was a beautiful view from the second floor and Amy moved her typewriter table to the living room window. She was once again in charge of McClure's correspondence and was also donating two hours a day to the hospital as a filing clerk.

All through the autumn months the pressures on McClure increased. The Kapit hospital was an emergency hospital which meant the doctor could be called any time of day or night. There were always hunting and fishing accidents with spears, guns, harpoons, knives, hooks, even blow pipes. Farmers would cut themselves carving the tapping grooves into rubber trees or slash themselves with their long-bladed *parangs* while hacking away jungle growth. Boys gathering coconuts or fruit would fall out of trees. Impalings caused by falls in which the victim was transfixed by broken branches caused wounds that McClure had not seen equalled since the war years in China. Many "emergencies" were simply terminal infections where jungle medicine had already failed before the victims were brought to Kapit and to McClure.

As time went by the government of Sarawak began to talk about the possibility of absorbing the hospital into the government services, not because the hospital was short-handed but as a matter of government policy. Once again it looked as though McClure might be presiding over the demise of a mission hospital, although if the government moved quickly it could also mean that he would be relieved from pressure and could use his time to work on public health. The government did not move quickly. Then Amy began to feel unwell. Her fingers swelled. She began to have intestinal trouble. Amy had been remarkably healthy in all the years following her major operation in 1952 but they had both watched carefully for any recurrence of trouble. The problem now was all the more worrying for being unclear. In the meantime the hospital work was increasing. The O.R. logbook showed a graphic picture of the pressure on McClure. Crisologo departed in early June and in July McClure performed a modest 11 major operations, plus 57 minor. But during August, September and October he performed more minors and majors than had been done in any previous three month period by himself and Crisologo combined. And then in November, as the other pressures were escalating, he performed 30 majors and 79 minors.

The ward nurses were unaware of any change in McClure

but the nurses in O.R. noticed he was beginning to tire by the end of the day. He was not quite as fresh for those night emergencies as he had been.

Everyone's affection for *Ah tong* was growing. He had shouted at nurses and he called them "Buffalo" when they were clumsy and on occasion threatened to operate on them without anaesthetic, but Miss Soeng had told him that they were all very fine girls and willing workers and that all he had to do was to explain what he wanted and they would all work hard without being scolded. *Ah tong* apparently had understood the message. In September, Miss Soeng discovered the date of Amy's birthday and on the 24th the staff threw a birthday party, complete with a Miss Soeng cake, singing, and gifts. The McClures resolved to keep *Ah tong's* birthday a secret but on the morning of November 23rd they were awakened at 6:30 in the morning by the melodic strains of "Happy Birthday" outside their bedroom window. The serenaders were off-duty nurses and a bevy of nurses' aides. That day brought more singing, more cake, and more gifts. It was difficult not to feel appreciated.

Amy's illness kept recurring. McClure sent her to Sibu to consult a government doctor but there was no definite diagnosis. She was hospitalized briefly in the Kapit hospital. McClure wondered if Amy's nerves were bothering her and it was quite possible they were. Her husband was carrying a load that would have crushed many a younger man and they were both willing to admit that he was no longer young. There were other things that could upset a Canadian housewife. Iban schoolboys killed a six-foot cobra near the house. Dick Schwenk spotted another one not long after and Amy watched her elderly husband join in the hunt through the underbrush armed with a *parang.* Amy herself was walking across the lawn one day when she nudged a black ball with her foot. It "reared up" at her, waving multiple legs, and turned into a scorpion about five inches in diameter. Being a grandmother she immediately worried about the Schwenk and Fowler kiddies so found a rock and disposed of the creature herself. And there was political unrest just below the surface of Kapit life. Guerrillas were reported on the edge of town and they eventually burned the utility shack at the town airstrip. Gunboats appeared on the river and helicopters dropped leaflets telling guerrillas to surrender. It was the potential for violence rather than the physical fact that made guerrillas, scorpions and cobras unnerving.

In spite of the accumulating stress the McClures found the energy to give a Christmas dinner at the hospital after which they joined in carol singing through the wards. They also attended the church Christmas dinner and survived a surprise party thrown by the nurses, evidence that Amy's system was still showing some resilience.

But 1972 came to an end and there was still no sign of another doctor. There was "hope" that Meganathon would be along soon but nobody knew when. In the meantime the government was still talking "take-over" and McClure was being drawn deep into those negotiations.

The nurses in the O.R. realized that McClure was now trying to avoid the heavier operations. He sent a woman who needed an enlarged thyroid gland removed down to the doctor in Sibu only to find that he was away. The patient returned to McClure who reluctantly performed the operation after confiding to the scrub nurse that he did not relish the thought of anything happening to the surgeon in the course of a heavy operation with no assistant to take over. The thought did not appeal to the nurse, either. Pharmacist Lorraine Gribbens was keeping an eye on the Chief. Occasionally, at the end of the day, he would have her take his blood pressure. Several times she found him at his desk with his head on his arms, resting, a most untypical McClure posture.

That January, 1973, Amy developed a sore on her leg that did not heal. The leg swelled. She developed a high fever and again was admitted into Kapit hospital. One evening, while Amy was in hospital, there was an emergency. The duty nurse 'phoned across to the doctor's house but got no reply. She tried again then finally left her post, called for help, and ran across to the house. They found McClure seated on a kitchen chair, sound asleep.

McClure would have found it ironic had he known that while he was struggling through one of the most difficult periods of his career the folk back home were beginning to assess him the way one does with public men who have reached the end of the road. The Rt. Rev. N. Bruce McLeod, who was now moderator of The United Church of Canada, had just penned a discerning summation of the McClure character without realizing his old friend was in deep trouble. "Energetic, highly skilled, ingenious," wrote Moderator McLeod, "aware of his own size in the scheme of things, with neither delusions of grandeur nor false modesty, at home on the earth which is our home, Dr. McClure is unquestionably one of the great men of our time."

While that letter journeyed through the Canadian mails one of the great men of our time was feeling remarkably small and unsure of himself. McClure was, in fact, in a classic dilemma. His own energy was waning, his wife was now seriously ill, but the hospital needed him. He was the only doctor south of Sibu in the only hospital south of Sibu. Where did his duty lie? To his wife? To himself? To the Iban and Chinese people of the upper Rajang? He and Amy wondered if Amy at least should go home, but McClure was not at all sure she could travel by herself. They thought of sending for Johanna Korlu (friend and nurse) to come and get her, then realized that Johanna herself was in hospital. Then Amy's fever subsided, still unexplained. She came out of hospital and they struggled on through January. The non-medical American missionaries—the Schwenks, the Fowlers and Miss Gribbens—were on the sidelines feeling helpless. It appeared to them that they were watching the elderly doctor and his wife being destroyed before their eyes while they stood by as spectators. Rev. "Andy" Fowler, who was watching it all from the inside as hospital padre, finally exploded. He was a small, quiet man with a gentle manner and a soft voice but he wrote a letter to church superiors that fairly roared with anger: "Dr. McClure has been on 24 hr. duty seven days a week since Dr. Crisologo left in June—more than seven months ago. Mrs. McClure is not well. Yet because of Dr. McClure's high degree of responsibility he has thus far stayed here beyond the call of duty . . . My view is that you . . . cannot simply leave the burden and the decision to Dr. McClure . . . The responsibility is on *your* shoulders. What are you going to *do* for the sake of the name and the service of Christ Hospital?"

There was not much they could do other than pray that the problems would solve themselves.

Finally, on Wednesday, February 7th, eight months to the day after Dr. Crisologo's last entry in the O.R. logbook, the *Express* from Sibu rumbled alongside the Kapit waterfront and disembarked a young Malaysian-Indian couple. The man was of stocky build and pleasant of feature. His wife was exceptionally pretty. She was also seven months pregnant and wearing polio leg braces. It was low water and she had to walk the plank from the *Express* to the old derelict, cross its deck, descend a steep plank to the large, slippery log, cross it to the firm ground and then toil up the steep path to the heights above. The Meganathons had arrived and one more uncomplaining missionary doctor's wife was accompanying her husband into the unknown.

During the months that followed, McClure, relieved of some of the surgical load and of much of the worry, was able to turn his energies toward establishing a mobile team to do family planning and public health work along the Rajang and up its tributaries. A nurse and mid-wife began making routine sorties with the Depro-provera contraceptive injections (and with the "loop" and the "ring" and the other devices) and wherever they went they discussed sterilization with those parents who had completed their families.

McClure had seen enough now to know that far more was involved than simple population control. There was a long-house custom that seriously affected the mothers of newborn children. For the first month after delivery the mother sat with her back to a fire to "dry out". During that period there was an almost total taboo on food; she ate only salt and rice. Under those conditions the fourth child almost destroyed a woman. For many of them it was as though they went through an instant aging. McClure unabashedly advocated tubal ligation for any Iban woman, regardless of age, after she had borne three children. During that year, 1973, the Kapit hospital performed 305 BTLs* as opposed to only 23 vasectomies.

There were other cultural habits among the Iban that created serious problems. When a baby was born in a longhouse the women would cut the umbilical cord with the sharp edge of a freshly split bamboo stick. They did not tie the baby's severed cord but would often "purify" it by rubbing on ashes from the hearth. Unfortunately dogs and cats liked to use the hearth as a latrine so the ashes were far from pure and many newborn infants contracted tetanus. When about eight days old they

*In 1978 the author visited two longhouses and in each one more than 50 per cent of the wives had had BTLs.

would stop nursing and would begin to cry in a thin, strange manner. "Lock-jaw" had set in. An hour or so after ceasing to nurse the infant would have convulsions and about an hour after that it would go into spasm and become rigid, its back bowed. At this stage a newborn infant could be stood upright in a corner like a pathetic wooden doll. About eighteen hours after the tetanus had struck the child would be dead. Even if parents in the *ulu* understood what the problem was they had less than eighteen hours to get their child to the hospital for treatment, an all-too-brief a time in a country where distance was measured by travel time on rivers where the hazardous currents of the wet season alternated with the dragging shoals of the dry.

If the child could be taken to hospital in time there was still a battle ahead involving continuing convulsions, constant intravenous feeding and day and night special nursing. The battle period could range anywhere from eight to fifteen days. The hospital in India had been unable to do much better than achieve a 70 per cent mortality rate when confronted with tetanus of the newborn. The hospital in Kapit, which was having more than its fair share of experience with the problem, was reducing the mortality rate to about 10 per cent but at terrific cost to the nurses in emotion and energy. It was a classic illustration of a problem where the only really effective solution lay in prevention.

Under McClure's eager encouragement the staff developed an anti-tetanus umbilical cord kit and in good McClure spirit gave it a catchy name, "ATUCK". The little kit was in a sterile package and contained a small pair of sterilized scissors, two pieces of sterilized tieing cord, and an antiseptic powder. The powder was carefully mixed to resemble as closely as possible the ashes from a hearth. Dick Schwenk and Andy Fowler, the agriculturalist and the padre, joined the act and suggested that an 8 mm movie be made showing how to use ATUCK. They both used film in their work and knew that the Iban loved it. McClure suggested such a film as a project to The United Church of Canada Women and $2000.00 was sent almost by return mail to buy film prints and a small projector. Then, as though Providence had heard the discussions, a young Canadian Jewish medical student, Lorne Direnfeld, turned up to donate two months of work and to gain invaluable experience. Not only was Direnfeld armed with a movie camera but he had had freelance experience with the Canadian Broadcasting

Corporation. With Direnfeld functioning as an enthusiastic volunteer cameraman and director a film was made showing how tetanus was contracted and demonstrating the proper use of ATUCK. McClure found the funds to provide hundreds of ATUCKs and the Depro-provera team added the film and the kits to their arsenal. Within a few months there was a significant decline in tetanus of the newborn. Once again Christ Hospital was reaching into public health in the *ulu*.

McClure did not go on the public health trips. He did go on one extended longboat weekend trip and came back exhausted from helping drag the forty-foot craft over the shallows and was almost an emergency case from sunburn. His feet were so burned and swollen he could not wear shoes for several days and Meganathon tried, unsuccessfully, to confine him to barracks. McClure learned as much as he could, however, from the Iban patients and from the staff. He was struck by the fact that wherever they went the public health team found a toe-hold in Christian longhouses and gradually it dawned upon him that the missionaries in Sarawak had been responsible for an amazing achievement. They had trained lay pastors at the coast and had had the faith to send those pastors into the *ulu* without constant guidance and oversight from the institutional church. The result was that among the peoples of the longhouse there was a vigorous tribal Christianity that was refreshingly free of rigid doctrine and almost oblivious of denominationalism and of hierarchical structure. McClure was even more impressed when he realized that the enlightened mission philosophy that had made such a development possible had been practised by evangelical fundamentalists, a type that had in the past so frequently irritated him. He began to revise his opinions.

Everything was going well and McClure was once again in fine fettle. One day a large cobra reared up near the front door of the house and he demonstrated there was nothing wrong with his seventy-two-year-old reflexes. He seized a *parang*, faced the swaying hooded reptile, and with one blow removed its head. Direnfeld commissioned an Iban craftsman to commemorate the event on a wooden plaque. Amy, too, was feeling much better and in August when the Schwenks went away for a few days she undertook to water, four times a day, a small experimental rice plot beside the Schwenk house. She, too, was intruded upon by a cobra but thereafter Amy simply carried a large stick and continued to tend the rice. There still was iron under that calm exterior.

The government came to terms with the church and announced that it would take over the hospital sometime in 1974. It would also pay compensation on condition the church used the compensation money in Sarawak. Meganathon, Miss Gribbens, Schwenk and McClure embarked upon hours of discussions exploring ways in which the medical work of the church might continue without competing with government.

The conversations bore fruit. The Government of Sarawak finally took over the hospital in July of 1974 and shortly after that the church, building on the work already begun by McClure's public health team, launched a programme designed to help the longhouse dwellers of the *ulu* attack the problems of safe water, proper diet, sewage, tetanus, family planning and all the other myriad items that came under the caption of "public health". The programme staff, mostly young, well-educated, keen Iban and Chinese Malaysians, were part cᶠ a larger team ministry that was also moving into the *ulu* to assist with agriculture and rural development, home and family life, schools, hostels, and evangelism.

The McClures left Sarawak early in May, 1974, before the final government take-over, but word of the team ministry reached them in Canada. For Bob McClure it was one of the most satisfying bits of mission news he had heard in years. A good hospital had been turned over to government and at a time when government was quite able to run it well. Most of the highly motivated staff had remained and the church had not withdrawn. Instead it had gone where the church was supposed to go, pioneering. And medicine had gone with it, where medicine was supposed to go, off into the *ulu* to help rebuild the whole man.

The McClures could take some quiet satisfaction that their own perseverance, their own determination to finish what they had undertaken, had played an important role in the transition. If they had not held the fort at Kapit for eight months the work might have collapsed and had it not been for McClure's catalytic influence in family planning and public health the new project might not have materialized. In the equation ($S = \frac{s}{i}$) McClure had no way to estimate the size of *service* but he knew that *income* was zero and that *Satisfaction* was enormous. The conclusion was simple algebra.

37

The Footsteps Falter

Young Lorne Direnfeld, the Canadian medical student who spent two months with McClure in Sarawak, continued his educational journeys in 1974 and visited a hospital in the jungles of eastern Peru. It was a hospital run by the Amazon Hospital Foundation, a joint Swedish-Canadian effort. Direnfeld found the hospital to be heavily devoted to surgery and to be in need of an associate surgeon who, most important, would be interested in organizing public health along a headwater tributary of the Amazon River. He passed the word on to McClure, who made inquiries. McClure found that the Hospital Amazonico, as it was known in Spanish, had been founded in the late Fifties by a Dr. Binder, a German agnostic who had been impressed by Albert Schweitzer and who wanted to honour Schweitzer without honouring religion. Foundations had been organized, principally in Sweden and Canada, but after some alleged irregularities on the part of the founder the latter had moved on leaving the Swedish and Canadian Foundations in charge of the hundred-bed, well equipped, surgical hospital. The hospital was intended to serve a large but scattered population of native Indians who, like the Iban of Sarawak, were river dwellers. And, yes, the Hospital Amazonico was indeed looking for an associate surgeon. McClure agreed to go. For awhile the wheels moved slowly but McClure was heavily involved in speaking engagements and did not worry.

Unfortunately, not long after Direnfeld's visit the resident doctor (from Canada) was forced out of Peru by political enemies

and his replacements allegedly were neither scrupulous in business nor skilful in surgery. If McClure received many warnings
he paid little attention, possibly because his own word had
already been given. One strong warning did come from a
member of Oxfam who had been a close associate of McClure's
during the China Convoy ambulance days on the Burma Road.
This person knew the hospital and the problems it had been
having. His advice said, in effect, "It's a bad set up. For God's
sake don't take it on. You'll be frustrated. Your direct approach
will be unsuitable."

A portion of that warning may have been heeded because at
least McClure went to Peru on his own. He arrived in late
November, 1975. If everything worked out, Amy was to follow
soon after Christmas. As it turned out, Amy never went.

McClure travelled the international air routes to Lima on the
west coast of Peru. From there he flew with a regional carrier
across the Andes mountains, travelling north-east. Below the
'plane one narrow, precarious, gravel road wound its lonely
way over the mountains, crossing the watershed through a pass
at 14,000 feet. That road led 526 miles to a single destination, the
city of Pucallpa, Peru. The 'plane reached the same destination
after a trip of some 325 miles.

McClure found Pucallpa to be a primitive city of about
80,000 people. The city had an inadequate electrical system, no
sewage disposal and was devoid of running water other than
that which flowed by in the muddy Ucayali River or descended
in torrents from the heavens. Apart from one portion of blacktop
the streets were unpaved and the roads ungravelled. There was
no gravel to be had. The town, being about 8 degrees south of
the equator in a climate where the humidity usually hovered
close to 100 per cent, enjoyed an average rainfall of some 200
inches per year and throughout the milleniums the waters of the
ancient Amazon flood plains had deposited sediment to such a
depth that drills could descend to 400 feet without striking rock.
It was not surprising that streets and roads became quagmires
during the six-month rainy season. It was the beginning of the
rainy season when McClure arrived.

If one followed the Ucayali River from Pucallpa north and
east some 400 miles as the condor flew, or some 900 miles as the
river flowed, one would come to the port of Iquitos, Peru. It was
a "seaport" at the head of the Amazon River and was 2600 miles

inland from the mouth of the Amazon on the Atlantic Ocean. Between Pucallpa and the Atlantic lay the entire formidable area of the dreaded Amazon jungle. Between Pucallpa and the Pacific rose the towering barrier of the Andes Mountains.

The hospital itself was located 5 miles from Pucallpa by the side of a lake that connected to the Ucayali River. The hospital was joined to the town by a dirt road, by river, and by a telephone line that had broken a year earlier and had not yet been repaired. By comparison, the hospital at Kapit in the Borneo jungle had been in the heart of civilization.

McClure, arriving as he did at the end of a period of chaos and maladministration, found that Hospital Amazonico was almost bankrupt. He was not the administrator but it was his hope to reduce the number of beds from 100 to 30, to charge reasonable fees for surgery if patients were capable of paying, and then to concentrate on public health as planned. He was overly optimistic. By the end of his first week the Foundation ordered the surgery to be locked. Only one person had the key and it was not McClure. From then on it seemed the only time the surgery was unlocked was when the custodian of the key wished to cast a few surgical instruments upon the waters of the black market. McClure was faced with turning a hospital completely around and moving totally to public health work with no financial base. During the next several weeks many employees had to be discharged. Termination pay was, by law, so heavy as to amount to a fine levied against the employer, giving rise to the same paradox as in India where a hospital could be too poor to shut down.

The situation was further complicated by the fact that the Canadian Foundation had elicited a promise from the Canadian International Development Agency (CIDA) to match $100,000 expected to be gained in a recent "Miles for Millions" march. The CIDA money was to be used exclusively for public health work. Unfortunately the "Miles for Millions" events fell far short of their targets and in February, 1976, less than three months after he had arrived, McClure reported wearily to family: "CIDA paid half of their share. Of that half only 30 per cent got to Peru for some reason or other and now the Canadian Foundation is trying to get CIDA to pay the 2nd half and CIDA seems to be a bit reluctant to do so. There are a lot of funny things going on in Canadian philanthropic organizations...

Nobody seems to do anything for love anymore." However, he reported in the same letter that there was enough money to carry on with a river health project until the end of June.

The backbone of the River Health Vaccination Project was provided by two Belgian nurses, who spoke fluent Spanish and almost no English, by a Swedish nurse-anaesthetist who had expected to work in the hospital but who unflinchingly took to the arduous river tours, by a married Swedish couple who were social workers, and by a French doctor who finally became completely and understandably frustrated and left. McClure considered them all to be heroic and was impressed by their physical endurance. He himself went on several river trips with the vaccination teams and found that weeks of travel in motorized dugouts, exposed to pouring rain, bugs and high heat, drained him physically. McClure's seventy-five years were beginning to tell, and no wonder. This jungle was the genuine green hell of the movies and many of its habitants lacked the hospitable nobility that had characterized the Iban of Sarawak.

McClure was also handicapped by language. English was of little use among the staff. He had to use Spanish socially, while working, and in writing case histories. He studied the language assiduously for several hours every day. He wrote home: "There is no doubt at all that older folks do not have such an easy time to learn a new language."

There was a larger, more destructive impediment than either jungle or language. It was the character of the hospital staff. McClure admired the river crew but when he returned to base after a river trip, sunburned, lice infested and weary, he missed the supportive atmosphere of a mission hospital. For the first time in his career he was working completely isolated from the psychological support and encouragement of the church. It was a lonely, frustrating experience. There was hostility and political in-fighting among the Peruvian administrative staff who pirated supplies and resented McClure. The staff would walk out of O.P.D. at 5 o'clock regardless of how many patients were still waiting. McClure looked in vain for the trusting, dedicated, caring people that he had come to expect as the basic requirement for a good hospital.

He had a brief moment of uplift in January when young Direnfeld, now a graduate doctor, interrupted his internship in

Vancouver to volunteer another few weeks of service to jungle medicine. Direnfeld was appalled by the "horrid situation" McClure had inherited. The young doctor went on a three-week river trip during which time the team vaccinated 1,000 children against tetanus, polio, diptheria, TB and whooping cough while Direnfeld held clinics to inspect an endless parade of skin and eye infections and diseased bowels. He marvelled that a seventy-five-year-old doctor had been able to survive such trips.

In February a French-Canadian doctor, Pierre L'Heureux, dropped in almost accidentally along with his wife, Michelle, a nurse. The L'Heureux couple stayed and went "on the river" thereby confirming McClure's faith in the medical professions.*

The frustrations of the whole experience were compounded by red tape. McClure reported home in a family letter that in Peru, "an 'honest doctor' is spoken of as a rare jewel that people have read stories about but have never met. . .". That was an exaggeration but the fact was that both the Peruvian executive committee of the Amazonian Foundation and the Peruvian government imposed an incredible amount of red tape and paperwork to make certain there could not be any more irregularities. It was unfortunate that those much needed regulations were applied just as they got a Chief who was one of the most scrupulously honest men ever to grace the medical profession. For McClure, it was a far cry from the days in India when the organization had complete faith in the hospital Chief and when, if wheels moved slowly, he could always draw on the McClure Fund. Here he used the McClure Fund, but reluctantly because he did not have enough faith in the system to be lavish with money from private Canadian backers who trusted him. He told the Peruvian committee that if they did not give him some measure of trust at least with Foundation and CIDA money from Canada (if it ever came through) then he was leaving. He pointed out that he was 75 years old and found no happiness in shoving paper around.

The money from Canada eventually arrived but the authority that would let McClure use it with some semblance of efficiency did not come through. On the contrary, word came from Lima that the Committee would not make the changes he de-

*Dr. & Mrs. L'Heureux toughed it for more than 6 months.

manded. McClure left, and all but two of the river staff left with him.

McClure had gone to Peru as a volunteer. While there he was paid no salary. His transportation down to Peru and into Pucallpa was paid by the Foundation. At the hospital he received a free room and a free bed. He bought his own bedding and paid for his own food. He paid for the stationery for his reports. He left during the first week in April, 1976, and since he had been there only four months he paid his own air fare home. None of this bothered McClure. What bothered him was that he felt that for the first time in his career he had not completed a project. He had been defeated. He had failed. His steps had finally faltered.

McClure took some heart from the knowledge that before he left more than 20,000 children had been vaccinated and most of them had received the additional two booster shots administered at intervals of several weeks. That alone had been a triumph of logistics and perseverance using delicate vaccine in the high heat and humidity of the jungle conditions. But there had been so much else he had hoped to do.

He came home to Toronto to a spate of newspaper speculation and to headlines like one in the Toronto Star which bannered, THE McCLURE CASE: WHAT WENT WRONG? It added a sub-heading, WHY DID CANADA'S SCHWEITZER QUIT HIS AMAZON HOSPITAL?

McClure's depression lifted eventually when he learned that the Swedish Foundation had enlisted a new team headed by a Belgian doctor and that this time the doctor was being given the authority and the freedom of decision that McClure had demanded. He told himself that as a senior citizen he should have known enough to explore the job ahead of time, and to make his demands before going instead of after. At least it proved that one was never too old to learn! He cheered up and was soon enthusiastically looking for portable refrigeration equipment he could send to his successor to help preserve vaccine during the river trips. He was delighted to find the ideal thing in a yachting magazine.

38

– and Again

While McClure was busily shopping for a portable refrigerator and tiny generator to send to the new doctor in Peru word came, via the Ontario government, that the government of St. Vincent, a tiny island in the Windward Islands of the Caribbean, about 100 miles west of Barbados, was looking for a surgeon who might also be interested in family planning and public health.

This time McClure reacted with more caution. The Prime Minister of St. Vincent, Mr. Milton Cato, visited Toronto and he and McClure had a long conversation. The little island, which had a population of about 100,000 people, had a two-hundred-bed government hospital in the capital, Kingstown, plus a couple of branch hospitals and many outlying health clinics. The main hospital had several staff doctors but was weak on surgery having recently lost a highly qualified surgeon to local private practice. It was hoped that McClure would help with surgery and also organize a public health survey involving sophisticated blood tests for sugar. The island had a high incidence of diabetes and no one knew exactly why, or how serious the problem might actually be.

The McClures went to St. Vincent on a scouting trip in June. They liked what they saw. Everyone from the Prime Minister and the Minister of Health on down was enormously friendly and hospitable. There seemed to be no colour tensions whatever, although the McClures, as whites, were very much in the minority. The hospital had four staff doctors, three from India and one from St. Vincent, all highly qualified, with specialties that ranged from surgery, to gynaecology, to internal medicine. One doctor was working on family planning under a UN grant.

McClure was told that if he decided to accept the invitation to work as a volunteer he and Amy would be given the use of a small house in the hospital compound. True, it had a 'phone that was not working and a toilet that would not stop running and taps that dripped but all that, he was assured, would be put right. Besides, there was a marvellous bonus; the island of St. Vincent was beautiful. It was a volcanic island, extremely hilly and heavily forested with sub-tropical growth. Its valleys were dotted with tiny villages. Bananas and coconuts grew in abundance. The central hills rose to a towering 4,000 foot peak in which nestled the mandatory crater lake. Winding roads ribboned the coast and linked pretty fishing villages. Hikers wandering from the beaten paths could find startling vistas of green-blue ocean lapping miles of deserted beach composed of beautiful black volcanic sand. Kingstown itself boasted the oldest botanical garden in the western hemisphere; one which included a bread fruit tree planted by Captain William Bligh at the end of a second expedition that had been more successful than the first on board the *Bounty*. The St. Vincent police band, looking incredibly pukka in dark blue uniforms with white helmets, gave band concerts in the lush botanical gardens. St. Vincent seemed to be an island oasis in which men and nature were in harmony with the soft Caribbean air.

Bob and Amy McClure returned to St. Vincent in the middle of October, 1976. McClure was to work for at least a year as a volunteer. As in Peru the agreement was that he would receive free transportation down (and back, if the term were completed), and free housing. Everything else, including food, would be at his own expense. The McClures had one major personal item shipped down also at their own expense; a refrigerator.

The McClures arrived in Kingstown to find that the 'phone had not yet been connected, the toilet still ran endlessly and the taps still dripped, but the little house had been painted from top to bottom and was spotlessly clean and the yard had been groomed and manicured. They were given a royal welcome and one of the welcomers was Sister Agneta Asp, the Swedish nurse-anaesthetist who had been "on the river" in Peru and who had left at the same time as McClure. She, too, was working at the St. Vincent hospital and would be living in the compound next to the McClures.

Work went well. McClure moved easily into the operating room and assisted with major operations. Because of his presence they began undertaking heavier gynaecological operations; total hysterectomies and large fibroids that normally would have been referred elsewhere. McClure was making no charge for his services and the hospital itself was charging very little. The hospital was booming. Therein lay disaster.

McClure knew that a St. Vincent surgeon had left the hospital and had set up private practice in his own hospital but McClure had not been briefed on Island politics. On some of the small Caribbean islands political divisions ran very deep and had more to do with cliques and families and old village power structures than with social policies or theories of government. The group that had formed the previous government of St. Vincent were now in opposition and it was said that they were sympathetic to the surgeon who had gone into private practice. McClure, a white foreigner, had come in, was working free, and was undermining the local surgeon. Never mind that the latter's fees were alleged to be exploitative, that was beside the point. The Chinese had a term for it. McClure was breaking the man's rice bowl. And not just McClure; the Indian doctors, too, were interlopers. Already there had been great pressure put upon the Indian Chief Surgeon. It was pressure that might have been simple vandalism but was too persistent. Frequently he had found the air gone from his car tires. Sometimes his tires had been slashed. There had been a rash of break-ins. The doctor now kept a watch dog. By now, the harassment against him, if harassment it was, was lessening. He was of no mind to leave and he always carried a pistol to prove it.

The McClures were assured that the police were always on the watch and that the compound had a twenty-four hour guard. There was some doubt of this, however, when one night in late November they heard Sister Agneta screaming. McClure rushed over to find that she had awakened in time to see a thief leaving her room. She had been cleaned out of tape recorder, camera, watch, and money. Whether it was theft or harassment no one could say.

A week later McClure made a major purchase. He bought a

second-hand Mini-Austin. He drove it home. That night he was awakened by Amy. The house was so doll-like that McClure and his wife, for the first time in their lives, had separate, tiny bedrooms. While they slept a thief entered the house by noiselessly removing a window. He opened all his exits. He then unfastened all the McClure baggage and ransacked all their clothing. He took a watch from within eighteen inches of McClure's head. Having completed all the actions that could be attributed to simple theft he then went further. He returned to Amy's room and began to maul her.

It was then that Amy awoke, screaming.

McClure charged into the room and the man vanished out a window.

It was 2 a.m. The 'phone was still not hooked up so they could not call the police. It seemed unwise to venture out together and McClure could not leave Amy alone. They sat together until morning, Amy terribly shaken and McClure feeling angry and suddenly elderly. It occurred to him that now, at 76, he no longer viewed this kind of adventure with the same exhilaration as he would have done in China.

By morning Amy had made up her mind and McClure was in agreement. They were going home. The Prime Minister, the Minister of Health and the Chief of Police all reasoned with them. The 'phone would be fixed, the windows would be barred, the patrol would function, a watchdog would be provided, and McClure would be issued with a .38 revolver. McClure had never shot a man in his life but he knew that if he had had a gun that night the intruder who had mauled Amy would now be dead. That was no solution. Amy agreed. "No," she said, "there'll be no .38s around our place. We had that in China."

McClure turned in the car for resale. He had put four and a half miles on it. They abandoned the refrigerator. They caught the first 'plane going north, which happened to be to New York, and by November 10th were back home in Toronto.

McClure did not feel that St. Vincent had been a personal failure but it certainly had not been a satisfactory venture. The *service* had not been long enough to be significant and although the income was negative the *Satisfaction* was naturally minute.

It was not long before he rallied from any sense of despondency. The McClures had liked St. Vincent. They had liked the people they had come to know. McClure admired the colleagues with whom he had practised and whole-heartedly approved of their work. He made family planning in St. Vincent a personal project and enthusiastically raised money to send to the island for that work. Private Canadian donors were still giving money "to Bob McClure's work" and it was still being administered for him by the United Church. Although he had decided that St. Vincent was not the place for him personally to serve he put some of the McClure Fund to work in St. Vincent as though by proxy. He knew it would be well used.

39

The Journey Resumes

One Sunday morning in February, 1977, the McClures were in a pew as usual at Bloor Street United Church. There was a visiting minister that morning. McClure found him to be very poetical and utterly boring. During the sermon McClure took out his notebook and started making notes, a device he had used for years to unnerve the preacher and, with luck, to help him (the preacher) concentrate his mind. On this particular morning McClure abandoned the notes and proceeded to read a pamphlet that he found in the hymnbook rack. It was a reprint of a letter from a missionary in Zaire, Africa, who was sponsored by the Bloor Street congregation. His name was Dr. Robert Hilliard. He told of the work that was being done in the "Institut Medical Evangelique", a hospital at Kimpese about 120 miles from Kinshasa, the capital of Zaire. Dr. Hilliard mentioned that the Church of Christ in Zaire, that operated the hospital, was looking for a surgeon to fill in for a few months while the staff surgeon took a much needed furlough.

On the way home from church that day McClure told Amy he had decided he should go to Zaire. Amy did not turn cartwheels of delight. She was beginning to think it was time her husband hung up his scalpel and stayed home in Canada. She told him to make enquiries. It was always possible they needed a younger man.

McClure landed in Kinshasa airport on July 6, 1977. He had come to Zaire by invitation of the Church of Christ in Zaire and once again he had come as a volunteer. This time he was paying his own air fare out of his personal pocket because he did not think a mission board should pay it and he was certain the African church in these nationalistic days would rather use the money to pay a local than to pay air fare for a foreigner. (Amy had thawed enough to suggest that by foregoing a summer holiday in '77 and by taking it easy at holiday time in '78 the family budget could be bent to accommodate the air fare.)

The Institut Medical Evangelique (I.M.E.) near the village of Kimpese had been established by Baptists and in its formative years there had been strong input by American, Canadian, British, Swedish and New Zealand Baptists. When the African church gained autonomy the Baptists had submerged their identity in that of the Church of Christ in Zaire and had embraced the co-operation of Mennonites, Christian Church (Disciples of Christ), The United Church of Canada, and other denominations. The hospital administrator was African and the staff was the usual cross-section of the United Nations. The language of work was French. McClure had a shaky but long-standing grounding in French and had been studying hard in recent weeks. He found he could get along. With friendly help he was literate enough to write his case histories in French. He also found that the out-going surgeon, not wishing to leave a large assortment of post-operative cases for the new man, had left a large backlog of cases waiting for surgery. McClure set to work with a will.

The I.M.E. hospital covered many acres of land about two miles from the rather primitive village of Kimpese. The hospital was not fortified with walls or barbed wire but was self-sufficient and self-contained. It was a four-hundred-bed hospital with a TB ward, a surgical ward, an obstetrical ward, an orthopaedic ward and a large paediatric ward (Dr. Hilliard's specialty). The various doctors came from a variety of backgrounds and were versatile. There was a good laboratory, a well-stocked blood bank, a large central supply room and a medical storehouse. The hospital also had its own airstrip from which the Missionary Aviation Fellowship flew a specially equipped Cessna 185 on regular trips to up-country clinics and on frequent mercy flights.

In the O.R., McClure found excellent equipment and a well-trained African nursing team, both male and female. He found them to be precise and meticulous. He soon decided that their operating standards were the highest of any hospital he had ever worked in on an overseas field. He found one of the team's habits, however, to be quite unsettling. He made the discovery one day while in the midst of a hysterectomy.

The operation had been going about fifteen minutes and McClure was deep into the pelvis and concentrating mightily when he realized that the scrub nurse was humming as she handed over scalpels, forceps and swabs. He was turning over in his mind how to ask her, politely, and in French, to desist, when he managed to unravel words in the midst of the humming. It was a French version of *Jesus Lover of My Soul*. Before he had decided how to react he noticed the music swelling and to his consternation realized that the anaesthetist was now joining in. Then the circulating nurse, over in a corner of the room by the shelves, added a third voice to the chorus. It was, of course, in harmony, since no self-respecting African would think of singing in simple unison. The hysterectomy was completed to a cappella music with the surgeon unable to find the off switch. While closing up he apologized for not having made it a quartet but said he had had other things on his mind.

A few days later he was removing an uncomplicated ovarian cyst under a spinal anaesthetic when the scrub nurse again felt musical. This time McClure recognized the tune more quickly and translated the words with ease. It was the hymn *Nearer My God to Thee*. The patient was conscious and McClure felt that less prophetic words could have been selected but before he could protest he heard the anaesthetist join in, again followed immediately by the harmonizing voice of the circulating nurse. The voices of the trio gently bathed the O.R. ". . . Still all my song would be . . ." they sang, never missing the slightest nuance in the surgeon's commands. "Forceps," ordered McClure, ". . . darkness be over me . . ." lilted the singers, their tones gentle and subdued, only snatches of the words surfacing through the melody, like the crests of warm waves. "Clamps!" exhorted the surgeon, ". . . in mercy given . . ." responded the trio. "Scalpel!" barked the surgeon, ". . . bright with thy praise . . ." sang the nurses. "Sponge!" said the harried doctor, only to be answered by the sweet refrain, ". . . still all my song shall be 'Nearer, my God to thee' . . ."

McClure had the patient's abdomen wide open and was burrowing after the cyst when his astonished ears heard four-part harmony. The patient, too, was singing. She had a beautiful alto voice. It had taken fifty-four years but McClure had finally practised surgery long enough to hear a patient singing on the table. It was surely time to hang up his scalpel!

McClure returned home in the first week of November, 1977, and he had stars in his eyes. He had seen a big *transplant* hospital that had made a smooth transition to becoming *adaptive*. He had seen dedicated staff of many colours and races working in harmony (in more ways than one) and with efficiency. He had seen a hospital of the kind that too often turned inward upon its own size and efficiency still functioning with compassion and reaching out to rural clinics. (He wrote to the Amazonian Hospital Foundation and told them, in all sincerity, to get observers to Kimpese to see what a Third World hospital was all about.) He had treated refugees flowing up from the war zones of Angola and had seen wounds and had heard stories that could break a strong man's heart but he had observed, once again, the indestructability of the human spirit. He had seen an indigenous church that was innocent of denominationalism and whose members seemed to consider their Christian religion to be a thing of joy. He had discovered that he himself had been able to take four months of heavy surgery without flagging and he had kept at it until the day he left. On his final day at the Institut Medical Evangelique he gave away his stethoscope, his measuring tape, his blood pressure apparatus and his diagnostic kit. He was about to climb into the mission car to head for Kinshasa and the airport but returned to the O.R. for another hour and a quarter to handle an emergency.

When McClure arrived in Toronto he announced, both mixing his blades and his metaphors, that he was hanging up his skates. His friends and his wife devoutly hoped that that was true. He had ventured farther and served longer in the name of his maker than most mortal men. There was nothing now he need prove to himself or to God. He had had a heart warning before going to Zaire and upon returning went into hospital for a hernia operation. The sunset years were indeed here, thought his friends. He should spend them quietly in Toronto, holding hands with his wife.

McClure had other plans. The McClure Fund was still flourishing and he was being constantly challenged to keep abreast of the most efficient ways to put the money into practical, humanly productive use. He and Amy were in constant contact with individuals and institutions in India, Sarawak, St. Vincent, Zaire, and Canada, sometimes as administrator of the McClure Fund, and often simply as private donors themselves, dipping into their own finances to help Third World students complete their education. In addition, McClure was in heavy demand as a speaker. He was appearing more frequently now on radio and TV talk shows than he had done even in the high profile days as moderator. In addition to media appearances, during the first half of 1978 he made fifty-five platform speeches with engagements as far apart as Newfoundland and British Columbia.

The only sunsets recognized by the McClures were those seen during the late summer evenings of July and August, 1978. They were viewed from the remote Indian village of Port Simpson, on the coast of British Columbia, where McClure went as a volunteer for two months while the regular doctor took a break. There were two clinics there, one run by government and one by the United Church, and he was the doctor for both. There was action but no surgery. Amy accompanied him; wife, homemaker, secretary. It was the first time they had ever lived so far north.

At Port Simpson the summer sun did not set until after 10:30 p.m. The McClures liked to walk together, quietly, at sunset time. Nowhere else on earth had they seen a more beautiful sight than that made by the sun's final rays lighting the mountain peaks to the east as its warm colours bathed the Pacific to the west. Their thoughts followed the sun at such times and imagined its morning rays beginning to caress the mountains of Taiwan and the fertile fields of China. In the heart's eye they could see the sun's new beams sweeping the jungles and rivers of Sarawak before moving on to the great interior plains of India and on and on to the orchards of Gaza by the blue Mediterranean then across Africa to Zaire and eventually full circle to the Western hemisphere, to Canada and home.

And for all the places and people whom kind memory visited, the McClure thoughts were as warm as the thoughts of home.

Epilogue

It was Thursday, December 7th, 1978. Winter had come early to Toronto but the first cold spasms had abated, yielding to a day that was miserably raw rather than snappingly cold. During the morning, snow had been falling half-heartedly; by noon it was disintegrating into rain lashed by an unpredictable east wind. In Queen's Park, the Ontario Legislative Building sat in the midst of its inner city oasis, its red stone giving a touch of sombre colour to otherwise grey and white surroundings.

Within the depths of the Legislative Building, in the brightly coloured, cheerfully decorated parliamentary restaurant, there was warmth, bustle, and noise. It was noon-hour and the inhabitants of the building—staff, parliamentarians and their visitors—were enjoying their noon meal. The diners were in a Christmas mood and roast turkey headed the menu. The tables were crowded.

One table accommodated eight people; four parliamentarians and four visitors. Two of the visitors were elderly. One was cheerfully spinning a yarn from China days. There was laughter and interpolated remarks and, since the story-teller's voice was strong and his tale entertaining, inhabitants of other tables were eavesdropping. The story-teller was Bob McClure and he was in good form. He and Amy and their two friends were guests that day of a non-partisan group of parliamentarians.

After completing the leisurely and somewhat noisy meal, during which the conversation and the stories had ranged the surface of the globe, the party rose and moved upstairs. They crossed the marble hallway of the main floor and then mounted the regal expanse of the red carpeted stairs, flanked by the stately sweep of carved oaken banisters, that led to the Ontario Legislature. One of the hosts, the Member for Victoria-Haliburton, ushered the guests past a uniformed commissionaire and into the Members' Gallery.

The House was already in afternoon session and as the McClures sat down the elegant old Victorian chamber was ringing with the sound of heated questioning from Her Majesty's Loyal Opposition. A Cabinet Minister was on his feet, making heavy weather of his answers. One Honourable Member kept interjecting the word "Nonsense". Another told the Minister that his tie was running away with his tongue. Yet another loudly informed the House that the Minister's answers were being "made up".

The Speaker, the Honourable John E. Stokes, issued a call for order. He addressed the House:

"It has been brought to my attention that we have under the Speaker's Gallery, the west section, a gentleman who has made a tremendous contribution, not only to the people of Canada, but to many trouble spots throughout the world. I would draw your attention to the fact that we have, as a very distinguished guest and visitor, Dr. Robert McClure."

There was a thunder of desk-pounding from both sides of the House after which the rowdy Question Period continued. It was a minority government these days in Ontario and behind every question and answer there gleamed a well-honed partisan knife.

At 3:15 p.m. the Question Period ended and the Press Gallery emptied. It was time for Private Members' Public Business. The first Public Business was a resolution by the Member of Brant-Oxford-Norfolk, Robert Nixon,* Liberal Party:

"That this House recognizes the outstanding achievements of Dr. Robert McClure whose life of service at home, in China and elsewhere in the world exemplifies the most commendable aspects of the human spirit. And that a suitable message be inscribed and forwarded to Dr. McClure."

As a resolution it was open for debate. Robert Nixon had the floor first:

"...In my view Dr. McClure's life, his attitude to life, and

*Former Leader of the Liberal Party of Ontario.

his service to mankind, ranks him in the first order of both good hero and good example..."

Ten minutes later Mr. Nixon zeroed in on the point that was at the heart of his resolution. It was a delicate point to make:
"... that has to do with a colleague of Dr. McClure's, a well-known medical practitioner in China, Dr. Norman Bethune. We have heard a lot about Dr. Bethune. Certainly the government of China had seen fit to make him a hero, as it might properly do so...

"I simply say to members that Dr. McClure... had a different motivation. It was not a political motivation. It was a broader one, in my view, than a political motivation... a more admirable one... I submit to you, Mr. Speaker, that we have in our presence this afternoon a man whose record puts him in the forefront of those of us who want to recognize a life of service and a life of altruistic concepts... Dr. McClure's wit, his motive and his energy must be examples to all of us if we are to have a better world."

Mr. Nixon was followed by speakers representing all three parties and all spectrums of political opinion.

The Member for Parkdale, Dr. Jan Dukszta, New Democratic Party:
"... The western experience in China is very peculiar, because it started in a rather obnoxious fashion since the westerners really went to China to rob. But there has been another element, which started with the Protestant churches—some Catholic members too but largely Protestant—which sent missionaries to China to give something to China... social services, medicine and other things... They were the precursors of the present social change in China, although they may not have fully realized nor fully accepted the degree to which they were precursors...

"I pay my respects to Dr. McClure as a man who both directly and indirectly contributed to the revolution of 1948 in China and to the tremendous work that the Chinese people are doing right now in modifying, changing and building a new society."

The Member for Yorkview, Mr. Fred Young, New Democratic Party:

"... We so often look at the rich and the powerful and say these are in the vanguard of civilization. They are not. All too often they are the ones who are preventing progress in our civilization... Progress depends upon the McClures, those who dedicate life and ability to save men and to change institutions so that the concept of unselfish service gradually replaces that of greed and lust for power..."

The Member for Scarborough-Ellesmere, Mr. David Warner, New Democratic Party:

"... this is a rare moment in our House. It is so entirely civilized the press are absent. It's not likely the moment will be reported by the press because there is no political animosity here. There is no partisan politics in this discussion. It's one of the rare moments when legislators have the opportunity to say publicly to a fine gentleman, ... 'thank you... we appreciate what you have done and we hope that your strength of spirit, the principles which you've held fast to over the years will be an example to others to follow...'

"We don't know the prospects for cloning these days, but we need more Dr. McClures, and the more the better."

The Member for Wellington-Dufferin-Peel, Mr. Jack Johnson, Progressive Conservative Party:

"... Though this occasion is a time to honour Bob McClure, it is appropriate to recognize his wife, Amy, too. Bob quite rightly has received much attention for his outstanding service to mankind. Without Amy though, who has understood him and his purposes; who has supported him, made him a home and given him her love, the way for Bob would have been very much harder. Indeed it has been said that Amy must be a saint, and I'm sure the good doctor would be the first to agree with this assessment."

The Member for Victoria-Haliburton, Mr. John Eakins, Liberal Party:

"... Dr. Bob McClure has spent his life as a Christian missionary surgeon; his service has been extended unstintingly to people of all religions. His hand, his heart, and his scalpel have always been ready to assist Buddhist, Hindu,

Moslem, animist, Protestant, Jew, or Catholic. Today in
Toronto, if Zoroastrians want a sympathetic ear they come
to Bob McClure. He has the knack of seeing the good in all
persons, regardless of nationality, race or creed, while at
the same time affirming, through action, his own uncom-
promising position as a Canadian and as a Christian."

The Member for Scarborough North, the Honourable
Thomas L. Wells, Progressive Conservative Party:
" . . . He has been a man of dedication, a man who has lived
his Christianity, has shown that it is the layman, acting in
the community, speaking and doing those deeds on behalf
of Christ that really is Christianity at work. He has shown
that is how you change lives, and that is how you change
society . . . I am pleased to support this resolution today,
Mr. Speaker."

The resolution, so enthusiastically supported, was unani-
mously passed. It had called for "a suitable message to be
inscribed and forwarded to Dr. McClure." When that message
eventually came, in the form of a hand-scripted scroll, it con-
densed seventy-five minutes of fulsome oratory into one precise
statement:
"The Legislative Assembly of the Province of Ontario in
Parliament assembled recognizes the outstanding
achievements of Robert McClure, C.C., M.D., D.D., whose
life of service at home, in China and elsewhere in the world
exemplifies the most commendable aspects of the human
spirit."

In the park outside the old red stone parliament building
the wind had dropped and the rain had turned to a light drizzle
when Bob and Amy McClure came out of the north exit. She was
wearing a turquoise-blue coat that set off the grey of her hair. He
was wearing a lightweight, beige, burberry topcoat. They
walked to Queen's Park Crescent and waited for the crossing
light. The December day had become almost balmy.

McClure was in high spirits. He had enjoyed the whole
"debate". The obituarial overtones had tickled his fancy. His
only regret was that he had not been permitted to rise to his feet

and pay a few tributes of his own. He would have liked to tell them how much he owed to Dr. Gushue-Taylor for instilling in him the urge for professional excellence; to the little Buddhist, Mr. See, as a model of true humility; to Dr. Donald Hankey for demonstrating absolute selflessness; to the Moslem, the Sheik of Majdal, for insisting on the importance of prayer; to the Hindu, Manohar Nagpal, for helping him understand the meaning of forgiveness; to Amy, the remarkable woman standing here beside him, waiting calmly for the light to change, just as she had stood beside him, physically and in spirit, throughout all these many years. And how about all the others with whom he had worked, the doctors and the evangelists, the technicians, the agriculturalists and the teachers? How about the nursing sisters? Loving Lotus, Sheila Yu, Margaret Briggs, Dorothy McIntyre, Sonu Canara, Soeng Hai King—where and how could one end such a list? And how about all those anonymous Canadians, and Americans, English, Germans, Swedes, Dutch, New Zealanders and so on who throughout the years had dug into their pockets and had given so that people like him could function? How could one man, any man, ever express his debt to all those others who had left their imprint upon him?

The light changed and the McClures crossed Queen's Park Crescent. A cruising taxi slowed down as its driver watched to see if the elderly couple wished to seek sanctuary but the drizzle was now a mere spatter and the December chill was invigorating. Bob and Amy McClure struck east along Wellesley Street, walking briskly.

McClure Chronological Table 1948-1978

1948 May. The state of Israel is created by the UN and is attacked by six Arab armies. The Palestinian refugee "problem" is in the making.
December. McClure leaves China and arrives home in
Toronto on Christmas morning.
1949 McClure enters group practice in a private clinic in Toronto. Finds the experience frustrating.
1950 October. McClure goes to Egypt en route to Gaza. Works
for acclimatization period at the Harper Memorial Hospital
in Old Cairo.
1951 March. McClure arrives on the Gaza Strip and takes up his
post as Chief Surgeon at the Anglican C.M.S. hospital in
Gaza City.
1952 McClure "sells" technicians into Libya. The Egyptian revolution takes place. He performs sex-change surgery.
October. McClure is summoned home and Amy under-
goes cancer surgery.
December. Amy returns to Gaza with McClure.
1953 April. The McClures and friends visit Jerusalem.
June. Amy returns to Toronto.
Fall. Following instructions McClure is trying to sell the
Gaza hospital.
1954 February. American Baptists take over Gaza hospital.
March. McClure arrives in Ratlam in Central India to head
a United Church of Canada supported hospital.
1956 March. McClure goes to Canada for short furlough. His
father, Dr. William McClure, celebrates 100th birthday on
April 9th and dies on July 16th.

September. McClure returns to India.

Fall. The Suez Crisis and the Hungarian Revolt take place.

1957 January. Amy arrives in India via Calcutta.

June. In Canada, Diefenbaker becomes Prime Minister.

1959 July. McClure studies new sterilization technique in Singapore.

1960 April. The McClures return to Canada for a major furlough. Their friends the Anklesarias visit Canada.

1961 April. McClure returns to India. Amy follows later.

1962 October-November. Border war between China and India.

1963 April. In Canada, Pearson becomes Prime Minister.

1964 May. In India, Prime Minister Nehru dies and is succeeded by Shastri.

1965 Sir Winston Churchill dies. A Soviet astronaut "walks" in space. The McClures take a summer holiday in Canada.

1966 January. India's Prime Minister Shastri dies and is succeeded by Mrs. Gandhi. There is drought and famine on the Malwa Plateau.

1967 June. The "Six-Day War" between the Arab states and Israel.

November. The McClures leave India to "retire".

1968 April. Trudeau becomes Prime Minister of Canada.

August. McClure is elected the first lay moderator of The United Church of Canada. The Biafran War is underway in Africa.

December. American astronauts circle the moon.

1969 January. Moderator McClure has traumatic meeting with Toronto Zionist Council.

May. Moderator and Mrs. McClure visit Scotland to attend 200th anniversary of Church of Scotland. During the year the McClures travel extensively in Canada.

1970 February-April. Moderator McClure visits mission fields in Africa.

May. He visits the Maritimes.

Summer. He pays official visit to the Middle East.

October. Crisis in Quebec. Ottawa proclaims the War Measures Act.

1971 January. McClure's term as moderator comes to an end.

April-July. He tours South-East Asia carrying out a family planning survey for Oxfam of the U.K.

July. The Governor General names McClure a Companion

of the Order of Canada.

December. McClure goes to Kapit in Sarawak, Malaysia, to work as a volunteer assistant surgeon at a Methodist jungle hospital. Amy accompanies him.

1972 June. Dr. Crisologo goes on furlough and McClure is the only doctor in an emergency hospital serving a large jungle area.

1973 February. Dr. Meganathon joins McClure.

Summer. Canadian medical student, Lorne Direnfeld, works with McClure as a volunteer.

1974 May. The McClures' term expires and they return to Canada.

Direnfeld visits Hospital Amazonico, a jungle hospital in Peru, and reports to McClure.

1975 November. McClure goes to Peru to work as a volunteer doctor at Hospital Amazonico on head waters of the Amazon River.

1976 April. McClure, frustrated, leaves Peru.

October. The McClures go to idyllic St. Vincent in the Caribbean where the doctor is again volunteering his services. Quarters are broken into, Amy is attacked, and they leave on November 10th.

1977 July-November. McClure works in Zaire, Africa, as a volunteer surgeon. Has thoroughly rewarding experience.

November. *McClure: The China Years,* the first volume of a biography of Dr. Bob McClure is published in Toronto.

1978 Summer. McClure works as a volunteer doctor at clinics in Port Simpson, an Indian community in British Columbia. Amy is with him.

December 7th. The members of the Legislative Assembly of the Province of Ontario in Parliament assembled pay public tribute to Dr. Robert Baird McClure. The McClures are present.